SCHOOL COUNSELING PRINCIPLES

ETHICS AND LAW

BY CAROLYN STONE, Ed.D.

AMERICAN
SCHOOL
COUNSELOR
ASSOCIATION

1101 King St., Suite 625, Alexandria, VA 22314
(703) 683-ASCA, (800) 306-4722, fax: (703) 683-1619
www.schoolcounselor.org

ISBN 1-929289-05-7

Dedication

To my fellow school counselors and counselor educators. Thousands of you have helped me develop the information presented in this book by questioning, challenging, searching and inspiring. I dedicate this book to you.

Acknowledgements

I want to recognize Julie Van Norstrand, Amy L. Colvin, Esq., and Dorothy Wagener for their extraordinary efforts and loyalty in helping me research and edit this book. There were many other faithful supporters, contributors and readers. Thank you to my colleagues Lynne Carroll, Rebecca Schumacher and Shunda Brown who read and edited. A sincere thank you to others who gave suggestions: Janet Brown, Carol Dahir, Amanda Davis, Lorene Gibson, Kristen Nocerino, LeAnn Pollard, Laura Price and Michael Varady. Twenty-two people contributed to case answers under the Getting Started case at the beginning of each chapter: Mary Ann Dyal, Cynthia Esielionis, Pat Estes, Mary Hermann, Alexia Huart, Fran Meffen, Brenda Melton, Sherry Merrill, Paul Meyers, Doug Morrissey, Pat Partin, Krylyn Peters, Kevin Quinn, Theodore P. Remley Jr., Russell Sabella, Rebecca Schumacher, Angie Stansell, Jan Tkaczyk, Richard Tutunick, Bob Tyra, Claire Wayne and Robert Weiss. Richard Wong, ASCA executive director, believed in this project, proposed it and supported me to complete it.

Thank you to my husband, Doug Stone, whose support literally made the difference between success and failure in meeting the book's deadlines and to my mother and father, Elsie and Silas Bishop, who taught me perserverence, which was sorely needed for this project.

Finally, thank you to Kathleen Rakestraw, the editor of so many fine ASCA publications; you are the consummate professional.

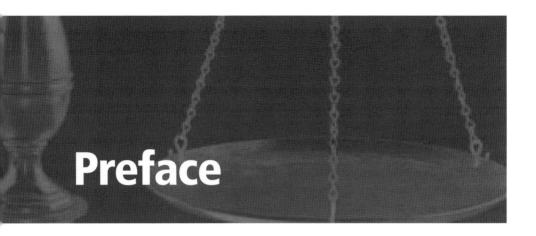

Preface

Welcome to "School Counseling Principles: Ethics and Law." As all school counselors can attest, the profession offers many unique, interesting and often formidable legal and ethical challenges and responsibilities, primarily because we are working with minors in a school setting. School counselors live and work in an increasingly litigious society and are called to a high ethical standard. Professionals who work with minors are sensitive to the fact that issues for counselors who work with adults are far different. Each day school counselors have to consider the legal and ethical ramifications of their work in fostering academic, personal/social and career growth with students, while being faithful to their obligations to parents, administrators and the community.

This book is written for practicing school counselors and candidates for the profession. It is intended to raise awareness of legal and ethical issues and reduce the risk of unethical or unlawful behavior that might result in legal complications for school counselors. Although avoiding legal liability is a common thread throughout the book, the larger purpose is to enhance our obligations and responsibilities to students. School counselors are rarely at the center of a lawsuit but daily are called on to act in the best interest of students and their families. Creating sensitivity to legal and ethical issues will heighten our awareness and help us examine the implications of our professional behavior for students.

Throughout this book we will examine the legal and ethical complications involved in working with minors in school settings primarily through the use of case study. Case studies help school counselors reflect on possible consequences before they actually have to deal with real-student situations, so that when in the throes of a dilemma, school counselors can ethically and legally justify their courses of action. The case studies represent a wide range of circumstances and situations. They were developed from actual situations that American School Counselor Association members posed to the ASCA Ethics Committee and from ethical dilemmas the author encountered when practicing as an elementary counselor, high school counselor and director of guidance. The more than 100 cases presented here will help the reader connect the reality of school counseling to critical federal and state statutes, ASCA's Ethical Standards for School Counselors (American School Counselor Association, 2004), the American Counseling Association's Code of Ethics and Standards of Practice (American Counseling Association, 2005), case law and school board policies that shape work with minors in schools.

The Organization of this Book

The chapter titled "Introduction to Legal and Ethical Issues" gives an overview of challenges and dilemmas school counselors face on a daily basis when working with minors in a school setting. As leaders and advocates, school counselors must choose the best path to support and assist students, and the ethical dilemmas and legal interpretations can at times make this feel overwhelming. This chapter presents key principles that are integral to ethical and legal understanding and are applied throughout all 11 chapters that follow.

Chapters 2-12 follow a template that will help you understand the concepts presented and will maximize effectiveness of the case study format as a learning tool. Each chapter follows this outline:

- Objectives
- Introduction
- Ethical Standards Addressed in This Chapter
- Getting Started: What Would You Do?
- Working Through Case Studies
- Points to Consider
- In a Position to Know: A School Counselor Speaks
- Making Connections
- Key Terms
- References

Here is brief description of these organizational items.

OBJECTIVES

The objectives section contains the intended learning outcomes that the reader will take from each chapter. As an example, listed below are the overarching goals of the entire book:

- Examine the legal and ethical obligations of the school counseling profession through application of case studies.
- Raise awareness about and implications of professional behavior and professional actions.
- Examine case law, court decisions and legislation that impact practice.
- Become familiar with legal and ethical terminology.
- Apply legal and ethical professional reasoning to concrete examples.
- Create sensitivity as to the difficulties and complexities of working with minors in a school setting.
- Increase tolerance for ambiguity.
- Lower the risk of legal liability in terms of professional practice.

INTRODUCTION

This section gives a brief overview of salient points that will be discussed in the chapter and sets the stage for learning.

ETHICAL STANDARDS ADDRESSED IN THIS CHAPTER

Each chapter highlights the most salient codes that address the ethical dilemmas presented. The American School Counselor Association's Ethical Standards for School Counselors (ASCA, 2004) and the American Counseling Association's Code of Ethics and Standards of Practice (ACA, 2005) provide direction to school counselors for answering the cases by applying the ethical codes. Discussion will also include reference to ethical codes, interpretations and practices formulated and promulgated by other professional organizations. However, the emphasis is on how to apply the ASCA and ACA codes to the resolution of cases.

GETTING STARTED: WHAT WOULD YOU DO?

This section presents an ethical dilemma to be answered at the end of the chapter by a practicing school counselor, administrator or community member who has a special interest, understanding or experience. The intent is to generate interest and excitement for the material you are about to read and to have you develop your own resolution to the case before seeing how a colleague chooses to answer it.

WORKING THROUGH CASE STUDIES

The case studies are the heart of each chapter. In five or more case studies, this section presents common daily dilemmas school counselors face, as well as a few obscure legal and ethical pitfalls. We will also look at some cases whose answer can be found in the law. We will consider the Constitution, statutes, regulatory law and case law. We will talk about some cases where counselors have been found negligent under civil liability. Some of the cases presented will have both a legal and an ethical dilemma. The cases in the upcoming chapters are designed to challenge you and make you uncomfortable as you wrestle with problems that defy easy answers.

POINTS TO CONSIDER

Following each case presented, this section gathers court cases and legislation that impact the answer and allows you to apply some of the principles of ethics or law in context. This section does not offer a black-and-white, right-or-wrong, concrete answer.

IN A POSITION TO KNOW: A SCHOOL COUNSELOR SPEAKS

This section provides you with a response from a practicing school counselor or someone who is in a position to know and understand how to approach the case in "Getting Started: What Would You Do?" School counselors, administrators or community members respond to the case based on their own personal and professional experience.

MAKING CONNECTIONS

These questions give you an opportunity to extend your learning as you consider five to eight questions posed to help you apply what you learned in the chapter.

KEY TERMS

This section identifies the key terms and phrases used in the chapter, giving you a chance to review your understanding and reflect on what you learned.

REFERENCES

Each chapter carries a reference list of sources used within it.

Table of Contents

CHAPTER 1

Introduction to Legal and Ethical Issues

IN THIS CHAPTER

Objectives

By the time you have completed this chapter, you should be able to:

- Define the difference between laws and ethics.
- Apply the ethics of the school counseling profession.
- Describe 13 of the most complicating factors of working with minors in schools.
- Understand the courts' stance toward parental rights to guiding their children.

Introduction

A working knowledge of the ethical standards and codes of our counseling profession enables us to develop an understanding of what are considered the norms, customs and practices of the ethical counselor. An understanding of laws, elements of negligence, and principles established by courts informs us as to the implications and consequences of our work with minors in school settings. An ability to reason ethically and to understand tenets of laws governing the school counselor's work affords us a greater comfort level with the ambiguous and situational dilemmas that are part of our profession. We hope this book will guide school counselors toward strategies for handling the ethical and legal dilemmas that are a daily part of life.

The intent of this book is not to leave you with the "answers," but to equip you with a working knowledge of certain principles of law and standards of ethical practice you can apply. By raising awareness, professional school counselors reduce their risk of backlash and develop a tolerance for ambiguity. Simple dogmatic solutions are seldom in the best interest of students, whose personal histories, developmental stages, family situations and problem-solving abilities are as complex as their conflicts. We will begin to appreciate the value of considering each ethical or legal dilemma in context.

Law and Ethics

The concepts we call *law* and *ethics* are ambiguous and contextual by nature. They seldom provide us with black-and-white answers, nor should they. As frustrating as it may be for counselors caught in a conundrum, there is always room for interpretation in each situation.

The U.S. Constitution, federal and state statutes, and regulatory and case laws are based on precedence or common law. Common law is judge-made law. This type of law is based on legal precedents developed over hundreds of years. Common law also has been referred to as the "body of general rules prescribing social conduct" (Alexander & Alexander, 2005). Because it is not written by elected politicians but by judges, it can be referred to as "unwritten" law.

Common law often contrasts with civil law systems that require all laws to be written down in a code. Judges look for prior cases that have similar law and facts to the case at hand – precedents – and render a judgment consistent with prior case law (A. Colvin, Esq., personal communication, January 12, 2005; Alexander & Alexander, 2005; Duhaime's Online Legal Dictionary, 2005).

The purpose of law is to codify a value or set of values. Law is the minimum standard society will tolerate. However, in our legal system, laws and their interpretation differ from one geographic location to another (Alexander & Alexander, 2005).

Ethics are agreed-upon values, norms, customs and mores that have withstood the test of time (Fischer & Sorenson, 1996). Ethical codes and behavior are the result of values within a profession or organization and bind those who, by membership, ascribe to them. Ethics provide a general framework for professional conduct. An ethical dilemma is not a clear-cut breach of the law, but a muddy situation from which positive or negative consequences can result, depending on how the problem is handled.

An ethical decision-making model empowers school counselors to make the best choices as they become more comfortable with ethical and legal ambiguity (Remley & Herlihy, 2005).

Cases presented throughout this book have both legal and ethical origins, specifically as regards the ethics of professionalism and confidentiality. Professionalism is the internal motivation to perform at the level of practice that represents the ideals of the profession (Remley & Herlihy, 2005). Confidentiality issues can have both legal and ethical implications. For example, a state statute may require confidentiality but cite exceptions that render the issue an ethical one. Conflicts between the law and ethics are not uncommon. In conflict, the law takes priority for school counselors. Remember, every decision a school counselor makes hinges on the context of a situation and deserves examination from multiple perspectives.

It is essential to keep in mind that school counselors do not practice in a protective bubble. Even our most well-founded and researched interventions can have unintended consequences (W. Bridges, Esq., personal communication, January 17, 2000). A thorough knowledge of the laws, ethical codes, school board policies and prevailing community standards arms the professional school counselor with tools to make difficult decisions. This book endeavors to help present and future school counselors become practitioners who not only accept risk but are willing to take steps to reduce it.

The Complications of Working with Minors in a School Setting

The legal and ethical complications of any human service profession are daunting; working with clients who are minors in a setting designed for academics only adds to the complexity. On any given day, a school counselor may navigate such charged, delicate subjects as abortion, harassment or suicide. In addition, the school counselor's influence extends well beyond the student to include parents, teachers, administrators, the school district and the community. Throw in legal and ethical complications and when all these elements converge, school counseling can feel like walking a tightrope in a hurricane.

It might help to remember the acronym COMPLICATIONS as it applies to the difficulties school counselors face. The acronym will remind you of the following 13 factors that bear on your work in the legally and ethically complicated setting of schools, with clients who are minor students.

Counselor's Values
Obligations Beyond the Student
Minors' Developmental and Chronological Levels
Privacy Rights of Minors
Legal Status of Minors
In Loco Parentis
Community and Institutional Standards
Academic Instruction
Trusting Relationship
Informed Consent
Opacity of Laws and Ethical Codes
Number of Student-Clients
Standard of Care

COUNSELOR'S VALUES

We are our values; we can't simply leave them at the schoolhouse door. However, professional school counselors are aware of the value-laden issues that sabotage objectivity, and they take proper steps to avoid those situations. For example, if a school counselor is vehemently opposed to abortion, he or she recognizes this personal bias and refers a student who is seeking help to another professional. It is unethical to impose our values on students; instead, our ethical imperative guides us to promote students' autonomy (Stone, 2001).

OBLIGATIONS BEYOND THE STUDENT

We owe our students a trusting relationship. The ASCA Ethical Standards dictate that school counselors have a primary obligation and loyalty to students. Yet, we also have an obligation to parents, teachers, administrators, the school district and the community. School counselors respect students' confidences and balance the rights of minors with the rights of their parents. Knowing when to invoke confidentiality at the expense of a parent's right to know is a daily struggle.

Our courts are continually vesting parents with legal rights to guide their children (*Bellotti v. Baird*, 1979; *H. L. v. Matheson*, 1981). In H. L. v. Matheson, the U.S. Supreme Court said "constitutional interpretation has consistently recognized that the parents' claim to authority in their own household to direct the rearing of their children is basic in the structure of our society." The Supreme Court emphasized that there are three reasons parents are the guiding voices in their children's lives:

- The peculiar vulnerability of minors to make life-altering decisions
- A minor's inability to make informed, competent decisions, particularly under emotional stress, and
- The concept that parents are the guiding voice in their child's life.

In *Quilloin v. Walcott* (1978), the Court expanded on this theme, "We have recognized on numerous occasions that the relationship between parent and child is constitutionally protected. See, e.g., *Wisconsin v. Yoder*, 406 U.S. 205, 231-233 [**1172] (1972); Stanley v. Illinois, [405 U.S. 645 (1972)]; *Meyer v. Nebraska*, 262 U.S. 390, 399-401 (1923). It is cardinal with us that the custody, care and nurture of the child reside first in the parents, whose primary function and freedom include preparation for obligations the state can neither supply nor hinder."

We have recognized that parents have an important "guiding role" to play in their children's upbringing, which presumptively includes counseling them on important decisions (*Bellotti* II, supra, at 633-639).

The desires, expectations and wishes of parents with regard to the welfare of their children can be varied and diffused, complicating our work. There may be no country in the world more intent than the United States on giving parents respect and legal latitude with regard to the care and upbringing of their children. The legal and ethical ramifications of this concept take on greater importance in those situations in which school counselors have to weigh the privacy rights of minors with parents' Supreme Court-given right to be the preeminent voice in their children's lives.

MINORS' DEVELOPMENTAL AND CHRONOLOGICAL LEVELS

The competency and developmental levels of minors cannot be attached neatly to a chronological age. Not all seventh-graders, for example, will behave the same way in the same situation. These middle schoolers may present themselves developmentally as mature 13-year-olds one day only to surprise us the next day with behavior typical of 9-year-olds. School counselors' sensitivity to the unique and holistic picture of each student is an important consideration when dealing with the ambiguities of legal and ethical issues.

PRIVACY RIGHTS OF MINORS

The privacy rights of minors belong to the student's parents or guardians. Our guidance for this is found in Family Education Rights and Privacy Act (FERPA, 1974) and the Health Insurance Portability and Accountability Act (HIPAA, 1996), two federal statutes. The parent, not the student, makes critical decisions about disclosure of personal information. Parents have the final word on who will know about certain details of their child's medical conditions, such as HIV-positive status.

LEGAL STATUS OF MINORS

The legal status of minors is difficult to define. A minor is generally defined as someone younger than 18. All minors share the legal characteristic that they are unable to make decisions on their own behalf. Minors are "a group of individuals with few responsibilities, many restrictions, and a complex legal status that maintains a dependency on adults for privilege and access to resources" (Sanger & Willemsen, 1992). Unemancipated teen-agers, even when living independently, cannot consent, rent or borrow, and still can be apprehended by police as runaways (Sanger & Willemsen, 1992).

The age a student can drive, marry and be held to contracts differs among states. Salo and Shumate (1993) in the American Counseling Association Legal Series defined juvenile and tort law as one of the difficulties of working with minors, because we are unable to rely on clearly stated principles of legal policy to guide us.

When in a secondary school setting a student turns 18 and becomes an adult, this student is not yet completely emancipated if he or she is still a dependent as defined under the federal income tax code. For example, even though adult students are now considered eligible to access their own educational records under FERPA, the parents also still have access to their children's educational records.

IN LOCO PARENTIS

Another complication of working with minors in a school setting is the interpretation of the common-law doctrine in loco parentis, which at times allows school personnel to act in place of the parent. Common-law thinking on this issue has prevailed for many years. There is a long history of recognizing that educators must be able to address the diversity of expectations placed on them and have sufficient control over the decorum and climate of the school to ensure that learning can take place (*Burpee v. Burton*, 1878).

"Inherent in this thinking is the necessity that educators, by virtue of their positions, have the authority to govern school in a reasonable and humane manner. {G}eneral education and control of pupils who attend public schools are in the hands of school boards, superintendents, principals, and teachers and [school counselors]. This control extends to health, proper surroundings, necessary discipline, promotion of morality and other wholesome influences, while parental authority is temporarily superseded" (*Richardson v. Braham*, 1933). Educators have an ethical obligation to promote harmony in the school while simultaneously advancing and protecting students' interests.

Though "*in loco parentis*" translated to English means "in place of the parent," the courts never intended that school authorities, teachers, or school counselors would fully stand in place of the parent in relationship to their children (Alexander & Alexander, 2005). The courts have recognized that although children's legal status is not identical to that of adults, they nonetheless are entitled to constitutional protection. Students also have an obligation to follow the laws and school rules, assume responsibilities, and follow the commands of school authorities (Imber & Van Geel, 2004). Current thinking suggests it may be more appropriate to view the school as an extension of the state rather than as a substitute parent (Imber & Van Geel, 2004).

Constitutional law that bears on the interests of students and protects their First and Fourth Amendment rights also reiterates the importance of *in loco parentis* in protecting children, and charges school personnel with the responsibility to protect the rights of the child when the child is in their care, control and protection. The Supreme Court, in *Bethel School District No. 403 v. Fraser* (1986), also reminded us of our obligation to protect children "from exposure to sexually explicit, indecent, or lewd speech." The school counselor owes a special duty to exercise reasonable care to protect a student from harm and intervene if necessary (Stone, 2001). *In loco parentis* is also explored in the two chapters on "Negligence" and "Obligations to the Courts."

COMMUNITY AND INSTITUTIONAL STANDARDS

As difficult as it may be to accept, ethics are situational. Your ethical behavior is determined in large part by your school's location.The prevailing community and institutional standards dictate to a large degree what school counselors can do and remain ethical.

We cry out, "The support we give students should not depend on the values of the community!" We fight against the notion of treating students differently based on their ZIP code. As much as it might bother us, we have to know and be respectful of the wishes of the community in which we work. In some communities the school counselor has the freedom to direct a student to a health clinic for contraceptives or recruit for a support group for gay/lesbian/bisexual/transgender students. In other areas of the country these activities are considered a breach of ethics and cross the line of community or institutional standards (Stone, 2001). Court cases have demonstrated that community standards often become the ultimate legal criteria to govern the outcome of a case. This does not mean, however, that we sit idly by and accept the status quo.

School counselors behave as change agents when community and institutional standards of behavior limit students' opportunities, at which point our ethical standards and codes give us a directive to act responsibly to try and change policies and practices that impede student success (ASCA, 2004). The message here is to understand the prevailing written and unwritten standards of the community, school district and individual work site, and to behave consistently within the parameters of those standards while working responsibly to change the ones that are detrimental to students.

When determining community standards, ask questions of everyone in the school's internal and external communities. Are you in an ultra-conservative part of the world, a bastion of liberalism, a solid middle-class suburb or an urban setting? Ask about hypothetical and real cases and what the prevailing standard would be for handling sensitive, value-laden cases. Counselors have to understand what threads comprise the community's fabric to discern how to behave ethically in a particular environment. Would you be able to encourage a student to go to a neighborhood health clinic if she tells you she is pregnant? It is important to have a feel for the local level of tolerance for school involvement in value-laden issues.

ACADEMIC INSTRUCTION

The setting in which school counselors work defines the student-school counselor relationship. School counselors work in a setting designed for academic instruction. Because we are not in a formal counseling setting as are our colleagues in private or agency practice, school counselors interact with students virtually everywhere from the bus loading zone to the privacy of their counseling offices. "For the purposes of the law, do these interactions constitute a counseling session …? No cases give us authoritative guidance on this matter" (Fischer & Sorenson, 1996, p. 18).

TRUSTING RELATIONSHIP

The school counselor must provide a safe and secure environment in which trust can be established and maintained. Without the assurance of confidentiality, many students would not seek help. Counselors must keep confidential information related to counseling services unless disclosure is in the best interest of students or is required by law (Fischer & Sorenson, 1996; Isaacs & Stone, 1999; Kaplan, 1996; Remley & Herlihy, 2001; Salo & Shumate, 1993).

INFORMED CONSENT

The ASCA Ethical Standards (2004) tell us that at the beginning of the counseling session, the professional school counselor must tell students in terms they can understand about the limits of their confidentiality so that students can decide if they want to participate in the counseling session. The counselee thus chooses to enter the counseling relationship fully aware of the purposes, goals, techniques and rules of procedure under which he or she may receive counseling – a process known as informed consent (Lee & Ekstrom, 1987). Counselors are obligated to keep confidences except when the student is a danger to self or others; child abuse is suspected; the student or parent requests that information be revealed; or a court orders a counselor to disclose the information.

OPACITY OF LAWS AND ETHICAL CODES

The multifaceted nature of working with minors in schools makes it difficult to develop law, ethical codes, written school board policies or procedures that cover all the potential situations school counselors might face. For example, laws that address malpractice, negligence and student privacy rights are complex (Levick, 2000). Laws often are defined case by case. Federal courts in each state can interpret the same law in different ways, and the interpretation will remain unresolved until a higher court can hear the matter – if ever. Although there is some legal guidance to be found in education law, state department regulations and local school board policy, school counselors often must practice in the absence of clear-cut guidelines.

NUMBER OF STUDENT-CLIENTS

The very nature of our role as school counselors impacts our legal and ethical obligations. As leaders, advocates and change agents, we are charged with reaching every student, but the multiplicity of our role and the obligations we have to so many students considerably reduce the amount of support we can give to each student; the extent to which we can document what we have done; and the effort we can undertake to see to each and every child's individual needs. Caseloads do not spell the difference between a counselor who behaves professionally, ethically and legally and one who does not; however, caseloads influence the thoroughness school counselors devote to each case. In its annual report, ACA's Office of Public Policy and Legislation showed an increase in the current U.S. student-to-counselor ratio of 478:1. Eighteen states showed a decrease in the number of counselors available to students (ACA, 2005).

STANDARD OF CARE

Standard of care is defined as what the reasonably competent professional would do. Negligence cases are founded on the assumption that the standard of care delivered by the professional was inadequate. If you find yourself in legal hot water, your attorney will want to demonstrate that you behaved as any other person in your profession would have. The following criteria are just a few types of information your legal counsel will gather to show that you behaved within the standard of care for your profession:

- Laws
- Ethical codes
- School board policy
- Case law
- Expert witnesses
- Length of career
- Professional development such as in-service training, professional conference attendance, and books and publications read.

Standard of care is explained more fully in the chapter, "Obligations to the Courts."

Ethical Codes

The American School Counselor Association's Ethical Standards for School Counselors (2004) is an attempt by the profession to standardize professional practice for the purpose of protecting students, parents and school counselors. The Ethical Standards are a guide to help us meet the needs of individual situations but seldom are appropriate for rote application. Appropriate application of the codes is content-specific. Only the school counselor, in consultation with other professionals, can determine how to apply an ASCA standard to further the student's best interest. Codes are guides or frameworks that require professional judgment in context to make each standard meaningful; they are not intended to provide answers, but are meant to guide.

ASCA ETHICAL STANDARDS FOR SCHOOL COUNSELORS

At a glance, here are the basic concepts found in the ASCA Ethical Standards for School Counselors (2004):

Standard A.1 discusses the responsibilities to students. This standard enumerates obligations to respect students and their values, to encourage students, and to be knowledgable of appropriate laws and policies regarding students.

Standard A.2 explores confidentiality and its limits. Although school counselors try to maintain confidentiality at all costs, there may be times when it must be breached, as in cases of potential suicide or risk of harm to another person. This standard also discusses the school counselor's responsibility in legal matters such as breaching confidentiality when required by a court order. Finally, school counselors must also balance the need to maintain confidentiality with their students against the right of parents to be involved in all aspects of their children's lives.

Standard A.3 concerns counseling plans and implementation of a school counseling program that is comprehensive and supports students' choices for a wide variety of postsecondary education options.

Standard A.4 is about dual relationships. Under this standard, counselors have the responsibility to remove themselves from dual relationships situations or proceed with extreme caution when such a relationship is unavoidable. This standard also addresses counselors' dual relationships with other school personnel that might harm the counselor-student relationship.

Standard A.5 addresses appropriate referral of students and parents to outside professionals and guides school counselors in the proper referral process.

Standard A.6 deals with group work. This standard guides the school counseling professional who works with students in groups and defines the selection, notification of parents (if necessary) and expectations of confidentiality for students in this setting.

Standard A.7 discusses the school counselor's responsibilities when students are a danger to themselves or others. These situations almost always require a breach of confidentiality, and this standard helps counselors seek to maintain the highest level of trust and confidence possible with the student in spite of the breach.

Standard A.8 covers the issues of records, both educational and sole-possession records, and gives the school counselor guidance about the disposition of sole-possession records.

Standard A.9 deals with the use of assessment instruments and the counselor's role in their administration, interpretation and use.

Standard A.10 is concerned with the appropriate use of technology.

Standard A.11 concerns the unique responsibilities school counselors have to students involved in peer-to-peer programs.

Standard B.1 requires that the school counselor respect the inherent rights and responsibilities of parents for their children and endeavors to establish, as appropriate, a collaborative relationship with parents to facilitate the counselee's maximum development. School counselors must be sensitive to cultural and social diversity among families and recognize that all parents, custodial and noncustodial, are vested with certain rights and responsibilities for the welfare of their children by virtue of their role and according to law.

Standard B.2 instructs school counselors to (1) inform parents of the counselor's role with emphasis on the confidential nature of the counseling relationship between counselor and counselee; (2) provide parents with accurate, comprehensive and relevant information in an objective and caring manner as is appropriate and consistent with ethical responsibilities to the counselee; and (3) make reasonable efforts to honor the wishes of parents and guardians concerning information that the counselor may share regarding the counselee.

Standards B through G are respectively: Responsibilities to Parents/Guardians; Responsibilities to Colleagues and Professional Associates; Responsibilities to the School and Community; Responsibilities to Self; Responsibilities to the Profession; and Maintenance of Standards. This last section discusses procedures to rectify situations with individuals or groups that are in conflict with the ethical standards.

The standards demonstrate the scope and depth of the role of counselor to school personnel, parents and students. Members and nonmembers of the American School Counselor Association can find a great deal of information about professional behavior by carefully reading the standards. Furthermore, professionals in schools can use the standards to improve effectiveness, avoid ethical problems and escape legal entanglements.

The ASCA Ethical Standards guide school counselors in their ethical responsibility to students and parents but do not attempt to provide complete answers. Ethics are situational and must be considered in context of institutional and community standards, school board policy and individual circumstances. Ultimately, the school counselor has the responsibility to determine the appropriate response for individual students who put their trust in the security of the counseling relationship (Stone & Isaacs, 2002).

Ethical Decision Making

Even more so than laws, ethical codes and standards are open to interpretation. Different professionals may implement varying courses of action in the same situation; there seldom is one right answer to a complex ethical dilemma. However, if you follow a systematic model, you can be assured that you will be able to provide a professional explanation for the course of action you chose. Van Hoose and Paradise (1979) suggest that a counselor "is probably acting in an ethically responsible way concerning a client if (1) he or she has maintained personal and professional honesty, coupled with (2) the best interests of the client, (3) without malice or personal gain, and (4) can justify his or her actions as the best judgment of what should be done based upon the current state of the profession" (p. 58). Following this model will help ensure that all four of these conditions have been met.

FIVE MORAL PRINCIPLES

School counselors need to develop sound ethical decision-making skills. Kitchener's (1984) five moral principles can serve as a guide to ethical decision making:

- *Autonomy* refers to promoting students' ability to choose their own direction. The school counselor makes every effort to foster maximum self-determination on the part of students.

- *Beneficence* refers to promoting good for others. Ideally, counseling contributes to the growth and development of the student, and whatever counselors do should be judged against this criterion.

- *Nonmaleficence* means avoiding doing harm, which includes refraining from actions that risk hurting students.

- *Justice, or fairness*, refers to providing equal treatment to all people. This standard implies that anyone – regardless of age, sex, race, ethnicity, disability, socioeconomic status, cultural background, religion or sexual orientation – is entitled to equal treatment.

■ *Loyalty, or fidelity*, refers to staying connected with your students and being available to them to the extent possible. School counselors often carry heavy caseloads, and loyalty takes on a different dimension in the school setting than at an agency. Loyalty for the school counselor does not necessarily mean 50-minute sessions once a week with students. Staying loyal may include connecting with students by encouraging them to stop by before and after school, visiting them at the bus-loading zone or briefly visiting their classrooms.

School counselors are confronted daily with ethical dilemmas that require the counselor to skillfully – and usually quickly – decide on an appropriate course of action. An ethical decision-making model for school counselors must give special consideration to the complicated and multifaceted work associated with minors and allow for the fact that our work setting is not intended primarily for individual therapy but for academic instruction.

ACA PRACTITIONER'S GUIDE TO ETHICAL DECISION MAKING

The American Counseling Association published A Practitioner's Guide to Ethical Decision Making (Forrester-Miller & Davis, 1996). The model presents a framework for sound ethical decision making and incorporates the work of Van Hoose and Paradise (1979), Kitchener (1984), Stadler (1986), Haas and Malouf (1989), Forester-Miller and Rubenstein (1992), and Sileo and Kopala (1993). The practical, sequential seven-step model has served counselors in all settings. Following the seven steps in this model, a counselor would:

■ Identify the problem.
■ Apply the American Counseling Association's Code of Ethics and Standards of Practice (2005).
■ Determine the nature and dimensions of the dilemma.
■ Generate potential courses of action.
■ Considering the potential consequences of all options, choose a course of action.
■ Evaluate the selected course of action.
■ Implement the course of action.

THE STEPS MODEL FOR SCHOOL SETTINGS

Stone furthered the ACA model by addressing the unique circumstances for counselors working in a school setting. STEPS, an acronym for

Solutions To Ethical Problems in Schools (Stone, 2001), adapts the seven steps in the ACA model and extends the conceptual and contextual applications. A nine-step model, STEPS addresses the emotional influences of a problem and considers chronological and developmental appropriateness as well as parental rights.

STEPS helps school counselors negotiate the nuances of ethical dilemmas arising within an environment significantly different from those found in agency, community, private, or hospital counseling settings. Counseling is another matter altogether when you primarily serve minors mandated by law to be in attendance in an environment designed for academic instruction.

Following are the nine steps in the STEPS model. Although the model is presented sequentially here, ethical decision making seldom follows a sequential, lock-step approach in practice.

1. Define the Problem Emotionally and Intellectually
How do your emotions define this problem (your initial reaction)? What does your heart tell you should happen in this case? File this initial reaction away for later reference.

How does your intellect define the problem unemotionally, objectively? What are the facts? Separate the hearsay, but remember rumors often inform.

It is important to acknowledge our first reaction to the problem. When a student in need comes through the door crying and in pain, our initial reaction generally is, "What can I do to help this student?" Our emotional reaction and supportive instincts are important because they help us protect our students' confidences. Because we care about our students, we don't want to discard the emotional reaction, but use it to guide us along with a healthy combination of reason and judgment.

In defining the problem, school counselors are careful not to act on emotion without considering the other ethical decision-making steps. Make the necessary effort to gather the facts while weeding out innuendoes, rumors, hearsay and hypotheses. Remember, however, that in school settings we cannot rule out hearsay or rumors, as they are often a source for school counselors to discover the truth about situations involving their students.

2. Apply the ASCA and ACA Ethical Codes and the Law
Ask yourself whether your code of ethics or the law offers a possible solution to the problem. Ethical dilemmas are often complex, and we will not

usually find a definitive answer in the codes or laws. The very nature of an ethical dilemma means there is more than one acceptable answer, so we must apply good judgment by proceeding with all steps of the ethical decision-making model and paying careful attention to steps 6 and 8, which emphasize seeking consultation supervision.

3. Consider the Students' Chronological and Developmental Levels
How does the student's developmental level impact the dilemma and how you will approach it? This step is critical, yet it has been left out of decision-making models. A child's age, and the ability to show that he or she can make informed decisions, matters. Also, school counselors must remember that the younger and more immature the child, the greater our responsibility is to the parents or guardians.

4. Consider the Setting, Parental Rights and Minors' Rights
You must consider the rights of parents to be the guiding voice in their children's lives, especially in value-laden decisions. You must also honor parents' rights to be informed and involved when their children are in harm's way. Clear and imminent danger can take many forms.

Furthermore, you must consider the dilemma in the context of the school setting. Ethical dilemmas in a school take on a different meaning from ethical issues in other contexts. Students come to school for academic instruction, and when they enter into the personal or emotional arena we cannot dismiss that this will carry obligations to other educators and to parents.

5. Apply the Moral Principles
Consider the basic moral principles of autonomy, beneficence, nonmaleficence, justice and loyalty (Kitchener, 1984) and apply them to the situation. It may help to prioritize these principles and think through ways in which they can support a resolution.

Decide which principles apply and determine which principle takes priority for you in this case. In theory, each principle is of equal value, which means it is your challenge to determine the priorities when two or more of them conflict. Review the relevant professional literature to ensure that you are using the most current professional thinking in reaching a decision.

6. Determine Your Potential Courses of Action and Their Consequences
Brainstorm possible solutions. Be creative. Try to enlist the assistance of at least one colleague to help you generate options. Consider probable courses of action, write down the options and discuss them with another per-

son if you can. Examine the consequences of various decisions. Ponder the implications of each course of action for the student, for the school district, for others who might be affected, and for you. List the good and bad consequences of each decision.

7. Evaluate the Selected Action
Considering the information you have gathered and the priorities you have set, evaluate each option and assess the potential consequences for all the parties involved. Eliminate the options that clearly do not give desired results or cause even more problematic consequences. Then decide which combination of options best fits the situation and addresses the priorities you have identified.

Review the selected course of action to see if it presents any new ethical considerations. Stadler (1986) suggests applying three simple tests to ensure the decision is appropriate. In applying the test of justice, assess your own sense of fairness by determining if you would treat others in this situation the same way. For the test of publicity, ask yourself if you would want your behavior reported in the press. The test of universality asks you to assess whether you could recommend the same course of action to another counselor in the same situation (Forrester-Miller & Davis, 1996).

If the course of action you have selected seems to present new ethical issues, then you'll need to go back to the beginning and re-evaluate each step. Perhaps you have chosen the wrong option or identified the problem incorrectly (ACA, 2004).

If you can answer in the affirmative to each of the questions suggested by Stadler – thus passing the tests of justice, publicity and universality – and you are satisfied you have selected an appropriate course of action, then you are ready to move on to implementation (Forrester-Miller & Davis, 1996).

8. Consult
Discuss your case with an experienced fellow professional, preferably a supervisor, to help you illuminate the issues. As your colleague reviews the information with you, he or she may see other relevant issues, offer a new perspective, or identify aspects of the dilemma you are not viewing objectively. Consult your state or national professional associations to see if they can help.

When caught in an ethical dilemma it is sometimes difficult to see all the issues clearly. School counselors must often do their ethical problem solving on the run; it is not always feasible for school counselors to close their office doors, sit with paper and pencil, and follow the ethical decision-making model. Consultation, if at all possible, is one step that you should never skip (Stone, 2001).

In fact, consulting is such a critical part of ethical behavior that you should routinely and confidentially consult with a network of professionals when difficult situations arise. School counselors need to be constant consumers of legal and ethical information by seeking the counsel of colleagues, administrators, supervisors and school attorneys. When you routinely consult with other professionals, you will find the complexity of the legal and ethical world less daunting. More importantly, consultation can help counselors provide increased safety and security for students.

9. Implement the Course of Action
Go forward with your decision after you have considered the previous steps. Regardless of your decision there will be risk, but you will have made the best decision based on the advice and information you had at the time. School counselors cannot practice risk free, but we can reduce our risk and raise our support for students by using ethical reasoning.

You may find taking the final step in the ethical model disconcerting. In a real-life ethical dilemma the final step never will be easy, but by strengthening your confidence through continuous professional development you will find it easier to carry out your plans. After implementing your course of action, it is good practice to follow up on the situation to assess whether your actions had the anticipated effect.

Making Connections

1. Discuss your opinion of the premise that a thorough knowledge of the laws, ethical codes, school board policies and prevailing community standards better prepares the professional school counselor to make tough decisions.

2. Why is the school counselor's job so much more difficult legally and ethically than that of fellow counselors in agency and private settings?

3. Discuss how you as a school counselor have an ethical imperative to promote the autonomy of your minor students.

4. Discuss each of the points that the courts stress as reasons children's rights are not the same as adults' rights:
   ■ The peculiar vulnerability of minors to make life-altering decisions

- A minor's inability to make informed, competent decisions, particularly under emotional stress, and
- The concept that parents are the guiding voice in their child's life.

5. Why is it impossible to develop laws, ethical codes, written school board policies, or procedures that cover all the potential situations school counselors might face? How should we proceed, in light of the fact that we cannot always find guidance in laws, codes or policies for all the situations we face?

Key Terms

Dogmatic solutions
Common law
Precedents
Tolerance for ambiguity
Laws
Ethics
Federal statutes
State statutes
Common law
Civil law
Counselors' values
Developmental levels
Chronological levels
Privacy rights
Legal status
Community standards
Institutional standards
Informed consent

Standard of care
Personal bias
Opacity of law
School board policy
Case law
Expert witnesses
Vested with rights
STEPS
Moral principles
Autonomy
Beneficence
Nonmaleficence
Justice
Loyalty
Potential courses of action
Consequences

References

American Counseling Association. (2005). *Code of ethics and standards of practice.* Retrieved February 21, 2005, from http://www.counseling.org/ Content/NavigationMenu/RESOURCES/ETHICS/ACA_Code_of_Ethics.pdf

American Counseling Association. (2005). *United States student-to-counselor ratios.* Retrieved February 21, 2005, from http://www.counseling.org/ Content/NavigationMenu/publicpolicy/resourcesforcounselors/ACA_Ratio_ Chart_03-04.pdf

American School Counselor Association. (2004). *Ethical standards for school counselors.* Alexandria, VA: Author.

Alexander, K., & Alexander, M. D. (2005). *American public school law* (6th ed.). Belmont, CA: Thomson West.

Bellotti v. Baird, 443 U.S. 622 (1979).

Bethel School District No. 403 v. Fraser, 478 U.S. 675, 106 S. Ct. 3159 (1986).

Burpee v. Burton, 45 Wis. 150, 30 Am. Rep. 706 (1878).

Duhaime's Online Legal Dictionary. (n.d.). Retrieved January 13, 2005, from http://www.duhaime.org/dictionary/dict-c.aspx

Family Educational Rights and Privacy Act, 20 U.S.C.§1232g (1974).

Fischer, L., & Sorenson, G. P. (1996). *School law for counselors, psychologists, and social workers* (3rd ed.). White Plains, NY: Longman.

Forester-Miller, H., & Davis, T. (1996). *A practitioner's guide to ethical decision making.* Alexandria, VA: American Counseling Association. Retrieved February 21, 2005, from http://www.counseling.org/Content/NavigationMenu/RESOURCES/ETHICS/APractitionersGuidetoEthicalDecisionMaking/Practitioner_s_Guide.htm

Forester-Miller, H., & Rubenstein, R. L. (1992). *Group counseling: Ethics and professional issues.* In D. Capuzzi & D. R. Gross (Eds.), Introduction to group counseling (pp. 307-323). Denver, CO: Love Publishing Co.

H. L. v. Matheson, 450 U.S. 398 (1981).

Haas, L. J., & Malouf, J. L. (1989). *Keeping up the good work: A practitioner's guide to mental health ethics.* Sarasota, FL: Professional Resource Exchange, Inc.

Health Insurance Portability and Accountability Act of 1996, 45 C.F.R. 164.530. Retrieved November 30, 2004, from http://www.hhs.gov/ocr/hipaa

Imber, M., & Van Geel, T. (2004). *Education law* (3rd ed.). Mahway, NJ: Erlbaum.

Isaacs, M. L., & Stone, C. (1999). School counselors and confidentiality: Factors affecting professional choices. *The Professional School Counselor*, 2, 258-266.

Kaplan, L. (1996). Outrageous or legitimate concerns: What some parents are saying about school counseling. *The School Counselor*, 43, 165-170.

Kitchener, K. S. (1984). Intuition, critical evaluation and ethical principles: The foundation for ethical decisions in counseling psychology. *Counseling Psychologist*, 12(3), 43-55.

Lee, V. E., & Ekstrom, R. B. (1987). Student access to guidance counseling in high school. *American Educational Research Journal*, 24, 287-310.

Levick, M. (2000). Privacy rights of minors. In F. W. Kaslow (Ed.), *Handbook of couple and family forensics: A source book for mental health and legal professionals* (pp. 105-119). New York: John Wiley & Sons.

Meyer v. Nebraska, 262 U.S. 390, 399-401 (1923).

Quilloin v. Walcott, 434 U.S. 246 (1978).

Remley, T. P., Jr., & Herlihy, B. (2001). *Ethical, legal, and professional issues in counseling*. Upper Saddle River, NJ: Merrill Prentice Hall.

Remley, T. P., Jr., & Herlihy, B. (2005). *Ethical, legal, and professional issues in counseling* (2nd ed.). Upper Saddle River, NJ: Merrill Prentice Hall.

Richardson v. Braham, 125 Neb. 142, 249 N.W. 557 (1933).

Salo, M. M., & Shumate, S. G. (1993). Counseling minor clients. *The ACA Legal Series*, 4, 73-78.

Sanger, C., & Willemsen, E. (1992). Minor changes: Emancipating children in modern times. *University of Michigan Journal of Law Reform*, 25.

Sileo, F., & Kopala, M. (1993). An A-B-C-D-E worksheet for promoting beneficence when considering ethical issues. *Counseling and Values*, 37, 89-95.

Stadler, H. A. (1986). Making hard choices: Clarifying controversial ethical issues. *Counseling & Human Development*, 19, 1-10.

Stanley v. Illinois, 405 U.S. 645 (1972).

Stone, C. (Speaker). (2001). *Legal and ethical issues in working with minors in schools* [Film]. Alexandria, VA: American Counseling Association.

Stone, C., & Isaacs, M. (2002). Confidentiality with minors: The effects of Columbine on counselor attitudes regarding breaching confidentiality. *The Journal of Educational Research*, 96(2), 140-150.

Van Hoose, W. H., & Paradise, L. V. (1979). *Ethics in counseling and psychotherapy: Perspectives in issues and decision-making*. Cranston, RI: Carroll Press.

Wisconsin v. Yoder, 406 U.S. 205, 231-233 [**1172] (1972).

Professionalism

IN THIS CHAPTER

Objectives

By the time you have completed this chapter, you should be able to:

- Define professionalism.
- Define what professionalism means for your behavior, attitudes and beliefs.
- Identify standard of care and the behavior of the reasonably competent professional.
- Apply your ethical standards of behavior.
- Discuss how personal behavior impacts professional standing and determine when your personal behavior has crossed the line of professionalism.
- Reflect on your group membership and the additional responsibilities school counselors carry to be inclusive with all faculty and staff.
- Define professional competence and discuss how it should influence your behavior.
- Identify the difference between defamation and qualified privilege.
- Discuss dual relationships, professional distance, and how to protect students from possible harm that can result from dual relationships.

Introduction

Defining professions and the process of professionalization has long been a topic for numerous journal articles, with as many definitions of professionalism as there are journals. The core characteristics that distinguish the professions from other occupations are that professionals have special skills and competence in the application of knowledge, and that their behavior is guided by a code of ethics (Clark, 2003).

In this chapter we will help define professionalism for school counselors. We will look at the behavior, attitude, beliefs and philosophy of school counseling that shape professionalism, and how those forces are in play as school counselors manage their day-to-day functions.

The guiding principles of professionalism for school counselors are used to maintain a counselor's standing with his or her peers, teachers, staff members, administrators, parents and students. These principles are formed by adherence to local, state and federal laws; school board policy; ethical standards; and prevailing community standards.

The American School Counselor Association developed its Ethical Standards for School Counselors (ASCA, 2004b) to clarify the ethical responsibilities of its members to students, parents, colleagues, the profession, the community, and to themselves. Each counselor has the responsibility to become knowledgeable about the ethical standards and to understand them.

School counselors develop their principles of professional behavior through membership in organizations, continuing education through journals, and attendance at workshops and conferences. All school counselors are responsible for seeking professional development opportunities through conferences, regional meetings, district in-services, networking with peers, training sessions, reading and research. The latest research, techniques and knowledge will help school counselors protect their professionalism, remain current and serve students' needs.

Unprofessional behavior is usually handled through school districts' due process procedures, the courts, principals' annual evaluations of school counselors or other local procedures. Rarely are ethical violations brought to the ASCA Governing Board. However, ASCA has developed a means to revoke membership. The ASCA Membership Revocation document allows members to be expelled for reasons such as violation of the association's ethical standards or failure to pay membership dues. Further, ASCA's Governing Board can also revoke membership for "any other reason deemed…to be in the best interests of ASCA" (ASCA, 2004a, p. 1).

The process of membership revocation is straightforward. Individuals must submit in writing, along with the support of other ASCA members, a request to expel a member. The member in question has a right to remediate the situation within a specified period of time and the right to respond to the charges in person, including the option of questioning witnesses. The ASCA Governing Board must approve revocation of membership by a two-thirds majority, and the decision of the panel is considered final.

This chapter will discuss how to avoid conflicts with our professional organizations, school district or larger community. But more importantly, this chapter will help school counselors act in the best interest of their students. Here we will wrestle with the meaning of school counselors' professional conduct, and we will explore personal conduct and how it impacts our professional standing with fellow faculty members and our larger school community. At the heart of a number of case studies is the way we exercise professionalism in our consultation roles by safeguarding confidential information. We will discuss how professionalism intersects with preparation and competence, and how dual relationships with parents and students can compromise professionalism.

It would be impossible to address all the possible pitfalls and complications that can threaten professionalism, but this chapter will address many of the guiding principles of professional behavior essential for effective school counseling.

Ethical Standards Addressed in This Chapter

Professionalism means knowing your professional associations' codes and adhering to them. Those ethical standards from ASCA that are most germane include the following:

- The professional school counselor avoids dual relationships that might impair his/her objectivity and increase the risk of harm to the student (e.g., counseling one's family members, close friends or associates). If a dual relationship is unavoidable, the counselor is responsible for taking action to eliminate or reduce the potential for harm. Such safeguards might include informed consent, consultation, supervision and documentation. (A.4.a)
- The professional school counselor avoids dual relationships with school personnel that might infringe on the integrity of the counselor/student relationship. (A.4.b)
- The professional school counselor establishes and maintains professional relationships with faculty, staff and administration to facilitate an optimum counseling program. (C.1.a)
- The professional school counselor treats colleagues with professional respect, courtesy and fairness. The qualifications, views and findings of colleagues are represented to accurately reflect the image of competent professionals. (C.1.b)
- The professional school counselor is aware of and utilizes related professionals, organizations and other resources to whom the student may be referred. (C.1.c)
- If a student is receiving services from another counselor or other mental health professional, the counselor, with student and/or parent/guardian consent, will inform the other professional and develop clear agreements to avoid confusion and conflict for the student. (C.2.c)

- The professional school counselor advocates that administrators hire only qualified and competent individuals for professional counseling positions. (D.1.f)
- The professional school counselor monitors personal well-being and effectiveness and does not participate in any activity that may lead to inadequate professional services or harm to a student. (E.1.b)
- The professional school counselor conducts herself/himself in such a manner as to advance individual ethical practice and the profession. (F.1.b)
- The professional school counselor does not use his/her professional position to recruit or gain clients, consultees for his/her private practice or to seek and receive unjustified personal gains, unfair advantage, inappropriate relationships or unearned goods or services. (F.1.f)
- The professional school counselor contributes to the development of the profession through the sharing of skills, ideas and expertise with colleagues. (F.2.b)
- The professional school counselor provides support and mentoring to novice professionals. (F.2.c)

The full text of American Counseling Association and ASCA ethical codes can be found at these Web sites: ACA at http://www.counseling.org and ASCA at www.schoolcounselor.org.

Getting Started: What Would You Do?

The following case is answered at the end of this chapter by practicing school counselors. Before you read their responses, formulate in your own mind how you would approach this ethical dilemma.

GIFT TAKING

Dear School Counselor:
You are cordially invited to an all-expense-paid trip to Central University. Accommodations will be in a bed-and-breakfast. Activities will include golfing at a country club and a trip to the racetrack, and you will receive $50 for gambling at the horse races. The purpose of the trip is to familiarize you with our university. It is not our intent to unduly influence your college advising role or to seek an unfair advantage for our university. Our intention in having you visit our university is to see that you have a good time and to have you learn about our university so that you will be able to speak with firsthand knowledge about the fine programs we have

to offer your students. We still want you to provide students with trust-worthy, objective advice.
Sincerely,
Your College Admissions Representative

Is it unethical to receive perks with more than a token monetary value if you know the gifts are being offered to influence you? For elementary and middle school counselors, consider a parallel situation. Can you accept gifts from parents whom you know want to influence you to gain advantage for their child, such as placement with certain teachers?

Working Through Case Studies

PROFESSIONAL COMMUNICATION: QUALIFIED PRIVILEGE

Greg was not promoted to the ninth grade because he did "nothing all year," according to his eighth-grade teacher. His parents argue that he should be promoted because his failure to do work was the result of his disability (he has been diagnosed as mildly ADHD). Greg's parents, the principal, his teacher and you hold a joint conference. During the course of the conference, you explain to Greg's parents that he is "lazy and interested only in his social life." Greg's parents bring suit against the school district, and they also name you in the suit for defamation. How will the court rule on the defamation charge?

Points to Consider

Administrators and other educators may say unpleasant things about students, but only when it is necessary to fulfill their obligations to educate and care for students while student are in their charge (*in loco parentis*). A school counselor may say that a student is "lazy and failed because the student did not complete work." "Lazy" was not the best choice of words, but it was legally tolerable since this was, in the opinion of the counselor, a true statement based on her observations. When this counselor was named in a larger court case involving many other issues, the case was thrown out with due speed because, as educators, school counselors have qualified privilege, or the right to say things about students that are not flattering but necessary to fulfill their duties. In the course of doing your job, you may have to make unflattering statements, but do so only in the context of the situation at hand (Imber & Van Geel, 2004).

Let's extend the discussion of professionalism and the language school counselors use while doing their jobs. The counselor in the preceding case used the word "lazy" to describe a student. Although the court would uphold the counselor's right to use unflattering language, were the needs of the student addressed in the best way possible? To simplify, had the school counselor left out the word "lazy" during the meeting, might there have been a different outcome? Using terms like "lazy" can serve only to make parents and students defensive and angry.

Collaboration with parents cannot proceed effectively in a climate of hostility and defensiveness. Using "lazy" to describe the student might have been accurate and precise, but it might also have been construed as mean-spirited. The choice of words school counselors use can be powerful, positive or negative motivating factors. Failure to recognize the power of words in conveying difficult information diminishes opportunities for growth and moves people away from rather than toward good resolutions. When conveying difficult information, professional school counselors should choose their words judiciously in an effort to maintain optimal communication with parents and students.

PROFESSIONAL COMMUNICATION: SENSITIVE INFORMATION

You are aware that a student has been sexually abused. During a child study meeting in which Exceptional Student Education is being considered for Robert, you become convinced that it is in Robert's best interest if you reveal to the child study team that he was a victim of sexual abuse. His parents, who did not attend the child study team meeting, find out about this revelation and sue you and the school district. Will Robert's parents prevail in court?

Points to Consider

Qualified privilege is the key consideration in this case. In the case of *N.C. v. Bedford Central School District* (2004), social worker Reulbach and school counselor Mackie help us answer this case by defining and refining the limits of our qualified privilege.

The parents have a strong interest in keeping the details of the student's abuse private because of the nature of the offense and their desire to prevent further trauma to their child, which might ensue from disclosure to his peers or other members of the community. However, Dr. Reulbach and Ms. Mackie, in their respective responsibilities as social worker and school counselor, have a substantial interest in revealing relevant details about events, which likely impact the student's emotional well-being. All of the communications cited by the parents occurred during the course of the child study team evaluation, which was conducted at the parent's request. The communications took place only between the educators so they could adequately determine the student's need for Exceptional Student Education.

The parents were upset because Reulbach was the only school district employee that they had informed about the abuse; when Reulbach told Mackie, the parents said he relayed incorrect information about N.C.'s sexual abuse history. However, the court said the facts provided no basis to infer that Reulbach and Mackie were engaging in "gossip" rather than professional communication. No communications had occurred outside of a professional setting, outside of the scope of the psychological and emotional evaluation of the student, or among individuals without a significant interest in communicating about the student's sexual abuse history. Therefore, the court found that the defendants' interest in professional communication for the student's benefit outweighed the student's and the parents' rights to confidentiality (*N.C. v. Bedford Central School District*, 2004).

We may often find it necessary to share information among other professionals in the same school, or as in this case, in the same school district. If the information about this child's sexual abuse had not occurred during professional discussions intended to help N.C., then the court might have ruled differently. We are cautioned to reveal such private and potentially prejudicial information in a formal setting and with parent permission if at all possible, or only to educators who have the "need to know," and to be able to defend our actions as critical to the well-being of the student.

PROFESSIONAL COMMUNICATION: DEFAMATION

At the faculty holiday party, a group of colleagues are engaged in a heated debate about teen-age pregnancy. You reveal that one of your students, Randall, has impregnated two girls, refused to accept responsibility and seems quite proud of his "accomplishment." Your comments reach Randall. He and his mother seek legal counsel about whether or not you have committed slander. Have you?

Points to Consider

Gossiping about a student's behavior in a social gathering is defamation of character and not qualified privilege. "Information should not be conveyed to other teachers or administrators unless the motive and purpose is to assist and enhance the educational opportunities of the pupil. Transmittal should be made in the proper channels and to persons assigned the responsibility for the relevant educational function. Gossip or careless talk among teachers which is not calculated to help the student, may be shown to be malicious and not protected by the cloak of qualified privilege" (Alexander & Alexander, 2005, p. 621).

In other words, qualified privilege is defined by the setting and circumstances in which we discuss a student, not by our job titles. This educator is in a tough spot because the parent has decided to take up the issue with the administration and pursue a lawsuit. It is unworthy of our professional standing to mishandle information that we have obtained in the course of doing our work. Social settings are the time to be especially discreet about sensitive, confidential information. Remember the "need to know" rule: School counselors may only reveal sensitive information with great reluctance and care to make certain the recipient has a "need to know" and is in a position to benefit the student if they have the information we share (ASCA, 2004b).

COLLABORATION: GROUP MEMBERSHIP

You are trying to develop a place for yourself in a deeply divided faculty. Three very strong faculty members control much of the group dynamics, deciding who will be accepted and who will be ostracized. The "in" group has a great deal of fun together, socializes on the weekends, and takes care of each other. However, a small group of teachers branded as "outcasts" spend some very lonely hours at the school. It is not apparent to you why some are accepted and others are not; it just appears that the leaders decide who will be included and everyone goes along. You have been chosen to be included, and you love having the warmth and camaraderie of a large portion of the faculty. However, the fun you are having is tempered by the constant reminder that good people are being ignored. You have made a few suggestions about including the others without much response, and you fear being pushed out. You feel you are not being true to yourself by participating in a group that snubs others, and you fret over your behavior that you view as weakness in not standing on your principles. How can you deal with this ethical dilemma?

Points to Consider

Group membership can be very difficult, yet success as a group member is critical for school counselors to develop a place as collaborators and team builders. Collaborative skills are a building block for the development of leadership skills (Idol, Nevin, & Paolucci-Whitcomb, 2000). Relationships with fellow teachers and other critical stakeholders pave the way for an effective school counseling program. The title "school counselor" adds the additional responsibility to be inclusive of all faculty to the fullest extent possible.

A school counselor should reflect on the implications of having or not having membership in this group. Reflect on the following:

- In an effort to fit in and not be ostracized, do you try to match the behavior of others even though it is against your better judgment and your own feeling of self-respect?
- Have you grown past peer pressure and the need to be accepted at the expense of your own inner voice?
- Can you preserve your place within this group and still reach out to the ostracized faculty members?
- Do you believe your self-respect is your primary consideration in this situation?
- Can you fight through your own inhibitions and fears and learn how to be a better group member?
- Do you have the ability to survey a person's situation and decide how best to support that person?
- Do you challenge yourself to step out of your comfort zone?
- Do you expend more energy on trying to find the good in people than you do trying to point out their flaws?

This case can only be answered by each individual professional in the context of his or her situation. There are no hard and fast rules of behavior that say a school counselor must abandon new friends, or seek to include the marginalized, or speak out on behalf of others. However, guidance in ethical codes and a history of practice imply that school counselors adhere to a higher standard of professionalism in our interactions with fellow professionals. School counselors should aspire to the standard of demonstrating strong interpersonal skills and the ability to successfully move within and among the different "camps" that can be found in schools (Cark & Horton-Parker, 2002; Kern, 1999). School counselors want to be bridge builders, helping all members of the school community find emotional safety (Hernández & Seem, 2004).

COLLABORATION: ADMINISTRATORS

Occasionally, the principal shares sensitive information with you. Last summer, he told you that he interviewed a recent graduate and hoped to hire her for a counseling position, but he explained that he had to temporarily drop the position out of the budget so as not to have to hire a surplussed counselor who is considered very weak. He explained that he would pick up the new school counselor by reinstating the position after the surplus counselor is placed at another school. At the 12-day count, the position is reinstated and the new counselor is hired. The teacher's union is filing a grievance and asks what you know about the entire situation. What should you do in a situation like this? Are you bound by your ethical standards to keep this confidential? Must you tell the union what you know?

Points to Consider

Principals and counselors need to be able to collaborate with the assurance that their confidences will be respected. The best recourse for this counselor would be to explain to the union representative that he or she is in a special relationship with the principal. Further, the counselor should explain that it is his or her regular practice to discuss with the principal sensitive information with the understanding that it will be kept confidential. This situation is no different than other conversations in which the principal's confidence has been respected. The school counselor could try this approach until someone in authority demands more information, in which case the counselor should seek legal counsel.

There is a general principle called *privity* involved in this case. Privity is defined as having an interest in a transaction, contract or legal action to which one is not a party, but where the interest arises out of a relationship to one of the parties of the legal action. There is no privity here. The counselor does not have a legal obligation to tell the union anything. However, if the counselor is a union member, he or she may have agreed to cooperate with union investigations as a condition of membership. The counselor would have to consult the union handbook.

COLLABORATION: TEACHERS

Over the course of time you have learned a great deal about different teachers' classroom management effectiveness. You believe that certain students assigned to one particular teacher are suffering academically and emotionally, because this teacher has chronic behavior problems. It also seems that the school administration is unaware of her ineffectiveness with many students. What is your role in this situation?

Points to Consider

The school counselor cannot afford to come across as an informant or align too closely with anyone's "camp." The school atmosphere is not unlike the United Nations, and in cases where potentially divisive situations arise the school counselor is advised to remain like Switzerland: neutral and nonjudgmental. Like a good ambassador, the counselor's job is to develop relationships with administrators and teachers, listening to the concerns of each and helping warring factions arrive at compromises. Having a solid, professional relationship with the principal benefits the students, teachers and support personnel. Regarding the above case in which a teacher's conduct may be a concern, the counselor's role is not to spy and report to the principal, but to glean as much information from different sources as possible, assess the problem, and share potential solutions with the principal without compromising confidentiality of sources or damaging the teacher's reputation (ASCA, 2004b).

Key to success in difficult situations such as the one described here is to genuinely respect and support teachers with their difficult jobs. Also essential is to make the effort to build trust between counselor and principal, firmly establishing respect of confidences. It will help if you know how information will be used, so that you feel secure that it will be used to help the teacher make strides toward a better academic and social environment. If you are uncertain the principal will deal deftly with a delicate situation, you may have to develop another plan. Identifying allies early on, such as the assistant principal or someone else who will use compassion and a nonjudgmental approach to problem solving, will help once in the throes of a dilemma. Remember, think like an ambassador and be neutral to the extent you are able.

COLLABORATION: FELLOW COUNSELORS

You are a school counselor serving the eighth-graders in a 7-12 school counseling department. Certification authorizes you to counsel elementary and middle school students, grades K-8. During your five years at the school you have earned a wonderful reputation, especially among the students. During your second year, about a dozen ninth-graders who were former students came back to you after they reported feeling dismissed by their high school counselor. This practice has continued for four years and now you have far too many students and the stress is wearing you down. Although you encourage these students to seek help from their own counselors or from outside agencies, they are reluctant and continue to see you. Are you behaving unethically or illegally? What do you do?

Points to Consider

The intention to support former students is admirable, but the counselor has unwittingly set up an unmanageable workload and everyone suffers. Tough as it is to admit, the counselor has enabled students to rely on their former counselor too much, and in the process may have needlessly alienated the rest of the counseling staff and imperiled his or her own well-being by taking on too much. The professional school counselor is obligated to be aware of her or his limitations (ASCA, 2004b), hence the need for certification and a manageable caseload. Although this counselor may be an intuitive counselor for preteens, older teen-agers bring with them a different set of developmental issues – issues the counselor is not certified to address and may not be qualified in skills to handle.

It is important to find a way to ease out of a relationship with the older students who have been receiving counseling. Be honest. Set time limits so these students are gradually able to make the transition. Tell the students, "I can only meet with you two more times, but I have set up an appointment for you with Mrs. Jones, who is terrific with people your age. With your permission I can sit down with Mrs. Jones and brief her about some of the things we've been talking about the past couple of years so she can have a sense of who you are."

Once the counselor creates boundaries, students will respect them. If they balk at consulting another counselor in the school, offer them the option of seeing someone in an outside agency. It is advisable to develop a relationship with an agency ahead of time so the students can be best informed about what they might expect. Perhaps an agency counselor could be repositioned – by special grant – to work out of the guidance office, or maybe that person could arrange to be available during school hours. The primary objective is to provide students with the most professional service available.

Inform the other school counselors about what has been happening and include them in a solution. By fostering cooperation, you may be able to avoid conflicts that can create fissures in the department.

Practice within the parameters of your certificate (ASCA, 2004b). If counselors are accused of wrongdoing, negligence or incompetence, legal counsel will have a difficult time defending them if they are practicing outside their certification, especially when the school district did not hire them to be out of field and did not sanction their out-of-field practice.

PROFESSIONAL INFLUENCES: YOUR COMPETENCE AND PERFORMANCE

A colleague, Randolph, seems very well-meaning, and the students like him. He is good with students but indifferent to the paperwork involved in his job, and he seems to lack basic organizational skills. Randolph's happy-go-lucky attitude is attractive to the students, but his lack of attention to detail has meant that several of his students almost missed tests they needed for graduation. Randolph's inability to maintain solid recordkeeping is bound to catch up with him and cause a problem that can't be fixed. You are not his boss nor do you have any authority over him, but as his colleague do you have an ethical or legal obligation to do anything more to help Randolph or his students? Can the school district fire Randolph? Must the school district offer remediation for Randolph before firing him?

Points to Consider

In the case of *Carroll v. Rondout Valley Central School District* (1999), the school district in Ulster County, N.Y., fired a tenured school counselor of 19 years. The dismissal was a result of the counselor's (1) failing to maintain required records; (2) failing to arrange required remedial assistance for students who failed the Regents Competency Test; (3) failure to schedule students for required courses; and (4) falsifying a student's educational record. These charges were brought by the board of education in a hearing against the counselor after several students did not graduate with their class in June 1998. The counselor in turn sued to overturn the hearing panel's decision.

The counselor was found guilty of seven charges, three of which involved failure to arrange remediation for students who failed the Regents Competency Test in global studies. Those students testified that they requested the counselor to arrange remediation on several occasions, beginning in June 1996. Under the education department regulations in effect at that time, students failing the RCT must be notified of test results, along with their parents, and plan for remediation. Remediation was to begin no later than one semester immediately following the semester in which the test was administered. The students must be placed in this remediation, regardless of scheduling conflicts, unless there is written consent from the parent to be exempted from the class. Since the counselor did not schedule remediation for these students and there was no written exemption consent from the parents, the counselor was found guilty of these charges.

Two charges stemmed from failure to ensure that students completed English 11 so they could graduate with their class in June 1998. One student did not graduate because she was short .25 physical education credits. The counselor was charged with failure to schedule this student for additional physical education credits in her senior year after she failed physical education during her junior year. While the counselor claimed that the student had a medical excuse, there was no proof of this, so the counselor's claim was unsubstantiated.

Finally, the counselor was charged with and found guilty of falsifying a student's record. The counselor untruthfully indicated on a student's plan card that the student had passed a course in the 1997-1998 school year. The counselor claimed that the plan card was a planning tool merely showing a projection of what the student's record would be if said student passed the course. On the contrary, a guidance secretary testified that the plan card was actually considered to be a part of a student's permanent record. Additionally, the notations on the plan card could be interpreted that the student passed and received a grade for the course. The social studies teacher also testified that she and the counselor discussed how the student could receive credit for the course without actually taking it. All of this evidence was definitive proof that the counselor did indeed falsify student records.

School counselors have a duty to maintain records on behalf of their students. The following are some recommendations for counselors to enhance their recordkeeping abilities.

1. Keep scrupulous records.
Students, parents and administrators routinely rely on the school counselor to keep abreast of the academic progress of students. The ethical codes for school counselors state that counselors "maintain and secure records necessary for rendering professional services to the student as required by laws, regulations, institutional procedures and confidentiality guidelines" (ASCA, 2004b).

2. Set up redundancy systems.
With the computer capability available in most schools today, a redundancy system is likely already in place. Get to know the technical expert in your building and ask him or her to help you create and maintain a system that is fail-safe for students. This type of collaboration with colleagues can be very powerful for students, help free up your time to attend to other counseling responsibilities, and give you and the other counselors ample warning should a red flag occur.

3. Involve the students.
While it is your obligation to maintain good records, it is also a good counseling and learning opportunity for students. Professional ethics for counselors mandate that they assist students to "move toward self-direction and self-development" (ASCA, 2004b). By partnering with students and giving them the chance to chart their own progress, counselors can become an empowering force for young people.

4. Consult often with other counselors and teachers.
When in doubt it is always best practice to consult with another professional. School counselors who choose to act alone have the greatest chance of landing in legal trouble.

Are we responsible for our colleagues and their successes or failures as school counselors? Professionals work hard to portray the fraternity of education and to support each other to be competent counselors. We are not entirely responsible for our fellow counselors, but it is ethical to exhaust our options in trying to help colleagues.

PROFESSIONAL INFLUENCES: SCHOOL DISTRICT POLICY

You believe that the school district's policy for calculating grade-point averages is unfair. If a student fails a course but subsequently retakes the course and passes, the original F is permanently removed from the student's record and is never factored into the final grade-point average. This practice has impacted rank in class and has given students who failed and retook a course a better class rank than students who passed the course the first time with less stellar grades. To get this policy reviewed and possibly changed, you have tried to go through the correct channels in the district but no one seems to be listening. You resort to writing a letter to the editor of the local newspaper criticizing the policy, hoping that public opinion will bring needed change. Does writing a letter to the editor constitute a legal or ethical concern?

Points to Consider

It is legal for educators to write a letter to the editor critical of a school district's practice or policy. The Supreme Court supported educators' right to voice their opinions in the public forum of newspaper editorials in *Pickering v. Board of Education* (1968). Marvin Pickering was dismissed for writing and sending for publication a letter to the editor critical of the superintendent and the board of education. The board said it could dismiss Pickering under Illinois statute because the letter was detrimental to the efficient operation and administration of the district's schools. The Supreme Court ruled in Pickering's favor because it said the statements in the letter were neither false nor recklessly made, and that educators exercising their right of free speech on issues of public importance is not basis for dismissal from public employment (Imber & Van Geel, 2004).

However, newspaper editorials are not considered an appropriate way for educators to air their concerns about a school district. Educators work extremely hard and are sometimes judged harshly by public opinion and the media. When a fellow educator criticizes the school district in a public forum, it can be disheartening or embarrassing to many in the district. It is best practice to portray the fraternity of education by working within the boundaries of professional behavior to change policy and procedures (ASCA, 2004b). An alternative method might be to send an e-mail to district-level administrators and continue to make the case internally. Taking the case to the press is subject to public misinterpretation on this and related issues, and your colleagues and supervisors may view you with suspicion.

The counselor who is an advocate will naturally want to raise awareness of barriers that adversely stratify students' opportunities. However, knowing how to negotiate the political landscape is also critically important. Frustration with ridiculous policies is understandable, but failure to understand the political climate resulting in inappropriate advocacy is just as damaging as not advocating at all. Acting in this manner will almost certainly minimize the school counselor's effectiveness in all future dealings with certain school district officials. School counselors should use finesse and diplomacy to navigate the political landscape and to determine how to get what students need.

In the case study above, the school district is not doing anything illegal or unethical. School districts are allowed to establish a pupil progression plan, and it often includes a forgiveness policy whereby a student can retake a course and be held accountable only for the passing grade or higher grade. Although you may disagree with the policy of grade forgiveness, professional behavior requires a school counselor to abide by the district policy.

PROFESSIONAL INFLUENCES: PREVAILING COMMUNITY STANDARDS

You are new to the community, and you have just accepted your first counseling position. Prior to becoming a school counselor, you were a teacher in four other school districts. You continue to be surprised by this school's approach to working with students, particularly those practices you consider to be harsh, punitive and stressful. The general routine of communication includes yelling, threatening and general negativity. However, nothing prepared you for the practice, sanctioned by the administration, of summoning parents to the school to administer corporal punishment to their child in front of the class. This community also condones the administration's practice of using corporal punishment. You are distressed by the disciplinary practices of this school, but leaving the district or transferring to another school are not options for you right now. What do you do?

Points to Consider

Ethics are situational. Community and institutional standards can differ significantly from school to school and community to community. It is difficult to accept that professional behavior varies according to the prevailing standards of the community, but our ethical imperative is to be aware and respectful of the school's community standards. For example, it is acceptable behavior for school counselors in certain schools and communities to refer pregnant students to Planned Parenthood, yet in many other communities, this would be considered a serious breach of ethics, infringing on parents' rights to be the guiding voice in their children's lives.

Acknowledging the prevailing standards of a community does not mean we unconditionally accept the standard. If we believe a practice, policy or law of a particular school or community is in any way detrimental to students, it is our ethical obligation to work in a responsible manner to try to influence a change so that students are protected. "The professional school counselor supports and protects the educational program against any infringement not in students' best interest" (ASCA, 2004b).

School counselors are respectful of the values of their students and their families, vigilantly avoiding the temptation to impose their own values on students and parents. However, school counselors practice as systemic change agents, challenging all internal and external stakeholders – such as families, parents, guardians, administrators and teachers – and advocating for change when practices adversely stratify students' opportunities. It is therefore an appropriate, indeed an ethical, responsibility for school counselors to ask tough questions in a respectful way and to encourage fellow educators to evaluate their stance on controversial topics such as corporal punishment.

How can this school counselor begin the change process needed for the well-being of all students, as well as for a happier place to work? The school counselor could explore what would be a good approach to impact the culture and climate of the school. Perhaps the school counselor could discuss with the administration the idea of forming a committee to develop a revised discipline approach for the school.

The school counselor could also interview supervisors in Child Protective Services to determine what constitutes abuse; the incidence of abuse in the community; the number of students who have been removed from homes for abuse and the number of children who have died at the hands of parents as compared to other parts of the United States; and other relevant information. This data could show how a community that believes corporal punishment is appropriate compares to other geographical locations where the practice is considered inappropriate.

The American School Counselor Association position statement on corporal punishment (2000) advocates for abolishment of corporal punishment in schools. The rationale reads, "Professional school counselors believe that corporal punishment teaches children violence is an acceptable way to resolve differences. In many states, children are the only individuals who officially may be punished, under law, by physical force. Corporal punishment seriously compromises self-esteem and contradicts the fundamental right of all children to be free from bodily pain and injury" (ASCA, 2000, p. 1). Further, ASCA declares that "the professional school counselor acts as a resource person to school personnel for the implementation of effective intervention strategies that facilitate positive individual development" (ASCA, 2000, p. 1).

"It is school counselors' professional responsibility to actively influence public and legislative bodies to abolish corporal punishment in schools. Professional school counselors encourage public recognition of the consequences of corporal punishment, disseminate research on alternatives to corporal punishment and encourage legislation prohibiting continued use of corporal punishment in states where such use exists" (ASCA, 2000, p. 1).

Engaging others in examining important issues and using advocacy skills, school counselors can initiate important conversations around topics that need to be more thoroughly examined (Stone, in press).

DUAL RELATIONSHIPS: STUDENTS AND PARENTS

You love being a school counselor, especially for a select group of students you describe as bright, engaging and accomplished. This group receives most of your time and attention. You attend select students' piano recitals, tennis tournaments and soccer games. You treat these students as your adult friends – encouraging them to call you by your first name, giving them your home phone number and your home e-mail address. You go out of your way to be extraordinarily responsive to their parents and you encourage their praise, gifts, invitations and personal favors. One parent who is an attorney helped you with your house closing without charging you. Are you behaving ethically and legally?

Points to Consider

School counselors have an ethical imperative to maintain a professional distance from students and parents. Professional distance is the appropriate familiarity and closeness that a school counselor engages in with students and their family members. When professional distance is violated, then dual relationships occur (ASCA, 2004b).

Dual relationships involve personal gains. While professional school counselors work diligently to make certain that they do not even give the appearance of gaining any unfair advantages through their work, unethical counselors cross boundaries for personal gain, a disturbing ethical violation. Examples of personal gain might include using the relationship to boost one's ego, sense of self-worth, self-importance, or image with select parents. For others the gain might be the need to nourish the belief that the counselor is the only one in the school who is a student-centered advocate.

Professional school counselors must continually examine their actions and ask the question, "Whose needs are being met by my behaviors?" If the answer is "only a select few students in my charge" or "I am feeding my own personal needs by my behavior," then the counselor is in the throes of a serious ethical violation.

School counselors, more than any other group of educators, have a responsibility to ensure the emotional safety of minor students. It is a strongly recognized and respected tenet in the profession that counselors should avoid dual relationships since they have the potential for harm to the students and the profession; additionally, they put our employers in jeopardy. The power differential between the school counselor and student makes it impossible for students to give equal consent to the extraprofessional relationship. It is considered exploiting the relationship when a school counselor crosses the boundaries and tries to establish friendships with students (Remley & Herlihy, 2001; St. Germaine, 1993). Violating professional distance with students suggests that a counselor is engaged in a dual relationship.

Dual relationships, which are addressed in Code A.4 of the ASCA's Ethical Standards for School Counselors (2004), evolve in many ways. To avoid such interpersonal conflicts, the school counselor must maintain professional distance with students and parents.

Accepting an invitation to attend a special event may simply be a show of support for a student who needs to know someone cares. However, when you also exhibit behaviors such as singling out a few on whom to lavish attention, you have breached professional distance. Professional distance or appropriate familiarity with clients and their family members will help avoid dual relationships that violate trust in the counseling relationship.

Currying favor with students or their parents or establishing yourself as the hero for students is unethical. It's not cool to be part of the "in" crowd as a school counselor, nor is it advisable to accept in-kind services from family members of your clients. While counselors may convince themselves that they are performing good deeds, the truth is no one benefits from the school counselor as hero – especially the students who have been excluded from selective acts of altruism. Sometimes in addition to showing favoritism, a counselor will feel the need to massage policies, ignore school practice and hound administrators and teachers to make certain that selected students get all the benefits, and therefore see the counselor as the hero.

Heroism can be intoxicating, especially for the school counselor who craves attention and celebrity. The parents of the chosen few may even act like fans, creating a loyal, vocal support system. But such backing never comes without a price. Inevitably the school counselor who campaigns for a select few will be indebted to these parents at the expense of others. What happens, for example, when the parent who provided free legal services asks you to pull strings for his son, the one just suspended from school for drug use?

A compromised school counselor loses her or his effectiveness. No one loses more from a lack of professional clarity than the neglected children. All students should receive our services, not just the select few.

DUAL RELATIONSHIP: THE COMMUNITY

You have lived in the same small tight-knit community your entire life, and you know nearly every person in the town through religious affiliation and the fact that your father was a very popular coach who always had a houseful of people. You worry that you will never feel comfortable working with students on a personal or emotional level, as you will probably know too much about their parents and family history. Do you have reason for concern?

Points to Consider

School counselors should avoid dual relationships with students if at all possible, but in some instances it is impossible. When a school counselor works in a small community where everyone knows everyone else, dual relationships may be unavoidable. The counselor is responsible for taking action to eliminate or reduce the potential for harm. Such safeguards might include informed consent, consultation, supervision and documentation (ASCA, 2004b). Dual relationships also involve a differentiation in power, with the student seeking services from the counselor having less power, and all the possible negative ramifications that can occur with power differentials.

The best practice is for the school counselor to be vigilant about recognizing when she or he is engaged in a dual relationship, and being prepared with steps to minimize negative implications. The personal relationships this counselor has with many of the families and their children will sometimes require that the prudent professional refer students to others with a more objective eye. For example, if a friend's child asks you for help with her or his schedule, and you are treating this child the way you would any other, then you have minimized any negative impact on this student or others. If the same child seeks your help during a relationship crisis with her mother (your close friend), then you will need more objectivity than you are able to deliver in this situation. Referring students to another counselor, if possible, may be the most ethical response.

Some safeguards against dual relationships can be established in advance. For instance, a counselor may want to stay clear of the teacher's lounge, where students and their families are often discussed. When it comes to dual relationships, school counselors must exercise caution and handle each situation on a case-by-case basis.

In a Position to Know: School Counselors Speak

The case presented at the beginning of the chapter is revisited here and answered by practicing school counselors. Read their opinions carefully to see what you can learn. Compare their answers with your approach.

GIFT TAKING

Dear School Counselor:
You are cordially invited to an all-expense-paid trip to Central University. Accommodations will be in a bed-and-breakfast. Activities will include golfing at a country club and a trip to the racetrack, and you will receive $50 for gambling at the horse races. The purpose of the trip is to familiarize you with our university. It is not our intent to unduly influence your college advising role or to seek an unfair advantage for our university. Our intention in having you visit our university is to see that you have a good time and to have you learn about our university so that you will be able to speak with firsthand knowledge about the fine programs we have to offer your students. We still want you to provide students with trustworthy, objective advice.
Sincerely,
Your College Admissions Representative

Responses from School Counselors

This hypothetical case took an all-too-real twist when *The New York Times* ran the article "Wooing of Guidance Counselors Is Raising Profiles and Eyebrows" (Winter, 2004). Shift your focus from the hypothetical case study to the responses of ASCA members who addressed the issues raised in this newspaper article. The article talked about school counselors receiving expensive perks such as trips to Vail, hockey tickets, nights at luxury hotels, spa treatments and other presents with monetary value in return for favorable or preferential treatment toward their universities. In the words of Mr. Davolt, a Denver College admissions representative who has been playing host to high school counselors, "It makes a huge difference as to how they're going to convey our university" (Winter, 2000). Although the writer interviewed only one school counselor at a private school, the article read as if lavish trips were the norm.

The ASCA membership debated whether the article was intended to make school counselors look as if they were committing ethical violations, or if the intent was to criticize practices of college admissions personnel. *The New York Times* is one of the most respected newspapers in the world; therefore, when it states that counselors are willing partners in accepting perks designed to influence their college advising role, counselors' ethics are being called into question. Whether *The New York Times* intended to place the focus on admissions representatives or on school counselors, the situations described require cooperative agreement between them. Consider the rules and regulations about limits in campaign contributions. "We question a politician who receives gifts and then votes for a law favorable to the gift giver," said Doug Morrissey, president of the New York State School Counselor Association, "If elected officials receive money in exchange for awarding certain companies lucrative contracts to build roads, we place them behind bars for racketeering." (D. Morrissey, personal communication, October 14, 2004)

Are there any standards applicable to the counseling profession that parallel those governing campaign contributions? Isn't it true that the overwhelming majority of school counselors would take these trips, learn about the schools' offerings, place the information in their memory banks and use it only in appropriate and fair ways? School counselors will do what is best for students; the only advantage the college can expect is that as a result of the visit to the campus and meetings with the college representatives, the school counselor will know more about the school. Previously, the college might have been simply a name in the college admissions guide.

However, there is the concern of perception. Since it is the nature of school counselors to provide students with trustworthy, objective advice, should we worry about the perception of others who may question the influence gifts will have? *The New York Times* stated, "First and foremost...guidance counselors are supposed to do just what their title implies: provide students with trustworthy, objective advice. By that logic, accepting gifts from the very universities they are paid to assess poses a conflict of interest that undermines the covenant between counselors and students" (Winter, 2004).

Richard Tutunick (personal communication, July 12, 2004) wrote, "I just finished reading *The New York Times* article and shared it with my colleagues. We had to laugh, and wanted to know what colleges were offering these perks. I think that the percent of colleges that are doing this is so small that we probably have a better chance of winning the lottery. I have been invited to several colleges. It has always been informative and I was always treated professionally but never have I received the kind of perks they mentioned in the article. I do sometimes get college banners and maybe even a cup or mug and I do display them in my office, but in no way does it cause me to change the way I counsel with students. I help them investigate the colleges that they are interested in and have the best programs to meet their needs."

ASCA board member Jan Tkaczyk (personal communication, July 12, 2004), wrote, "Our local association has our meetings hosted by colleges and universities from around the country, but I have never heard a school counselor mention anything other than that the update was beneficial and a chance to meet someone from admissions most informative."

Sherry Merrill (personal communication, July 12, 2004) wrote, "I would only hope that any guidance counselor who participates in college visits shares their ethical commitments, e.g., 'Thank you, but you are aware that this will not influence my recommendations for my students unless your school is the best placement for them.'"

Cynthia Esielionis (personal communication, July 12, 2004) wrote, "I am a bit put off that the profession is being accused (no matter how indirectly) of being unethical and biased. These are two things that we cannot afford to be and effectively do our jobs. Counselors spend their money and time to go visit places that do not offer these 'grand' perks. I have received invitations from colleges/universities that require a nonrefundable deposit if the counselor registers to visit the school. Personally, given the money, time away from students and the incredible catch-up of work when I return, I prefer to get information from the Web or through telephone contact. Some counselors may be influenced; however, I believe the vast majority of school counselors are genuinely interested in meeting the needs of students and would never guide someone to a college or university that is inappropriate for them because of a perk. My overall opinion is that it is okay to accept something as a 'thank you' if I visit an institution, but not something extravagant that could potentially be perceived as a bribe or payoff."

Making Connections

1. You are a school counselor who has a solid reputation as an effective professional. Your live-in boyfriend parties hearty on weekends, and along with a group of friends, you usually end up consuming large quantities of alcohol. Several times the police have come when the neighbors have complained about cars and loud music. Lately, the parties have been getting longer and wilder. Does your behavior pose an ethical question? Answer the case by discussing how your behavior is affected by "standard of care" or the behavior expected of the reasonably competent professional.

2. Your principal occasionally asks questions about the content of your counseling sessions. You worry about this principal's trustworthiness with information, as you have heard her repeat information that others have told her, embellishing the information to make herself look important. What do you do when the principal asks you for information? How would you use your ethical codes and qualified privilege to help you in this situation without alienating your principal?

3. Currently grant money for career programs is plentiful and your school is submitting a proposal. However, the equipment and expertise required to be in place at the time of grant submission are currently nonexistent. Administration tells you not to worry, that if your school receives the grant they will quickly gather the equipment needed and send you for training to acquire the needed expertise. Are there ethical violations here?

4. School climate is especially glum at your school. Your principal asks you if you will try to help her with the situation by conducting small focus groups with all grade levels to try to determine the causes. You are certain that you will find that many faculty members are discontented with the principal, as faculty members constantly exchange complaints that the principal is inconsistent, shows favoritism and micromanages. Do you agree to hold the focus groups? If you do agree, what must you consider in advance before conducting the focus groups? What are the pitfalls and the possible advantages of agreeing to help in this manner? What parameters must you set with the principal in advance? Discuss how confidentiality and informed consent should play a role in this ethical dilemma.

5. Your principal wants you to conduct focus groups to evaluate a disciplinary policy that is drawing much fire from faculty as too permissive. Defend one of these two statements:

- "A school counselor is an appropriate person to lead a focus group of this nature."
- "A school counselor should always try to avoid running a focus group of this type."

6. You are concerned about a policy that your school district has established for reporting students who express suicidal ideation. The policy requires that a three-part form be completed, with one part going in the educational record, one part going to the district level and one part staying in the school counselor's office. You think the policy is an invasion of your clients' confidentiality and that it eliminates counselor judgment. Discuss how you will address this situation. Whom would you involve? Who can help you advocate for a change?

7. One of your students, 11-year-old Erin, lost a parent to cancer two months ago. Throughout her parent's illness you tried to help Erin, but her grades continued to slip and she lost her enthusiasm for playing soccer. You have a very good relationship with Erin and you continue to see her as often as you can. The last conversation you had with her surviving parent turned flirtatious and you accepted a date. Are you involved in an ethical dilemma? Whose needs are being met?

Key Terms

Professionalism
Ethical standards
Qualified privilege
Professional communication
Privity
Maintaining student records
Falsifying student records
Self-direction

Defamation
Slander
Monitoring your competence
Prevailing community standards
Planned Parenthood
Corporal punishment
Dual relationships
Professional distance

References

Alexander, K., & Alexander, M. D. (2005). *American public school law* (6th ed.). Belmont, CA: Thomson West.

American School Counselor Association. (2004a). *ASCA governing policies.* Alexandria, VA: Author.

American School Counselor Association. (2004b). *Ethical standards for school counselors*. Alexandria, VA: Author.

American School Counselor Association (2000). *Position statement: Corporal punishment in the schools*. Alexandria, VA: Author.

Cark, M. A., & Horton-Parker, R. (2002). Professional development schools: New opportunities for training school counselors. *Counselor Education and Supervision*, 1, 58-75.

Carroll v. Rondout Valley Central School District (1999). Ulster County, New York.

Clark, J. (2003). *World apart: Civil society and the battles for ethical globalization*. Bloomfield, CT: Kumarian Press.

Family Educational Rights and Privacy Act, 20 U.S.C § 1232g (1974).

FindLawForLegalProfessionals (2005). Retrieved January 5, 2005, from http://dictionary.lp.findlaw.com/scripts/results.plco=dictionary.findlaw.com &topic=31/31of117c83da70f2987351c8893ce99d

Hernández, T. J., & Seem, S.R. (2004). A safe school climate: A systemic approach and the school counselor. *Professional School Counseling*, 4, 256-262.

Idol, L., Nevin, A., & Paolucci-Whitcomb, P. (2000). *Collaborative consultation* (3rd ed.). Austin, TX: Pro-ed Publisher.

Imber, M., & Van Geel, T. (2004). *Education law* (3rd ed.). Mahway, NJ: Erlbaum.

Kern, C. W. (1999). Professional school counselors: Inservice providers who can change the school environment. *NASSP Bulletin*, 603-10-18.

N. C. v. Bedford Central School District, NY decided 8/27/04, US District Court of NY, 04 CIV. 2627 (SCR), 2004 U.S. Dist. LEXIS 24198.

Pickering v. Board of Education, 391 U.S. 563, 88 S.Ct. 1731 (1968).

Remley T., Jr., & Herlihy, B. (2001). *Ethical, legal, and professional issues in counseling*. Upper Saddle River, NJ: Merrill Prentice Hall.

St. Germaine, J. (1993). Dual relationships: What's wrong with them? *American Counselor, 2,* 25-30.

Stone, C. (in press). Corporal punishment and community standards. In Tyson, L., *Critical incident in supervision.* Alexandria, VA: American Counseling Association.

Winter, G. (2004, July 8). Wooing of guidance counselors is raising pro-files and eyebrows. *The New York Times.* Retrieved November 28, 2004, from http://www.uh.edu/ednews/2004/nytimes/200407/20040708guidance coun.htmlW

CHAPTER 3

Family Education Rights and Privacy Act

IN THIS CHAPTER

Objectives

By the time you have completed this chapter, you should be able to:

- Discuss the federal legislation Family Education Rights and Privacy Act (FERPA, 1974).
- Identify your advocacy role in protecting the privacy of students' educational records and parents' rights to records.
- Define what directory information is and what implications it can have for schools, students and parents.
- Identify situations that involve FERPA laws and how to resolve them legally.
- Adhere to FERPA's right for noncustodial parents.

Introduction

The 1974 Family Education Rights and Privacy Act is federal legislation that governs education records and dictates how all written information regarding a student will be handled and disseminated for the protection of the student and her or his family (Alexander & Alexander, 2005; Fischer & Sorenson, 1996; Imber & Van Geel, 2004). FERPA, also known as the Buckley Act, is administered by the Family Policy Compliance Office, and has enacted safeguards so that parents can access their children's education records and have a voice in how that information is shared with others (Alexander & Alexander, 2005; Fischer & Sorenson, 1996; Imber & Van Geel, 2004).

Ideally, school counselors should not be in charge of managing education records, but should have a working knowledge of FERPA guidelines to support their advocacy role for the legal and ethical protection of any written information kept on a student (ASCA, 2004). There are multiple challenges faced by school counselors and other educators in complying with FERPA, and the challenges can be as varied as the students.

FERPA clearly identifies parents' right to view their children's education records and to decide, within certain parameters, who can have access to their child's records. Eligible students – those who reach the age of 18 while in secondary schools – may also have access to their records. Noncustodial and certain stepparents also have rights under FERPA (1974, 34 C.F.R. § 99.3).

The FERPA legislation allows for parents and eligible students to request that corrections to records be made, to remedy information that may be erroneous or potentially misleading. FERPA requires that parents be given due process so they can protest when they disagree on the accuracy of records. Due process refers to procedures or steps that the school district and parents must take to settle a disagreement (Alexander & Alexander, 2005).

According to FERPA (1974), schools must have written permission from parents or the eligible student before any information is released from a student's education record with the exception of disclosing information to:

- School officials with legitimate education interest (school counselors are considered school officials along with teachers and others)
- Other schools to which a student is transferring
- Officials for purpose of audit or evaluation
- Persons involved with the student's financial aid
- Those conducting specific research studies for the school
- Organizations involved in accreditation
- Holders of a judicial order or lawfully issued subpoena
- Persons involved with emergencies or in cases of health and safety, or
- Local and state authorities in the juvenile justice system, in compliance with specific state law.

FERPA further allows for the dissemination of "directory information," which is basic information about a student such as name, address and telephone number, without parent or eligible student consent. Within certain parameters, FERPA allows states to define what they will consider directory information. School districts can establish policies and procedures regarding the release of directory information and they may decide not to participate in releasing directory information. The military cannot be excluded from directory information unless a student's parents have signed to opt out of releasing directory information (Alexander & Alexander, 2005).

In this chapter, we will look at the many ways FERPA legislation impacts students and families in schools and its influence on a counselor's case notes in a school setting. We will examine the most-often-used FERPA guidelines through case studies and also respond to critical questions, such as when and how education information can be released and to whom. The cases presented will lead us through the primary FERPA guidelines and introduce us to other federal legislation that will help us understand that parents own the privacy rights of students in schools. We will examine the close relationship between student confidentiality and the FERPA legislation to better equip ourselves to protect students and their families and to avoid exposure of our school districts to unnecessary legal action.

Ethical Standards Addressed in This Chapter

Professionalism means knowing your professional associations' codes and adhering to them. Those ethical standards from ASCA that are most germane include the following:

- The professional school counselor maintains and secures records necessary for rendering professional services to the student as required by laws, regulations, institutional procedures and confidentiality guidelines. (A.8.a)
- The professional school counselor takes appropriate and reasonable measures for maintaining confidentiality of student information and educational records stored or transmitted over electronic media including although not limited to fax, electronic mail and instant messaging. (A.10.c)
- The professional school counselor informs parents/guardians of the counselor's role with emphasis on the confidential nature of the counseling relationship between the counselor and student. (B.2.a)
- The professional school counselor makes reasonable efforts to honor the wishes of parents/guardians concerning information regarding the student, and in cases of divorce or separation exercises a good-faith effort to keep both parents informed with regard to critical information with the exception of a court order. (B.2.d)
- The professional school counselor is knowledgeable about release of information and parental rights in sharing information. (C.2.d)
- The professional school counselor conducts appropriate research and reports findings in a manner consistent with acceptable educational and psychological research practices. The counselor advocates for the protection of the individual student's identity when using data for research or program planning. (F.1.c)

The full text of American Counseling Association ethical codes and ASCA ethical codes can be found at these Web sites: ACA at http://www.counseling.org and ASCA at www.schoolcounselor.org.

Getting Started: What Would You Do?

The following case is answered for you at the end of this chapter by two school counseling administrators. Before you read their responses, formulate in your own mind how you would approach this ethical dilemma.

REPORTING STUDENT INFRACTIONS TO COLLEGES

You gave a student a strong letter of recommendation regarding his character, service, leadership and academic record. The student, Mark, was accepted by his first-choice college, which subsequently received Mark's midterm report showing all A's. In April, school officials discovered that Mark and two others had exchanged papers during a test in the first semester of trigonometry. The school disciplined all three students, and once the zero grade was factored into the final grade, the result was a drop to a letter grade of B. Are you under any legal or ethical obligation to report the cheating incident to the college? Will you be breaching any legal or ethical obligation if you do report the cheating incident to the college? How would you handle this ethical dilemma?

Working Through Case Studies

DIRECTORY INFORMATION

Ms. Sheffield disappeared with her son Richard to escape an abusive husband; then she enrolled Richard in a new school without saying a word about their problems. The school published the honor roll of fifth-graders in the newspaper, and Richard's name was among them. A relative of Mr. Sheffield saw Richard's name in the paper and contacted Mr. Sheffield. Ms. Sheffield is furious; she feels she must uproot her family and seek a new town in order to hide. She maintains that the school acted improperly by publishing her child's name without her permission. Did the school act legally when it published Richard's name in the newspaper?

Points to Consider

It was legal for the school to print Richard's name in the newspaper to recognize his academic achievement. FERPA allows for the publication of directory information, which includes the acknowledgment of honors or awards received. In fact, under FERPA, the school could also legally have published Richard's photograph (U.S. Department of Education, personal communication, December 12, 2004).

FERPA requires that each year school districts are to notify parents that they can opt out of having their child's directory information made public (1974, 34 C.F.R. § 99.7). Directory information can include:

- Name
- Address
- Telephone number, if listed
- Participation in officially recognized activities and sports
- Weight and height, if an athletic team member
- Name of the most recent previous school or program attended
- Dates of attendance at schools in the district, and degrees and honors received
- Major field of study, and
- Date and place of birth.
(Alexander & Alexander, 2005, p. 622)

In other words, parents can keep private their child's directory information. Schools may use a variety of vehicles for this annual notification to parents of their rights under FERPA, such as the student handbook, PTA newsletters, school calendars, special letters, e-mail, Web sites or newspaper articles. Schools must offer parents or eligible students who wish to opt out of directory information a reasonable amount of time to respond.

Richard's situation is especially sensitive because of the circumstances surrounding his personal life. Although the school district gave Ms. Sheffield a brochure detailing FERPA guidelines, including her right to suppress information, they were not able to assure that Ms. Sheffield read and understood the implications. An overburdened parent like Ms. Sheffield may be too consumed with paying the bills and creating a safe home for Richard to read the fine print regarding FERPA. More and more school districts are now asking parents to sign an informed consent form as an added precaution, to safeguard privacy rights and prevent this type of situation from occurring. If the school counselor were aware of the family situation, it would be ethical and respectful of the counselor to follow up with Ms. Sheffield to be sure she understands the guidelines and implications of opting out of directory information.

In addition, if the school counselor knew of Ms. Sheffield's plight, he or she could also let her know about services available in the community to help battered women put their lives back together. The school counselor might also increase visibility with Richard and check in with his teachers periodically. Keeping the lines of communication open with Richard can foster a beneficial comfort level between him and the school counselor, cementing a trusting relationship where both Richard and Ms. Sheffield know they can turn to the school and the counselor in the future.

The Ann Arbor (Mich.) Public Schools district has established a Web site for parents to help them understand their rights under FERPA: http://www.aaps.k12.mi.us/aaps.forparents/ferpa_information. School counselors may find this Web site a helpful model for informing parents of their rights.

PARENT'S INFORMATION

John Smith, a middle school student, lives with his mother and not his father. Are his mother's and father's information considered directory information also?

Points to Consider

The student's address in this case is also his mother's address, and is part of the directory information. No other information for either parent is considered directory information. If John lives with his grandparents, then it is their address that appears as directory information, not his father's or mother's. In other words, directory information is limited to the student's information (Fischer & Sorenson, 1996).

ACCESS TO DIRECTORY INFORMATION

The school principal asks you to speak with local business owner, Mr. Achinson, who was denied a request for the class lists, names and addresses of the students in the local high school for a targeted marketing campaign. Mr. Achinson knows that the local school district gives the information to colleges and the military. He is irate because the school district has denied his request. Did the school district act within FERPA guidelines?

Points to Consider

FERPA directs that school officials can deny individuals and groups directory information but cannot discriminate within those groups. For example, they can deny Mr. Achinson a class list for the purpose of selling student a Caribbean cruise for graduation, but they cannot deny Mr. Achinson's request and then allow his competitors to have the directory information. In short, if access is denied to one, it is denied to all in that group.

Giving out directory information is a sensitive subject for school districts; many are choosing not to give out any directory information or allow only select groups to have the information. Class ring companies, yearbook companies and other entities considered necessary to the graduation process that have a history of not abusing class lists are usually provided information.

The No Child Left Behind Act (2002) requires any school district receiving federal money to allow military recruiters the same access to students that college admissions counselors or business recruiters have. Colleges and recruiters often are allowed access to students to discuss admissions, employment opportunities and so on; frequently, this takes place with the involvement of school counselors. Thus, if a school has a policy allowing colleges, college recruiters and employment recruiters on campus, then military recruiters must be allowed as well. Additionally, schools are required to provide recruiters with student directory information, such as names, addresses, and phone numbers, unless a parent or student has opted out (Alexander & Alexander, 2005).

LEGITIMATE EDUCATIONAL INTEREST

Your cousin coaches Little League baseball and would like information on a student in your school whom he coaches. He is very fond of the young man, who seems to be having vision difficulty. The coach asked the boy's parents about his problem and the parents dismissed it by saying, "He can see; he is just uncoordinated." Your cousin would like you to look at the vision screening results in this child's student record to see if a problem has been noted. Is there an ethical or legal dilemma here?

Points to Consider
FERPA guidelines delineate who may have access to education records without parental permission. School counselors and other educators who have "legitimate educational interest" (Fischer & Sorenson, 1996, p. 91)

can access education records. Legitimate educational interest means you may access an education record for the purpose of:

- Performing appropriate tasks within your job description
- Performing a task related to a student's education
- Performing a task related to discipline, or
- Providing a service or benefit related to the student or to the student's family such as counseling, health care or job placement.

School counselors have legitimate educational interest, not by virtue of their title, but in the context of doing their work. However, school counselors do not have unrestrained, unlimited access to education records. When a school counselor legitimately needs to access a record, it can be done without parental permission. Examining an education record out of curiosity, however, to figure out what your new next-door neighbor does for a living or to see how many people live in the house, is not a legitimate educational interest. Professional school counselors take great care to read records only if the action is within the parameters of legitimate educational interest (Stone, 2001).

The school counselor may not give the Little League coach vision screening results, as this is outside the boundaries allowed by FERPA unless the parents agree. However, it is legitimate for you to take the information learned from the coach and go into the education record to note if there are vision screening results, and contact the student's parents if the student needs attention. You can also suggest that the coach approach the child's parents a second time and make the case that a vision screening could be beneficial. Advocacy is important but not to the point that you jeopardize your job, or that you break a student's confidentiality by implying in any way that you consulted educational records to learn of a vision problem.

PURGING STUDENT RECORDS

A first-grader has just been adopted by her stepfather, and the natural father agreed to the adoption. Her mother requests that all information regarding the natural father be purged from the cumulative folder. The principal has appointed you as the principal's designee to handle this situation. Can the record be purged?

Points to Consider

FERPA provides that parents can challenge information in education records which they believe is "inaccurate, misleading, or violates the privacy or other rights of the students" (Fischer & Sorenson, 1996, p. 99). The meaning of these terms is not completely clear and they are open to interpretation, providing an opportunity for the school counselor to act as an advocate on the student's behalf. Records are not unalterable documents meant to be kept absolutely intact, since FERPA allows for purging of records. If the entry on the record no longer has a legitimate purpose and the parent wants you to alter the record for good reason, then you can comply and amend the record. Using good judgment is essential in cases like these. Maintaining the integrity of education records is important but so is respecting the parents' right to advocate for the privacy and accuracy of their child's educational record.

There will be times, however, when parents or eligible students will be denied their request to have an item purged from an education record. Parents can request due process. FERPA states: "An educational agency or institution shall give a parent or eligible student, on request, an opportunity for a hearing to challenge the content of the student's education records on the grounds that the information contained in the education records is inaccurate, misleading, or in violation of the privacy rights of the student" (1974, 34 C.F.R. 99.21). "If, as a result of the hearing, the educational agency or institution decides that the information in the education record is not inaccurate, misleading, or otherwise in violation of the privacy rights of the student, the parents will be informed of the right to place a statement in the record commenting on the contested information in the record or stating why he or she disagrees with the decision of the agency or institution, or both" (1974, 34 C.F.R. 99.21).

You can learn more by reading "Excerpts from a Letter to Parent re: Amendment of Special Education Records," which can be found in the FERPA Online Library at http://www.ed.gov/policy/gen/guid/fpco/ferpa/library/parent.html.

PARENTAL RIGHTS AND EXCEPTIONAL STUDENT EDUCATION RECORDS

The school counselor, the principal and the director of exceptional student education have had a long history of involvement, most of it unpleasant, with Mr. Markett, a particularly outspoken, demanding parent. His son, Shane, is in ESE and has academic, social and emotional problems. These problems are documented by the ESE teacher on the report card under work habits and personal interactions with others. Mr. Markett disagrees with the evaluations and wants them purged from the education record. He argues that as a result of an altercation he had with the ESE teacher, "she has it in for my son," and the information contained in these report card summaries is inaccurate and misleading. The principal has denied the request to purge the report card record and appoints the school counselor as the principal's designee to be in charge of the due process hearing that is required under FERPA and IDEA to determine if the record should be purged. How can you prepare for this hearing? Are there any legal or ethical issues with a school counselor being in charge of the due process hearing at the school level?

Points to Consider

Exceptional Student Education records also fall under FERPA and therefore are governed by the Family Policy Compliance Office. Additionally, the Individuals with Disabilities Education Act, federal legislation for ESE administered by the Office of Special Education, spells out parents' and students' rights with regards to ESE records (IDEA, 1990). Therefore, ESE records are subject to FERPA and the Confidentiality of Information regulations for Part B of the Individuals with Disabilities Education Act (1990), found at 34 C.F.R. §§ 300.560-300.577.

FERPA requires an educational agency or institution to give a parent or guardian the opportunity for a hearing to challenge the content of the student's records on the grounds that the information is inaccurate, misleading or in violation of the student's privacy rights. Regulations of IDEA (which governs ESE) specifically provide the same opportunity for a hearing to challenge the content of education records as provided in § 99.21 of the FERPA regulations, and further provides that a hearing held under IDEA must be conducted according to the hearing procedures contained in FERPA regulations. In other words, IDEA supports and reiterates that ESE records are education records subject to FERPA guidelines.

Parental rights to challenge information are not unlimited. A school is not required by FERPA or IDEA to give parents the right to seek to change substantive decisions made by school officials, such as grades or other evaluations, including decisions regarding special education students (Letter to Parent, 2004). Therefore, the work habit evaluation part of Shane's education record stands and due process is not necessary. FERPA is intended to require only that educational agencies and institutions conform to fair recordkeeping practices and that they not override accepted standards and procedures for making academic assessments, disciplinary rulings, placement determinations and other evaluations. Parents cannot challenge a grade or evaluation unless it has been proven to be inaccurately recorded.

IDEA and FERPA provide guidelines to help answer the question about the school counselor's being in charge of the due process hearing. To help ensure an unbiased and disinterested outcome, FERPA and IDEA guidelines say the hearing on changing education records should not be conducted by the supervisor or a colleague of the school official who made the initial decision not to amend the student's records. Furthermore, FERPA regulations state the hearing official may not have a "direct interest in the outcome of the hearing" (Letter to Parent, 2004, para. 4). While there are no specific guidelines, someone in a direct reporting or close collegial relationship with the individual who denied the grade change should not be the one to conduct the hearing.

If during a legitimate due process hearing parents are denied the right to remove or change information, then each time the contested part of the record is given out, the parents can require that their statement of protest be attached. Section 99.21(c) provides that an educational agency or institution must:

- Maintain the statement with the contested part of the record for as long as the record is maintained, and
- Disclose the statement whenever it discloses the portion of the record to which the statement relates.

STUDENT ACCESS TO RECORDS

One of your high school juniors comes in and asks to review her education records. Can you honor students' requests to review their own education records?

Points to Consider

Nothing in the FERPA legislation answers this question. A request by a student to view her or his records would most likely be addressed under the policies and procedures of a particular school or school district and, if allowed, would probably be conducted under adult supervision. The school counselor should consider the student's age and developmental levels. Students who are 18 have the right to review their education records.

ELIGIBLE STUDENTS AND THEIR RIGHTS

Peter is an 18-year-old college student who lives at home. His parents have requested copies of his records from you, his former high school counselor. Must you seek Peter's permission before releasing his records to his parents? The Army recruiting officer also wants Peter's records. Who must give consent: Peter, his parents, or both Peter and his parents?

Points to Consider

Parents continue to have rights when their child is still a dependent according to the federal tax code, so Peter's parents would not need to seek his permission before being allowed to see his records. The Army recruiting officer, on the other hand, wants more than just directory information, to which he would already have access under FERPA. The Army recruiting officer must seek Peter's permission to view his education records; permission from Peter's parents is not necessary.

MARRIED STUDENTS AND THEIR RIGHTS

Faye, a 16-year-old married student, wants to deny her parents access to her education records. Can Faye prohibit her parents from obtaining her records?

Points to Consider

All rights shift to the student if the married student is emancipated, but not all states emancipate minors at marriage. In addition, rights shift to a married minor who is no longer listed as a dependent on the parents' tax return. If the parent still claims the child who is a minor, then the parent still has access to secondary records (FERPA, 1974). Therefore, the answer to this case depends on the state's statutes.

THE SUPREME COURT DEFINES EDUCATION RECORDS

Mrs. Shubuta complains to you that her child is being humiliated and his privacy rights violated because his teacher has the students exchange papers to grade and the students then call out grades for recording. Her child has serious learning difficulties and his grades are always very low. She says her lawyer has explained that FERPA rights are violated because his grades are education records. Is her lawyer right?

Points to Consider

In the 2002 Supreme Court case of *Owasso Independent School Dist. v. Falvo* (2002), the court decided that homework assignments, tests and the grades assigned to them are not, strictly speaking, "maintained" by an educational agency or institution at that point and therefore fall outside the definition of education records. A student's interim tests and homework assignments are not highly personal matters worthy of constitutional protection. Once the grades are reported to the teacher and they are recorded in the teacher's gradebook, then the grades are "maintained" records, with gradebooks as education records only in limited circumstances.

The *Owasso* case is an example of ethics and law colliding. Legally she practice of grading and calling aloud grades is sanctioned, but ethically it begs for us to raise awareness. The ethical school counselor is concerned about creating a safe, respectful school climate for all students. Perhaps a conversation with the principal on staff development presentations can eliminate this archaic, demeaning practice.

VIOLATING THE PRIVACY OF EDUCATION RECORDS

You are in the front office copying a student's education record when the school nurse implores you to help with a child who is not breathing properly. You fly to the phone to call for medical assistance, and it is fully 25 minutes before you return to the copy machine. In the interim, sensitive health information in the education record is left open and apparently seen by a parent who tells other parents that this child suffers from schizophrenia. The child's parents intend to sue you for your part in breach of their child's privacy. How have the courts responded when confidential information from a student's record has been revealed? How does FERPA apply in this situation?

Points to Consider

The U.S. Supreme Court recently ruled that the Family Educational Rights and Privacy Act does not give individuals the right to sue educational institutions that violate the law's provisions by divulging confidential student information. In a decision involving a lawsuit against Gonzaga University, the justices held that the original purpose of FERPA was not to give individual students and their families litigious license to bring charges against educational institutions for violating the privacy of student records (*Gonzaga Univ. v. Doe*, 2002). Rather, FERPA was designed to hold institutions accountable to the federal government for following guidelines involving privacy issues and confidentiality of student records.

The justices held that the 1974 Family Educational Rights and Privacy Act intended that its privacy provisions would be enforced by the U.S. secretary of education, mainly by withholding federal funds to educational institutions that failed to change their policies to comply. Based on this recent Supreme Court case, the parents in the scenario above would not be able to seek damages for a breach in the confidentiality of their student's record (*Gonzaga Univ. v. Doe*, 2002).

RIGHTS FOR NONCUSTODIAL PARENTS

Justina has a history of conflicts with her mother, with whom she lives, and is often in your office distraught over their latest verbal round. A teacher comes to you worried about Justina, who "is not herself." When you talk to Justina, you too become worried as she appears withdrawn, distracted and depressed. You suggest that you need to involve her mother so that she can get some help, but she begs you to call her father. After consultation with your supervisor and much discussion with Justina, you honor her wishes and call her father, the noncustodial parent. He immediately responds by coming to the school to discuss Justina and picking up copies of her educational records to take to a psychologist whose help he will seek. He says he will contact Justina's mother and the two of them will set up an appointment for Justina. Justina's mother calls you furious that you contacted Justina's father, and says she is refusing to allow you or any other school representative ever again to contact the father or give him information about Justina.

Can you call the noncustodial parent about a social-emotional issue involving his or her child? Does Justina's father have the right to be included in parent-teacher conferences and to receive education records? Is the school obligated to notify the custodial parent before contacting the noncustodial parent?

Points to Consider

FERPA (1974) clarifies that custodial parent is a term used for the parent having primary physical custody of a child. Typically the child resides with the custodial parent. Noncustodial parent denotes the parent having the child for a lesser amount of time. Typically the child does not reside with the noncustodial parent except when the noncustodial parent exercises her or his visitation rights. Unless there is a court order expressly stating otherwise, noncustodial parents enjoy all the same rights as custodial parents. Noncustodial parents can participate in parent-teacher conferences, receive report cards and progress reports, and get copies of educational records (Alexander & Alexander, 2005).

You may contact the parent who is not the custodial parent and involve him or her in an academic or emotional issue. In an effort to preserve the relationship with the custodial parent, you may decide to inform the custodial parent that you have called the noncustodial parent. This is a judgment call that would depend on the context, history, and the student who is experiencing the problem.

Consider the court case *Page, Petitioner, v. Rotterdam-Mohonasen Central School District* (1981). First-grader Eric Page lived with his mother who was legally separated from his father. Mr. Page tried to meet with the educators in Eric's school and to review his son's education records so that he could stay involved in his son's academic progress. The school followed Mrs. Page's direction and denied all requests by Mr. Page. Mrs. Page's contention was that as a result of their separation and having been awarded custody of Eric, Mr. Page had "abandoned" any interest he may have had in Eric's education.

The lawsuit against the Rotterdam-Mohonasen Central School District resulted in Mr. Page being given full access to Eric's teachers and also to his records, in accordance with the Family Education Rights and Privacy Act allowing inspection of school records by either parent, irrespective of custody issues. The court held, "educators and school districts are charged with the duty to act in the best educational interests of the children committed to their care and although it may cause some inconvenience, those interests dictate that educational information be made available to both parents of every school child fortunate enough to have two parents interested in his welfare" (*Page, Petitioner, v. Rotterdam-Mohonasen Central School District*, 1981).

All 50 states and the District of Columbia have adopted the Uniform Child Custody Jurisdiction Act in an effort to support both parents' involvement in their child's life. When deciding custody, many states follow the Uniform Marriage Act, which encourages custodial decisions in part to favor the parent that is most likely to keep the other parent involved in the child's life (Commissioners of Uniform State Laws, 1997).

RIGHTS FOR STEPPARENTS

One of your seventh-graders, Joseph, is having a very difficult time adjusting to his new school. Joseph has just moved across the country after his mother sent him to live with his father and stepmother. You have worked with Joseph, but you have not been successful in getting his father involved. Joseph's stepmother is very receptive and offers to come to the school for a parent conference and to check and sign for his daily progress reports. Can you involve Joseph's stepmother in parent conferences, progress reports, report cards and other education records?

Points to Consider

Stepparents also have rights under FERPA, which defines parent in Section 99.3 as "a natural parent, a guardian, or an individual acting as a parent in the absence of a parent or a guardian." Additionally, the U.S. Department of Education has stated "that a parent is absent if he or she is not present in the day-to-day home environment of the child. Accordingly, a stepparent has rights under FERPA where the stepparent is present on a day-to-day basis with the natural parent and child and the other parent is absent from that home. In such cases, stepparents have the same rights to education records under FERPA as do natural parents. Conversely, a stepparent who is not present on a day-to-day basis in the home of the child does not have rights under FERPA with respect to such child's education records" (Commissioners of Uniform State Laws, 1997).

RESEARCH INVOLVING STUDENTS

You are the counselor of Gracian Howell Elementary School. A University of the West counselor educator has been working with you to implement a character education program and to assess its impact on discipline referral rates. You did not require parental notification before you and your colleague collected and analyzed aggregated data for the discipline referral rate for all students. Then, you disaggregated the data to determine which students were chronic discipline offenders, and you targeted for further research those 12 students responsible for the majority of discipline referrals. You and the counselor educator meet with the teachers of the 12 students and ask them to track student behavior on a rating chart. You plan to use the disciplinary records of these students to complete the data. In the final report, you will not identify students by name. Have you followed FERPA laws?

Points to Consider

The counselor violated FERPA throughout this research study. To understand how and why, we need to examine the case study step by step. In the study's first stage, collecting and looking at discipline referral rates of all students and then disaggregating the data by chronic offenders would be following FERPA if:

- All the data were collected and analyzed by the school counseling department without involving higher education
- All the data containing identifying information were absent from the file and non-personal identifiers (Student A, B, C...) were used when given to the university counselor educator, or
- The students' parents gave consent before the counselor educator looked at the files.

None of these avenues was taken in the case study.

In the second half of the case study, the counselor educator and the school counselor studied chronic discipline referral offenders and met with their teachers, who were to track the students' behaviors on a chart. This chart, along with the students' discipline records, was to be used to complete the data. At this stage, the study would be legal under FERPA if:

- The counselor identified the chronic discipline referrals and gave the counselor educator the list with all personally identifying information removed so that students remained anonymous, or
- The students' parents gave consent.

The last part of the study, the final report, came close to passing the FERPA test. Yes, it is against FERPA to identify students by name, but the report must make sure all other types of identifying information are also removed. For example, if the report discusses a 14-year-old Asian male in the sixth grade and there is only one student fitting that description, then the study has failed the FERPA test.

Additionally, all universities have internal review boards established to approve research projects in advance so that human subjects are protected legally and ethically. Most school districts have also developed their own guidelines. You can access an example at http://www.cssd11.k12.co.us/ aero/Evaluation/OutsideResearch/RelationswithEducationResearch Agencies.pdf.

LETTERS OF RECOMMENDATION

Evelyn is applying to a very competitive university and your letter of recommendation will be a critical part of her admission. Evelyn's freshman year was academically dismal. She confided in you that she was being physically abused by her boyfriend during her freshman year but ended the relationship after seven months. Evelyn has been a stellar student since her sophomore year and is no longer the same person who remained in an abusive relationship. You are considering explaining all this in your letter of recommendation in hopes that Evelyn will be judged only on what she has done since leaving the abusive relationship. Legally and ethically, can you include this information in a letter of recommendation?

Points to Consider

School counselors conscientiously work to behave legally in writing letters of recommendation, and they find their guidance primarily in FERPA. On the other hand, ethical considerations involving letters of recommendation are far more complicated for school counselors. In an informal survey of more than 2,000 school counselors (Stone, 2004), respondents overwhelmingly said they would consider it a breach of confidentiality to put sensitive, confidential information in a letter of recommendation without a student's permission. Most respondents said they would not put Evelyn in the position of having to make that decision, as the letter could convey triumph without giving the details of her past. Even when it comes to confidential information that, if known, would benefit a student, counselors would rather get the student's permission. Among other suggestions were to include in the letter an invitation to call the counselor to discuss the student's special circumstances regarding her ninth-grade performance.

In addition, many colleges require brief statements or an essay as part of the admission application process. This could provide Evelyn with an opportunity to explain or allude to the trauma she suffered in ninth grade. With the school counselor's assistance, Evelyn can also contact the admissions office and speak to an admissions counselor regarding her academic record.

It is important to note that what you write in a letter of recommendation is not addressed by FERPA. FERPA protects against improper disclosure of personally identifiable information from a student's education records. A letter of recommendation is temporary and not part of the permanent education record. Typically, you write a letter of recommendation because the student or student's parent has asked you to do so. Legally, school counselors can include anything in a letter that is common knowledge and observable such as, "Kennard has never let the fact that he is wheelchair-bound keep him from being an active and high-profile school leader, engaged in numerous school activities such as…. " It is best practice to leave out sensitive, confidential information; however, if in your judgment you believe such information would benefit the student, then secure student and parental permission to include what they might not want known.

In a Position to Know:
School Counseling Administrators Speak

The case presented at the beginning of the chapter is revisited here and answered by two school counseling administrators. Compare their answers with your approach.

REPORTING STUDENT INFRACTIONS TO COLLEGES

You gave a student a strong letter of recommendation regarding his character, service, leadership and academic record. The student, Mark, was accepted by his first-choice college, which subsequently received Mark's midterm report showing all A's. In April, school officials discovered that Mark and two others had exchanged papers during a test during the first semester of trigonometry. The school disciplined all three students, and once the zero grade was factored into the final grade, the result was a drop in grade to a letter grade of B. Are you under any legal or ethical obligation to report the cheating incident to the college? Will you be breaching any legal or ethical obligation if you do report the cheating incident to the college? How would you handle this ethical dilemma?

Responses from School Counseling Administrators

Ethically, this is a case that must be decided by the individual school counselor, as there are no hard and fast rules governing what a school counselor should do. Legally, the counselor is under no obligation to call or contact the university to inform them of changes in the status of students who have applied to their schools. Knowing this doesn't necessarily help you do what is right. Written below are some things to consider when making your decision.

A counselor may believe that the grade change or cheating incident should be reported to the university in the belief that their own integrity will be called into question if they do not directly inform the university. The line of reasoning is that this student did not deserve the glowing letter and that it would be wrong to let the recommendation letter stand without adding the new information.

However, if we follow this line of reasoning, where does it end? Is it then a counselor's responsibility to inform potential employers, military recruiters, community colleges, career and technical schools, and other postsecondary placements of any new and potentially damaging information that came to light since the writing of any letter or evaluation? And, perhaps more importantly, is cheating the only offense that would trigger a report to any of these agencies? What does a counselor choose to report or not report after an initial letter of recommendation or evaluation?

On the other hand, counselors might respond that they do not believe it is their responsibility to notify the university. A counselor believes that the letter was written in good faith based on the information available at the time, and no obligation exists to voluntarily provide additional information to the university. The drop in the grade or any additional discipline issued by the school should be consequence enough without the incident of poor judgment affecting a student's entire future.

A potential downside to not informing the university is that many university admissions counselors believe that they should be informed and could devalue future letters of recommendation written by the counselor. This could adversely affect future college applicants who have letters of recommendation from this counselor. Nevertheless, a school counselor's role is to be a student advocate, not a university advocate.

A third approach might work as an effective compromise. Upon the lowering of the grade, the counselor sends the university a corrected transcript with no explanation. It is then the university's responsibility to call and inquire if they choose to. If they do, the counselor can truthfully tell of the incident. The counselor could also inform the student of the possibility that the university would call to question the change in grade, and if they do, the counselor will provide an honest answer. The student may make the decision to "do the right thing" and inform the university in advance to explain the situation prior to the university calling the counselor.

One last consideration: FERPA. What impact, if any, does voluntarily providing confidential student information have on violating parent and student rights under FERPA? Notifying a university of a grade change probably does not violate FERPA. However, we would encourage you to read your state statues on education records to determine what confidential information can be provided to third parties.

In any case, it would undoubtedly help the situation if the school district had a policy in place regarding letters of recommendation and updates. A short paragraph to be included with a recommendation form or evaluation could delineate the district policy. This would effectively inform both the student and any recipient of a recommendation letter or evaluation of the guidelines in place to protect all parties involved.

Bob Tyra, consultant in school counseling for the Los Angeles County Office of Education
Paul Meyers, principal in Ferndale, Calif.

Making Connections

1. If you as a school counselor were allowed to define your own role with regard to educational records, what would it be?

2. Are there any current practices by your school that potentially violate FERPA?

3. What is the current method used by your school to tell students and parents about directory information and their rights? Is this a good method? If not, what changes would you suggest?

4. A licensed mental health counselor, whom you know to be a very reputable therapist, wants to write a book about student behavioral issues in middle schools. The counselor asks you to identify common behavioral issues in your schools and to supply quotes about these behaviors for the book. What can you do? What is best practice?

5. A teacher in your school makes a habit of making her students' grades public in an attempt to motivate them to perform better. You realize that this practice is quite hurtful to students and does not produce the outcome for which the teacher is aiming. What can you do to advocate for the students?

6. A parent wants to change an "inaccurate" notation in her child's file regarding her child's behavior because she claims that the teacher had personality conflicts with her child. You are the principal's designee for handling this matter. What are the due process procedures you must offer this parent?

7. A 14-year-old student tells you that her biological father, whom she met for the first time recently, has suddenly appeared in her life and wants

to be involved in her education. The father's name is on her birth certificate filed in her educational record. The student and the student's mother do not want him to be able to have any access to her education records or her teachers. Can you comply with their request?

Key Terms

Family Education Rights and
   Privacy Act
Directory information
Legitimate educational interest
Family Policy Compliance Office
Individual with Disabilities
   Education Act

Due process hearing
Noncustodial parent
Custodial parent
Uniform Marriage Act

References

Alexander, K., & Alexander, M. D. (2005). *American public school law* (6th ed.). Belmont, CA: Thomson West.

American School Counselor Association. (2004). *Ethical standards for school counselors*. Alexandria, VA: Author.

Commissioners of Uniform State Laws. (1997). Retrieved January 28, 2005, from Legal Information Institution Online Access: http://www.law.cornell.edu/uniform

Family Educational Rights and Privacy Act, 20 U.S.C. § 1232g (1974).

Family Educational Rights and Privacy Act and Gonzaga University. (June 18, 2002). *The Chronicle of Higher Education*, 48(42), A24.

Fischer, L., & Sorenson, P. (1996). *School law for counselors, psychologists, and social workers*. White Plains, NY: Longman.

Gonzaga Univ. v. Doe 536 U.S. 273 (2002) 143 Wash. 2d 687, 24 P.3d 390.

Imber, M., & Van Geel, T. (2004). *Education law* (3rd ed.). Mahway, NJ: Erlbaum.

Individuals with Disabilities Education Act, 20 U.S.C. §§ 1401-1485 (1990).

Letter to Parent re: Amendment of Special Education Records. (2004). Retrieved August 13, 2004, from FERPA Online Library at http://www.ed.gov/policy/gen/guid/fpco/ferpa/library/parent.html

No Child Left Behind Act of 2001, 20 U.S.C. § 6301 (2002). Retrieved February 19, 2005, from www.ed.gov/policy/elsec/leg/esea02/index.html

Owasso Independent School Dist. v. Falvo 534 U.S. 426 (2002) 233 F.3d 1203.

Page, Petitioner v. Rotterdam-Mohonasen Central School District et al., Respondents, Supreme Court of New York, 109 Misc. 2d 1049; 441 N.Y.S. 2d 323; June 3, 1981.

Stone, C. (Speaker). (2001). *Legal and ethical issues in working with minors in schools* [Film]. Alexandria, VA: American Counseling Association.

Stone, C. (2004). [Survey of school counselors attending legal and ethical workshops: September 2000 to January 2005]. Unpublished raw data.

Negligence

IN THIS CHAPTER

Objectives

By the time you have completed this chapter, you should be able to:

- Define negligence in school counseling.
- Understand the definition of malpractice in school counseling.
- Identify the components of standard of care.
- Understand *in loco parentis.*
- Identify the four elements of negligence.
- Discuss practices that lead to negligence in school counseling.
- Discuss how to prevent negligence in academic advising, suicide prevention and other potentially difficult areas.
- Apply the ethical standards that govern competency in school counseling.

Introduction

The fundamental basis for exploring legal concepts in this chapter is that we live and work in a litigious society: People sue. However, the chances that school counselors will be sued in the course of doing their jobs historically is slim (Parrott, 2001; Remley & Herlihy, 2001; Stone, 2001; Zirkel, 2001). This fact may provide little comfort, because the emotional and financial burden involved in defending against a lawsuit can be substantial.

As professionals, we should be familiar with certain legal terms and concepts that are part and parcel of work with minors in school settings. This chapter is designed to help familiarize you with our obligations to students in issues involving the court system, specifically with regard to negligence.

Constitutional law comprises two major categories, criminal law and civil law. A criminal wrong is a crime against society. The degree of the crime can be categorized as either a felony or a misdemeanor, with a felony carrying a longer prison term (Garvey, Aleinikoff, & Farber, 2004; Tribe, 2000). A civil wrong is a wrong against another person that causes physical, emotional or monetary damage and for which the plaintiffs can seek compensation. An individual can be exonerated of a crime yet be found guilty of breaching the plaintiff's individual rights (Tribe, 2000). School counselors who find themselves in legal difficulty are usually charged with a negligence or civil wrong; only rarely do we hear of a counselor being charged with job-related criminal activity.

This chapter will focus on civil wrongs such as negligence and malpractice. Negligence is a civil wrong – or in legal terms, a tort – in which one person breaches the duty owed to another. Malpractice, on the other hand, is the negligent rendering of professional services (Remley & Herlihy, 2001; Valente, 1998).

NEGLIGENCE

We will apply general legal principles regarding negligence to the school counseling profession. As a general legal principle, civil liability for negligence accrues if a school counselor is found to owe a duty to another person, breaches that duty by not living up to expected standards, and as a result of the breach of duty causes damages to another person. According to Prosser (1971), all four of the following elements must be present for negligence to be proven:

- The school counselor owes a duty to a student or parent/guardian of a student
- The counselor breaches the duty owed
- There is sufficient legal causal connection between the breach of duty and the injury, and
- The student or parent/guardian suffers an injury or damages, and an assessment is made.

Duty

Duty requires establishment of a relationship whereby the defendant owes the plaintiff a duty to act reasonably (Garvey et al., 2004). A school counselor who takes a group of student government students to the beach for their end-of-the-year party owes a different duty if a student enters the water and starts to drown than the lifeguard does. The stronger the duty (as with the educator who takes a student to the beach) the greater the legal responsibility and concurrent legal liability if something goes wrong (Alexander & Alexander, 2005; Imber & Van Geel, 2004).

Breach

The judgment as to whether or not a breach has occurred with regard to the duty owed is centered on the issues of reasonability and an agreed-upon standard of care. Reasonableness includes the precautions you take. When taking the students to the beach, did you have enough chaperones? Did you explain to the students that they could not enter the water for any reason? Did you position yourself so that you would know if any student wandered away? Did you take along someone trained in first aid? Another test of whether one has acted reasonably is the potential for harm and the possible magnitude of harm. There is significant likelihood of harm on field trips to locations with water, and the seriousness of harm – such as potential drowning – is great. School districts across the country have banned field trips to pools, beaches, rivers and lakes because of the likelihood of harm.

Reasonableness is difficult to define as it is person-specific and depends on an individual's background, education, profession, culture, nationality and experiences. What the court system tries to do is to answer the question, "What would the reasonably competent school counselor do in a similar situation?" The school counselor as defendant would have to show that he or she behaved with reasonable care. The American School Counseling Association provides us with ethical codes and our school districts provide us with written policies and procedures, to make standard of care more concrete and uniform in order to help define the elusive "reasonable man test" (Alexander & Alexander, 2005; Imber & Van Geel, 2004; Remley & Herlihy, 2001).

Causal Connection

There must be a causal connection between the school counselor's breach of duty and the injury that the student suffers. Liability in a negligence case hinges on causation. Proximate cause refers to the foreseeability of the harm, or whether the school counselor could have predicted the harm (Houston-Vega, Neuhring, & Daguio, 1997). The school counselor owed a duty to keep students safe, but another student carelessly pushed the student into the water. The school counselor might have been negligent in not properly supervising the students, but the student who pushed the other student into the water is more negligent since he directly caused the harm. In Alabama, North Carolina, South Carolina, Tennessee, Virginia, Maryland and the District of Columbia, the school counselor would be exonerated as compensation to the injured party would be denied in cases of contributory negligence, as here where the school counselor may have been negligent due to improper supervision, but the student who pushed the other student would likely be negligent. "Comparative negligence for all other states balances the school counselor's negligence with the percentage of blame assigned to others who contributed to the injury, thereby impacting the amount awarded in compensation" (L. Colvin, Esq., personal communication, January 30, 2005).

Injury Suffered

Assessment refers to determining monetary damages needed to compensate for the harm an individual suffers, such as injury, lost scholarship or death.

Nominal damages can be awarded in cases where actual cost cannot be determined (Houston-Vega et al., 1997). Punitive damages are awarded in cases where the intent is to punish the defendant and deter similar actions in the future (Imber & Van Geel, 2004; Remley & Herlihy, 2001).

The courts have rejected the vast majority of negligence cases against school counselors (Fischer & Sorenson, 1996). The courts have been reluctant to determine that school counselors owe a duty to prevent suicide, give accurate academic advice, or inform parents when their child is considering abortion (Fischer & Sorenson, 1996; Stone, 2001). Since the counselor does not owe a duty, liability for negligence cannot be imposed. Therefore, only a few court cases exist to give us guidance, and they appear throughout this chapter and this book.

EDUCATIONAL MALPRACTICE

In order to prove malpractice, there must be a comparison between the acceptable standard of care for the school counseling profession, and the specific act or conduct claimed to be malpractice. The testimony of an expert witness, another school counselor, or someone well versed in school counseling often helps determine whether or not the defendant met the professional standard.

In addition to expert witnesses, standard of care is established in a variety of other ways, including adherence to and participation in professional licensing and credentialing entities both locally and nationally, and educational degree preparation and continuing education programs (Caudill, 2004). For the school counselor, additional resources for establishing a standard of care include school board policies as well as participation with in-service opportunities on a local level. Using standard of care as the framework, the court will decide if the school counselor acted as the reasonably competent professional would have acted under the same or similar circumstances (Cottone & Tarvydas, 1998). Malpractice claims often result from dissatisfaction with services provided, breakdowns in communications between persons, anger with the professional, retaliation or personal greed, and not from substantiated grievances (Alexander & Alexander, 2005).

Historically, school districts have had governmental immunity or protection from civil or tort liability. In most states with regard to negligence, malpractice or civil liability, individual employees are protected from personal liability if they are not acting in a willful or wanton way (Cafaro,

2000). Most states have legislation declaring that public employers must defend, indemnify and hold harmless any employee who is named in a civil suit for an act of omission arising out of the employee's job (Collins, 2001). Further, according to these statutes, the employee cannot be fired because of an unintentional act that has harmful effects. This obligation does not extend to criminal acts or acts where the employee is intentionally harmful.

The state can abrogate governmental immunity but usually the rule is reinstated. "The rule prevails that the state and its agencies are immune from tort liability, their agents, officers, or employee, while engaged in school functions of a governmental nature" (Alexander & Alexander, 2005, p. 633).

However the state can qualify the immunity. For example, state statutes can limit immunity where the activities performed are:

- **Ministerial.** A ministerial duty is one that is plainly laid out and requires no discretion. Under ministerial duty, a state could require the district to have counseling services available in each school, but the state legislature could not dictate precisely what advice or information a counselor must dispense to students at the counselor's discretion. In one example, a Wisconsin school counselor's actions did not fall within the definition of ministerial conduct when he failed to provide correct advice to a student, leading to the student's loss of a scholarship. The counselor was obligated to provide counseling services but was not told what advice or information he was required to give to each student, and thus the advice he gave was discretionary in nature. The more relevant issue is whether the counselor was negligent in failing to provide correct advice (*Scott v. Stevens Point Area Public School District*, 2003).
- **Addressing a Known Danger.** A known present danger is a situation that requires a public officer or employee not merely to do something, but rather to act in a particular way. A school secretary moved a child off a bus after she received two reports that children on the bus were being fondled; she could have responded in many different ways, not just in one particular way. Therefore, she was immune from being sued (*Raquel R.S. v. Necedah Area Sch. Dist.*, 2002).
- **Professional Discretion.** The courts usually apply this exception to medical settings.
- **Malicious, Willful and Intentional Torts** (Alexander & Alexander, 2005). An intentional tort occurs when one acts in a determined way

to harm another individual. Some intentional torts may also be crimes, such as assault, battery, wrongful death, fraud and theft. While breaking up a fight, a school counselor loses control and starts returning punches to one of the students, continuing to hit him even after the student stops hitting the counselor back. This school counselor has committed an intentional tort.

An example of a malicious, willful and intentional tort involving a school counselor is found in *Doe v. Blandford* (2000). The counselor sexually abused a student, constituting a willfully harmful act or intentional tort. The students' parents brought a complaint against the school district, claiming that the district was negligent in hiring, failing to supervise, and failing to fire their child's abuser. In its decision, the court found that the intentional tort exception should be interpreted narrowly and that action in this case should be brought against the government.

Why are states hesitant to recognize educational malpractice? The courts have articulated five reasons:

- First, as discussed above, the standard of care is amorphous, lacking specificity and difficult to define.
- Second, it is difficult to determine amount of financial harm to the complainant. If a counselor misadvises a student about a required prerequisite college course, causing the student to lose an awarded scholarship, should the student be awarded the cost of tuition for the first year or for all four years?
- Third, the courts realize if they allow a few students to win educational malpractice suits, other students would be lining up to sue teachers, school counselors and school administrations concerning any wrongs they have endured in school, from suffering with bad teachers to failing to get into the colleges of their choice. The list would be as long as the imagination!
- Fourth, the courts do not want to be in the position of making decisions regarding internal operations of schools. No educational institution is perfect, and each school and staff must make the best decisions possible based on the circumstances and often meager resources available at a given time. Such operations should be overseen by school administrative agencies with expertise to judge appropriate actions made by a school.
- Finally, courts prefer that legislators define the standards of competency for educational malpractice in a statute, as they do with malpractice actions concerning doctors and lawyers (*Moore v. Vanderloo*, 1986).

In light of the above, school counselors understandably want the courts to shield them from educational malpractice. However, even though most states provide governmental immunity we should not relax, as the elements of negligence could well be proven in many instances if states begin to adopt the stance that governmental immunity is too generous in the face of blatant negligence. Additionally, courts may begin to view school counselors as professionals in the business of supplying correct information necessary to guide students. Therefore, the courts might perceive counselors as having a special advisory relationship with students and hold them accountable for correct advice (Willis, 2004).

With regard to negligence and school counselors, a unique relationship exists between the school counselor and the minor in school settings. We refer to this unique and special relationship with the term *in loco parentis* – Latin meaning "in place of a parent" – in which the person or entity takes on the standard of care attributed to a parent. A school has a duty to provide for the physical safety of its students. Teachers and other certified employees may step in as a parent would to discipline and correct a child's behavior, or alternatively to keep one child safe from another child or adult (*Gammon v. Edwardsville Community Unit School District*, 1980). In addition, a school board may stand in the place of a parent to ban sexually explicit material from the school library (*Bethel School District No. 403 v. Fraser*, 1986). However, the courts balanced a student's biblical condemnation of homosexual behavior and his assertion of First Amendment rights to freedom of speech against the school's responsibility to act as a parent would to protect the rights of other students and promote tolerance (*Doe and Doe v. Greendale Baptist Church and Academy*, 2003).

Ethical Standards Addressed in This Chapter

Professionalism means knowing your professional associations' codes and adhering to them. Those ethical standards from ASCA that are most germane include the following:

■ Each person has the right to privacy and thereby the right to expect the counselor-student relationship to comply with all laws, policies and ethical standards pertaining to confidentiality in the school setting. (Preamble)

- The professional school counselor is knowledgeable of laws, regulations and policies relating to students and strives to protect and inform students regarding their rights. (A.1.d)
- The professional school counselor will attempt to minimize threat to a student and may choose to (1) inform the student of actions to be taken, (2) involve the student in a three-way communication with parents/guardians when breaching confidentiality or (3) allow the student to have input as to how and to whom the breach will be made. (A.7.b)
- The professional school counselor adheres to laws, local guidelines and ethical standards of practice when assisting parents/guardians experiencing family difficulties that interfere with the student's effectiveness and welfare. (B.1.b)
- The professional school counselor accepts employment only for positions for which he/she is qualified by education, training, supervised experience, state and national professional credentials and appropriate professional experience. (D.1.e)
- The professional school counselor functions within the boundaries of individual professional competence and accepts responsibility for the consequences of his/her actions. (E.1.a)

The full text of American Counseling Association ethical codes and ASCA ethical codes can be found at these Web sites: American Counseling Association at http://www.counseling.org and American School Counselor Association at www.schoolcounselor.org.

Getting Started: What Would You Do?

The following case is answered for you at the end of this chapter by a counselor educator. Before you read his response, formulate in your own mind how you would approach this ethical dilemma.

NEGLIGENCE IN EATING DISORDERS

Karen, one of your seventh-graders, has been a regular in your office for the last two years. The student has serious problems, and you have implored Karen's stepmother – you can never get her father to respond – to get her some help. Lately, you believe she is now suffering from bulimia. Her teeth appear pitted, her skin is shallow and pasty-looking, she is losing weight and she appears more nervous than ever. When you confront Karen, she does not answer but rather starts a long diatribe about how you cannot tell her father because he is ready to send her off to live with her birth mother, and that phone call will give him the ammunition he needs. You know that Karen has all but admitted to you that she is bulimic and you also know that her assessment of her father's reaction is probably accurate. You decide to try to help Karen without calling her parents. The unthinkable happens and Karen suffers heart failure. You are sued for negligence. How do you believe the courts will react? Is it likely that your school district will pay for your defense?

Working Through Case Studies

FORESEEABILITY

You have heard positive reports from several sources including a few parents about Mr. Stevenson's success with difficult teenagers. Ms. Smith seeks your advice about Emily, her truant daughter who is also abusing drugs and alcohol. You give Ms. Smith the name of only one counselor, Mr. Stevenson, even though he is not on the district's approved list for agency referrals. If Mr. Stevenson turns out to be a sexual offender and abuses Emily, are you in any way legally responsible?

Points to Consider

In the case *Smith v. The School Board of Orange County, Florida* (1994), the parents sued the school district because a school counselor did not follow school board policy for making outside referrals. The school district requires school counselors to give a list of multiple district-approved resources. When K.W.'s mother sought help from the school counselor for her 14-year-old daughter's alcohol and substance abuse problems, the counselor allegedly gave only one name, that of Ron Markham. Markham ran an outpatient treatment center licensed by the Department of Health and Rehabilitative Services, but his name was not on the school district's approved list. Markham insisted he be given 24-four hour custody of the child, although his program was not licensed to have inpatient care or to place children in foster homes. K.W.'s mother immediately had misgivings when she placed K.W. with Markham and sought more information from a school employee, who said if the counselor thought Markham was "okay," he was "okay." Unknown to K.W.'s mother and apparently to the school counselor, Markham "placed" K.W. in his own home and for two-and-a-half months sexually abused her.

The majority of the justices in the Florida Court of Appeals dismissed the complaint for a rehearing but a dissenting justice issued this opinion:

> The foreseeability of K.W.'s injury – sexual battery by Markham – is a jury issue [meaning this justice wanted to send the case back to the lower court to be heard by a jury]. In my view, the school had at least a threshold duty to make a referral only to "approved" programs. ... Further, K.W.'s mother's specific inquiry about Markham, after meeting him, should also have triggered a follow-up by the school counselor, which was not done in this case. Had an additional conversation with K.W.'s mother taken place following her questions about Markham, the counselor might have discovered that Markham was not licensed to place children in foster homes on a twenty-four hour custody basis, and that the treatment being proposed for K.W. was inappropriate. I do not think the sexual battery of a young female child consigned to the twenty-four hour custody of an adult male (particularly one with a criminal record) is "unforeseeable" in the least. I would reverse for further proceedings (*Smith v. The School Board of Orange County*, 1994).

NEGLIGENCE IN ACADEMIC ADVISING

You are a school counselor who enjoys the role of accomplishing the impossible to help your high school students get scholarships. Bert, one of your seniors, is a talented rower who is being recruited by the six universities in the country that offer rowing scholarships. All of these schools require four years of science, including physics. Bert dropped physics in his junior year so that he could pick up weight lifting to help his rowing. Neither you nor Bert had any idea of the consequences of this decision. As a senior, Bert has the grades, SAT scores and talent to get into any of these schools, but not the physics course and certainly not the money. Efforts to right the situation have failed until you speak directly to one of the coaches recruiting this young man. The coach encourages you to "get physics on the transcript somehow." Physics would have been an easy A for this student. Bert needs this scholarship and a chance at having a bright future. You put physics on the transcript. Bert gets his scholarship. Did the end justify the means? Can you be sued and found guilty for giving Bert incorrect information?

Points to Consider

Before 2001, no jurisdiction had recognized that negligence could occur in the context of a school counselor giving academic advice to a student (Zirkel, 2001). In reversing a lower court's decision and remanding the case to trial, the Iowa Supreme Court in *Sain v. Cedar Rapids Community School District* (2001) determined that the school counselor owed a duty in this situation to advise a student with due care and attention.

IOWA

Bruce Sain, a senior in Cedar Rapids, Iowa, was a talented all-state basketball player. In 1996, he was awarded a five-year basketball scholarship to Northern Illinois University. However, in the summer prior to his freshman year, Sain was notified in a letter that he did not meet the National Collegiate Athletic Association regulations for incoming freshman athletes at Division I schools. The letter explained that he fell one-third credit short in the required English credits because his one-third English credit in Technical Communications was not on the list of classes his high school submitted to the NCAA for approval. Sain lost his scholarship and his family filed suit against the Cedar Rapids School District, citing the school district as negligent and the school counselor, Larry Bowen, as guilty of negligent misrepresentation in his role as an academic adviser (*Sain v. Cedar Rapids Community School District*, 2001). How did a scholarship opportunity for Bruce Sain turn into a shambles, with Larry Bowen at the center of a lawsuit?

In his senior year, Sain needed three trimesters of English. Dissatisfied with the second-trimester English course, he turned to Larry Bowen, his school counselor at Jefferson High School, and asked Bowen to place him in another English class. Bowen suggested Technical Communications and explained to Sain that it was being offered at the school for the first time but that the Initial Eligibility Clearinghouse would approve the high school course. Without further concern, Sain completed Technical Communications and graduated in the spring of 1996 with the prospect of a five-year scholarship at Northern Illinois University. Then the letter arrived from the NCAA Clearinghouse declaring Sain ineligible based on academic grounds. Sain and Jefferson High School requested reconsideration from the NCAA, but their request for a waiver was denied (Parrott, 2001; Reid, 2001; *Sain v. Cedar Rapids Community School District*, 2001; Zirkel, 2001).

With his scholarship offer voided, Sain turned to the courts. He filed suit against the NCAA (a suit he dropped shortly thereafter) and the school district but not the school counselor, claiming negligence and negligent misrepresentation. He alleged that negligence occurred when the counselor never submitted the course, Technical Communications, to the NCAA for approval. The suitability of the course was not at issue, since Technical Communications had been approved for other schools as a core English course. The problem was that it had not been approved for Jefferson High School because the school had not included it on the list that is annually submitted to NCAA Clearinghouse for approval. Sain claimed negligent misrepresentation by the school district because Bowen gave out erroneous information by telling him that Technical Communications would be an approved course (*Sain v. Cedar Rapids Community School District*, 2001).

The trial court initially rejected Sain's suit. In the past, courts have received a number of educational malpractice lawsuits, but they continually sided with school districts, rejecting the notion that school counselors owe a duty to a student to give competent academic advice (Fischer & Sorenson, 1996; Gladding, Remley, & Huber 2001). Courts recognize how difficult the role of academic adviser is for school counselors who are routinely required to manage large numbers of students, constantly changing rules and regulations, and fluctuating admissions and financial aid criteria. Courts have therefore been reluctant to determine that counselors owe a duty in the academic advising arena (Fischer & Sorenson, 1996; Gladding et al., 2001). Surprisingly, however, when Sain appealed to the Iowa Supreme Court, the Court remanded the case for trial (*Sain v. Cedar Rapids Community School District*, 2001).

It is important to note that the Iowa Supreme Court did not determine whether the school district was negligent; that was left for the lower court to decide. Rather, the state Supreme Court found that the claim of "negligent misrepresentation" possibly had merit and should not have been dismissed by the lower court. "Never before had any court, let alone one in Iowa, considered the liability of a school counselor for the tort of negligent misrepresentation without the ability to rely upon a tort immunity statute that protected school districts" (Willis, 2004, p. 7).

The Iowa Supreme Court remanded the case to the lower court for trial on the count of negligent misrepresentation. Justice Mark Cady of the Iowa Supreme Court wrote for the 5-2 majority that school counselors could be held accountable for providing accurate information to students about credits and courses needed to pursue post-high school goals (Parrott, 2001; Reid, 2001). The erroneous advice given by the counselor was equated to negligent misrepresentation in professions such as accounting, the law and others whose businesses require that they give accurate and appropriate information (*Sain v. Cedar Rapids Community School District*, 2001; Zirkel, 2001).

The court determined that school counselors have a similar type of business relationship and responsibility of giving accurate advice to students when the student has a need to know. The court explained that just as accountants and lawyers stand to gain financially from giving accurate advice, so do school counselors, since that is what they are paid to do. Therefore, negligent misrepresentation may be applied to the school counselor-student relationship when erroneous advice means a student loses a lucrative scholarship. This kind of lawsuit is more business-oriented than academic, and, according to the Iowa Supreme Court, is a classic case of negligent misrepresentation (*Sain v. Cedar Rapids Community School District*, 2001; Zirkel, 2001).

The court found that school counselors must use reasonable care in providing specific information to a student when (a) the counselor has knowledge of the specific need for the information; (b) the counselor provides the information to the student in the course of a counselor-student relationship; and (c) the student reasonably relies upon the information in circumstances where the counselor knows or should know of the student's reliance (Zirkel, 2001). Bowen claims never to have had a conversation with Sain about NCAA course eligibility, which Sain disputes.

Justice Linda K. Neuman, speaking on behalf of the minority, wrote that the Iowa Supreme court's decision "spells disaster for the law," explaining that the decision will open the "floodgates" and could be applied broadly to students in a variety of situations, and not just athletes who need counsel on NCAA rules (Reid, 2001, p. 3). Judge Neuman noted that the decision exalts logic over experience; it might appear logical that school counselors should give correct advice, but the reality of the expectations placed on school counselors makes this impossible. School counselors cannot have a command of everything there is to know about colleges and universities, admissions requirements, NCAA rules, financial aid and scholarships, and a multitude of other facts that change daily. In other words, the two minority-opinion Supreme Court justices expressed the fear that students could sue when they miss admission to Yale because they were not advised that there is a requirement of four sciences and they took only three. Judge

Neuman wrote, "Instead of encouraging sound academic guidance, today's decision will discourage advising altogether" (Reid, 2001, p. 3).

In its opinion by the majority, the court acknowledged that the ruling could have a "chilling effect" on academic advising by school counselors (Reid, 2001, p. 3). However, the court cautioned that the ruling should have limited effect, as negligent representation is confined to students whose reliance on information is reasonable (such as an inquiry as to whether a course meets NCAA eligibility). Additionally, the school counselor must be aware of how vital the information is to the student. This explanation was intended to reassure school counselors and to keep them from overreacting to the principles outlined by the Sain case (*Sain v. Cedar Rapids Community School District*, 2001).

While the case was never heard by the lower court, the findings of the Iowa Supreme Court in remanding the case to trial serves as a caution to the school counseling profession about providing accurate advice that could have an impact on a student's future financial opportunities. It is unusual for a tort claim of this nature to proceed to court, but by breaking with tradition, the Iowa Supreme Court has reinterpreted the nature of the school counselor-student relationship (Parrott, 2001).

CALIFORNIA

A similar case in California demonstrates the usual reluctance of the courts to impose the first element of negligence, a duty owed, against a school district. In the case of *Compton Unified School District* (1998), a high school student named Brown enrolled in Manuel Dominguez High School as a senior with the express purpose of taking the required classes to satisfy the NCAA eligibility requirements and of participating in the Manuel Dominguez High School basketball program. School counselor Rae Bonner advised Brown to enroll in a particular science course, but the course did not meet the NCAA requirements. After Brown had enrolled at the University of Southern California, the university revoked his basketball scholarship because of his failure to complete a required science class.

Brown's claim of negligence and breach of contract alleged that he lost an athletic scholarship to the University of Southern California because of the admitted mistake by Bonner and the high school. Brown argued that a special relationship existed between him and the school district because the district induced him to transfer and assured him that the Manuel Dominguez High School would allow him to satisfy the NCAA requirements for athletic eligibility. Brown further contended that he relied on the promise he would be placed in courses that satisfied NCAA requirements. According to Brown, the relative ease of calculating damages favored of imposing a duty. Finally, Brown argued that neither Bonner nor the school district was immune.

Reluctance to hold educators guilty of educational malpractice may outweigh the allegations by Brown. But even assuming a duty to Brown, both Bonner and the school district were immune from liability for misrepresentations. "Government Code n1 section 822.2 protects a public employee acting in the scope of employment from injury due to the employee's misrepresentation" (*Brown v. Compton Unified School District*, 1998, p. 6). A California court explained the court's reluctance to impose duty on educators. "The issue of duty owed is in question by this court and many other courts. To hold them [educators] to an actionable 'duty of care,' in the discharge of their academic functions, would expose them to the tort claims – real or imagined – of disaffected students and parents in countless numbers. They [educators] are already beset by social and financial problems which have gone to major litigation, but for which no permanent solution has yet appeared. The ultimate consequences, in terms of public time and money, would burden them – and society – beyond calculation" (*Peter W. v. San Francisco Unified School District*, 1976).

WISCONSIN

Another case made its way to the Wisconsin's highest court, which ruled that school counselors and school districts may not be held liable for giving students erroneous information – even when that information costs a student a full four-year college scholarship. Ryan Scott, a student at Stevens Point Area Senior High (SPASH), sued the school district after he was declared ineligible for an NCAA student-athlete scholarship. The Scotts sued the district with the arguments that (1) a counselor was negligent in advising Ryan of NCAA eligibility requirements, and (2) the district violated its legal obligation to provide students with counseling services. The district responded by filing a motion to dismiss the Scotts' claim on the grounds that the guidance counselor and the district are protected by a state law providing immunity for government employees when they exercise discretion in the course of their duties.

The plaintiff, Ryan Scott, and his parents met with school counselor Dave Johnson for assistance during Ryan's junior and senior years at SPASH regarding courses that met NCAA Division I hockey requirements. Ryan took Broadcast Communication and was told by Johnson that it was an NCAA-approved course. However, SPASH had several curriculum surveys from the NCAA that clearly indicated that Broadcast Communication did not satisfy NCAA eligibility requirements and after graduation and the receipt of a four-year hockey scholarship from the University of Alaska, Ryan learned that the NCAA had denied his eligibility certification because Broadcast Communication was not an approved course. The University of Alaska rescinded the scholarship offer. The Scotts sued the Stevens Point Area School District to recover the lost scholarship dollars, but the lower courts dismissed the case and the Scotts appealed to the Wisconsin Supreme Court.

The negligence claim hinged entirely on whether the district was immune from liability for negligence under Wisconsin's governmental immunity statute. The Wisconsin Supreme Court dismissed (but not happily) the law-suit because of governmental immunity. Although the justices were com-pelled to follow prior decisions, in their opinion, their decision was an injustice. Justice Bablitch stated, "This court should revisit these past cases....A doctrine of governmental immunity that has caused such injustice and inequity, in this case and others, cannot, and I predict, will not, stand much longer. In light of these sentiments, which appear to have growing support in many state courts, school districts should keep a watchful eye on the seemingly unstable future of the state's government immunity law" (*Scott v. Stevens Point Area Public School District*, 2003, n.p.).

RECOMMENDATIONS FOR ACADEMIC ADVISERS

The Sain, Brown and Scott rulings should not deter school counselors from career and academic advising, a role that has great opportunity for implementing a social justice agenda and leveling the playing field for many students. Following are some recommendations for counselors who are in the role of academic adviser.

- Continue to offer academic advising sessions to students. School counselors can help close the information gap between those students who know what they need to do to successfully access postsecondary education leading to wider economic opportunities, and those stu-dents who have not received even the most basic information. Students without a significant adult in their lives helping them under-stand how to access and be successful in postsecondary opportunities need the school counselor to be an advocate. Remember, in each case it was the school district that was sued, not the school counselor. It is unlikely that school counselors will have to face monetary liability in their work. You should not be deterred from academic advising on the slim chance that someone might level a charge of negligent misrepresentation against you.

- Act as the reasonably competent professional would. If faced with a lawsuit, school counselors who practice with care and caution will pass the standard of care test. The courts are not asking for extraordinary care, only reasonable care. Our ethical codes help professionals aspire to extraordinary care, but the courts do not demand this level. By exercising skill and care in every action taken as a professional, school counselors can demonstrate that they are behaving as reasonably competent professionals.

- Stay abreast of information needed for competent academic advising. You should be able to demonstrate a working knowledge of procedures, policies, laws, ethical standards and the school district's policies. By seeking professional development in the area of academic advising from many resources such as the school district, counseling organizations and literature, school counselors are demonstrating a good faith effort to stay informed.

- Empower others to take responsibility for having and giving the right information. Coaches could be responsible for advising students about NCAA regulations, and students could be encouraged to become their own advocates in gathering information about college admissions, scholarships and financial aid. You can teach self-advocacy for students through classroom guidance lessons in the computer lab, where students can conduct Internet searches and locate information on their own. As a manager of resources, the school counselor can equip others to be a key presence in the career and academic advising roles.

- Widely publicize academic information for all students and parents. Make use of newsletters, form letters and e-mail listservs in your advising role, thus demonstrating a proactive stance to disseminating critical, timely information.

- Require that students and parents sign off when they receive critical information. When you give seniors their personal credit check for remaining graduation requirements, for instance, have them sign an acknowledgment that they have been told and understand what they need to do – and have parents sign, too.

- Consult when appropriate. Best practice for school counselors is always to consult whenever they are unsure. School counselors never stand alone unless they fail to consult with others who are in a position to help, particularly school district legal counsel. You might review the *Sain*, *Brown* and *Scott* rulings carefully with your district legal counsel and ask how you should protect yourself. In addition, maintain a tracking system to document whom you consulted. Although the onus should be on the student and his or her parents, best practice is to verify information to the extent possible.

NEGLIGENCE IN SUICIDE PREVENTION

A student tells you that her friend Jocelyn, one of your counselees, is threatening suicide. When you call Jocelyn into your office, she vehemently denies any consideration of suicide, scoffing at the idea that she would ever harm herself. You are convinced that there is no basis for concern and you drop the issue without discussing it with anyone else. Do your actions pose an ethical or legal dilemma?

Points to Consider

The specter of teen-age suicide is an unfortunate reality for school counselors. And, counselors know all too well the damage to their effectiveness if they have the reputation of breaking confidences and calling parents. The ambiguity of protecting a student's trust in the school counselor as a confidant, and the need to respect parents' rights to be the guiding voice in their children's lives, are a constant source of tension for school counselors. This case underscores the conflict counselors face in trying to behave legally and ethically toward students, parents and their school district.

Let's look first at the legal aspects of this case. The law of negligence involves injury or damage to another through a breach of duty owed to that person. *Duty owed* means a legal responsibility one person has to another, such as a legal responsibility to drive with care so that you do not injure another person (Alexander & Alexander, 2005). As we noted earlier, negligence requires the presence of four elements: (1) a duty is owed; (2) the duty owed was breached; (3) there is a causal connection between breach of duty and injury; and (4) an injury has occurred. Until the *Eisel v. Montgomery County Board of Education* court case (1991), courts consistently found that school counselors did not "owe a legal duty" to prevent a student's suicide. Eisel strengthened counselors' legal obligation to students by satisfying for the first time the primary element of negligence, declaring that school counselors have a special relationship with students and owe a duty to try to prevent a student's suicide.

The Maryland Court of Appeals in the Eisel case ruled that school coun-selors had a duty to notify the parents of a 13-year-old student who made suicidal statements to her classmates. Nicole Eisel allegedly became involved in Satanism and told several friends and fellow students of her intention to kill herself. Some of these friends told their school counselor of Nicole's intentions, and this counselor in turn informed Nicole's counselor. The two counselors questioned Nicole about the statements and Nicole denied making them. The counselors did not notify either the parents or the school administrators about these events. Shortly thereafter, in a public park, Nicole and her friend tragically consummated their suicide pact.

The court in the Eisel case cited as critical the *in loco parentis* doctrine, which states that educators including school counselors legally stand in the place of parents. Furthermore, school counselors owe a special duty to exercise reasonable care to protect a student from harm. The court con-cluded school counselors have a duty to use reasonable means to attempt to prevent a suicide when they receive notice of a student's suicidal intent. With the Eisel ruling, the court redefined the school counselor-student relationship and declared that school counselors have a duty of care when placed on notice of a possible suicide. The court recognized the fact that school counselors hear a great amount of suicidal ideation and have the complicated task of trying to determine which threats are real, yet the court stated, "The consequence of the risk is so great that even a relative-ly remote possibility of a suicide may be enough to establish duty" (*Eisel v. Board of Education of Montgomery County*, 1991, n.p.). In other words, the court stopped just short of declaring that school counselors have an affirmative duty to notify parents in each and every case involv-ing a suicidal threat.

Does the Eisel ruling take away counselors' ability to exercise judgment with regard to student suicide? No, *Eisel* did not argue for *absolute duty* as in the case of child abuse reporting, in which counselors must report any and all suspected situations; the court stopped just short of declaring an absolute duty. However, the tenets established in *Eisel* set a precedent that counselors now have a legal obligation to try to prevent suicide. Counselors should not be paralyzed by the Eisel ruling. Rather, the ruling should serve to help counselors realize the importance of seeking supervi-sion and carefully deliberating decisions about breaching student confi-dentiality, as well as protecting parental rights. The duty of care is critical, as is the enormous consequence of breaching confidentiality. You should feel considerable discomfort with the weight of the decision to breach; if not, examine carefully your level of commitment to confidentiality.

The Eisel case did not deliver the final word. Following the Eisel case, courts in at least five states have rejected these kinds of cases. An Illinois appellate court in 1997 absolved a school counselor of legal liability when the counselor failed to tell the student's parents about his threats of suicide (*Grant v. Board of Trustees of Valley View School District*, 1997). "But courts in three other cases have ruled that in certain circumstances school employees' failure to act can make them or the school legally responsible for a student's suicide" (Simpson, 1999, p. 12). All of the cases that imposed liability, however, involved employees who failed to notify parents that their children had written or talked to others about killing themselves (Portner, 2002; Simpson, 1999).

Where does a school counselor's legal liability end? It ends when you have notified school authorities or parents that a student is at risk and you have recommended appropriate actions – and be sure to document your notification. The courts do not expect counselors to do the impossible and prevent all adolescent suicides. Rather, the court's message is that the consequence of the risk in not involving parents is too great and that parents must be allowed to try to intervene. However, a counselor's ethical obligation to a suicidal student may extend beyond parental notification if the parents do not enroll the student in counseling. If they do not arrange counseling when the suicidal student is first identified, the probability of attempts and completion increases. School counselors must make every attempt to supply parents or guardians with counseling referrals until placement is secured for that student (Capuzzi, 2002). In most cases, the counselor will need to notify Child Protective Services of a possible neglect situation if the parents do not pursue counseling.

Ethical standards provide guidelines regarding protecting students and others from potentially dangerous situations, but it is ultimately the responsibility of the counselor to negotiate the rights and privileges of students and parents with regard to issues of duty to care. The courts continually vest parents with legal rights to guide their children (*Bellotti v. Baird*, 1979; *H. L. v. Matheson*, 1981). The ASCA codes dictate that school counselors have a primary obligation and loyalty to students, but that parents need to be involved as appropriate (ASCA, 2004). Community standards, a counselor's own personal values, school board policy, the school setting, state and federal statutes, and school procedures all contribute to the complex nature of working with minors in schools.

GOVERNMENTAL IMMUNITY AND SUICIDE

Andrew was a freshman at St. Croix Falls High School in January 1996. One day his father, James McMahon, drove Andrew to school, but the boy did not attend classes that day. A district policy provides that if a student is absent from school, the school will call the parents at home or work to verify the absence, but the school did not call the McMahons. A classmate, Jamie Stocker, told a school counselor that Andrew "was planning to skip school that day," that he was probably at her house, and that someone should check on him or contact his parents. Stocker further said she thought Andrew seemed to be bothered by something because he seemed depressed and preoccupied, and that he had said something to the effect that he was "sick and tired of this life." Stocker's affidavit also indicates that she left school without permission that afternoon to check on Andrew at her home and discovered Andrew's body in her family's closed garage. An autopsy lists the cause of death as suicide from self-immolation; Andrew doused himself with gasoline and set himself on fire. According to the McMahons' affidavits, they were unaware that Andrew had received five failing grades, had been removed from the basketball team for those grades, and had been very upset in school and at times crying.

The McMahons appealed the dismissal of their wrongful death suit against St. Croix Falls School District for their son's suicide. The McMahons argued that the circuit court erred when it established a bright-line rule that a school district has absolute immunity for its negligent acts when a student commits suicide. The McMahons contend that contrary to Wisconsin tort law, the circuit court erroneously established that under no conceivable circumstances, no matter how egregious a school district's negligence, can a school ever be found liable for a minor student's suicide. They contend that the district breached its duty to call them and to follow up after a school counselor learned that Andrew was despondent and absent from school.

The appeals court rejected the argument and concluded that under *Bogust v. Iverson* (1960), Andrew's suicide constituted an intervening, superseding cause that breaks the chain of causation. In other words, for negligence to be determined there had to be a connection between the school counselors' breach of duty and the injury suffered. Most states follow the general rule that suicide is an intervening force, meaning regardless of what the counselor did or did not do (the wrongful act) before the suicide, the suicide itself broke any chain of causation. The district disputes the facts of Stocker's affidavit, but states that it is of no matter as they are immaterial to governmental immunity. The appeals court agreed with the district that such facts would not change the results.

In *Bogust v. Iverson* (1960), the Wisconsin Supreme Court dismissed a wrongful death action brought against a college guidance counselor by the parents of a 19-year-old student who committed suicide six weeks after counseling was terminated. Bogust cited that suicide constitutes an intervening force that breaks the line of causation from the wrongful act to the death and therefore the wrongful act does not render the counselor civilly liable (*Bogust v. Iverson*, 1960).

Another ruling provided a similar result. In *Lezner v. Shaw and Gresham School District* (1990), Lezner, an emotionally disabled student, was suspended from school for smoking marijuana on school property. The school unsuccessfully tried to reach the parents by phone to let them know of the suspension, then gave a copy of the suspension papers to the student and mailed the original to his home. The student did not inform his parents of the suspension and committed suicide. The parents claimed the school was negligent by failing to notify them promptly of their son's suspension. Following the *Bogust v. Iverson* (1960) precedent, the court ruled that a delayed suicide was not sufficiently connected to any act of negligence.

Even though case after case throughout the country finds that school counselors do not owe a duty to try to prevent suicide or that suicide is an intervening variable, we take little comfort in this. "Do no harm" means we should always err on the side of caution when we think a student may be in danger. Call parents. The breach of confidentiality is a minor transgression when weighed against the greater harm, the death of a child.

In a Position to Know: A Counselor Educator Speaks

The case presented at the beginning of the chapter is revisited here and answered by a counselor educator. Compare his response with your approach.

NEGLIGENCE IN EATING DISORDERS

Karen, one of your seventh-graders, has been a regular in your office for the last two years. The student has serious problems and you have implored Karen's stepmother – you can never get her father to respond – to get her some help. Lately, you believe she is now suffering from bulimia. Her teeth appear pitted, her skin is shallow and pasty-looking, she is losing weight and she appears more nervous than ever. When you confront Karen, she does not answer but rather starts a long diatribe about how you cannot tell her father because he is ready to send her off to live with her birth mother, and that phone call will give him the ammunition he needs. You know that Karen has all but admitted to you that she is bulimic and you also know that her assessment of her father's reaction is probably accurate. You decide to try to help Karen without calling her parents. The unthinkable happens and Karen suffers heart failure. You are sued for negligence. How do you believe the courts will react? Is it likely that your school district will pay for your defense?

Response from a Counselor Educator

We can learn many lessons from this counselor's unfortunate predicament. School counselors who want to make sure they are never sued for negligence could avoid such unfortunate experiences by always telling parents or guardians everything students tell them in counseling sessions. Of course, such counselors might have to find other jobs at some point, because few students would seek them out for help when they realize the counselors are informing parents and guardians of everything the students say. Every time a school counselor decides not to inform parents or guardians after students have disclosed something in a session that could possibly lead to the student or others being harmed, counselors take a legal risk. However, if they refuse to take such risks from time to time, they could not possibly be effective counselors.

In reality, school counselors have to decide on a regular basis when to inform parents or guardians of something students have told them in counseling sessions. When counselors determine that students may be at risk of endangering themselves or others, counselors have an ethical and legal duty to inform parents or guardians. But when should counselors tell parents or guardians, and when should counselors take a risk and not tell them?

No one knows the answer to that question, and statutes and case law do not offer much help. The general rule is that if a reasonable school counselor with similar education and training in a similar community would have foreseen harm to self or others in a similar set of circumstances, then counselors should disclose what they know from counseling sessions with their students to parents or guardians. Unfortunately, this is an "after the fact" test, and school counselors have to make their decisions on the firing line, often quickly.

The best advice for school counselors is to consult with other professionals if they are unsure whether they should disclose a student confidence to the student's parents or guardians. The more consultants counselors discuss the situation with, the better. If later, a school counselor's decision not to inform parents or guardians is questioned (as is the situation in this case study), and the school counselor consulted with others who agreed parents or guardians should not be informed, then the counselor has met the legal test stated above, "What would a reasonable school counselor with similar education and training in a similar community have done?"

Most school counselors reading this case study probably will conclude that the counselor should have told Karen's father of Karen's suspected bulimia because her condition was life-threatening, even though Karen's father was likely to react negatively in a way that would add more pressure to Karen's life. However, there might be special circumstances to this situation that could have led a reasonable counselor (and his or her consultants) to decide not to inform Karen's father, but instead to seek help for Karen in other ways. Telling the father of the counselor's suspicion of bulimia would have relieved the school counselor of any finding of negligence, but would it have been the ethical, moral and professional action to have taken? Should the counselor have taken a risk by not telling the father in this particular situation? No one knows for sure.

Will the school district pay for the counselor's legal defense in this case study? Probably yes. In this situation, both the district and the counselor most likely will be sued. The insurance company holding a liability policy for the school will hire an excellent attorney who specializes in defending professionals in negligence cases to represent the school district. That same attorney probably will represent the school counselor as well, but only if the attorney believes it is in the school district's best interest to do so. In most states, public entities cannot be sued because of sovereign immunity, or there are limits to negligence suits because of the sovereign immunity doctrine. If the attorney believes he or she could get the school district dismissed from the lawsuit, but could not get the school counselor dismissed, the attorney would have an obligation to do that.

Getting the school district dismissed from the suit would leave the school counselor in this case study legally and financially vulnerable. As a result, school counselors should always have their own personal professional liability insurance policies that would pay for their defense and any judgment rendered against them individually. If school counselors do not have such a policy as a benefit of their union dues, they should purchase a policy from professional associations such as the American Counseling Association or the American School Counselor Association.

Theodore P. Remley Jr., counselor educator at the University of New Orleans

Making Connections

1. Discuss the differences between negligence and malpractice.

2. What are the elements of negligence? Why is it so difficult to find that a school counselor owes a duty to prevent suicide?

3. What is standard of care? Who is the reasonably competent professional?

4. What is foreseeability? How should this guide your behavior?

5. What is governmental or sovereign immunity?

Key Terms

Constitutional law
Criminal law
Civil law
Negligence
Breach
Reasonableness
Causal connection
Injury suffered
Malpractice
Educational malpractice

Governmental immunity
Ministerial
Addressing a known danger
Malicious, willful and intentional torts
In loco parentis
Duty of care
Intervening, superseding cause

References

Alexander, K., & Alexander, D. (2005). *American public school law* (6th ed). Belmont, CA: Thomson West.

American School Counselor Association. (2004). *Ethical standards for school counselors.* Alexandria, VA: Author.

Bellotti v. Baird, 443 U.S. 622 (1979).

Bethel School District No. 403 v. Fraser, 1986 Supreme Court of the United States, 1986, 478 .S. 675, 106 S. Ct. 3159.

Bogust v. Iverson, 102 N.W.2d 228 (Wis. 1960).

Brown v. Compton Unified School District 68 Cal. App. 4th 114; 80 Cal. Rptr. 2d 171; 1998 Cal. App.

Cafaro, C. S. (2000). Student suicide and school system liability. *School Law Bulletin*, 31, 17-28.

Capuzzi, D. (2002). Legal and ethical challenges in counseling suicidal students. *Professional School Counseling*, 6(1), 36-46.

Caudill, C. O. (2004). *Therapists under fire.* Retrieved June 1, 2004, from http://www.cphins.com/riskmanagement/therapists_under_fire.htm.

Collins, K. L. (2001). *Guidance counselor liability for "negligent representation."* Retrieved December 12, 2001, from http://www.sai-iowa.org/901Report.html

Cottone, R., & Tarvydas, V. (1998). *Ethical and professional issues in counseling.* Upper Saddle River, NJ: Merrill Prentice Hall.

Doe v. Blandford, 402 Mass. 831, 835, 525 N.E.2d 403 (2000).

Doe and Doe v. Greendale Baptist Church and Academy, 327 F.3d 492 (Wisconsin 2003).

Eisel v. Board of Education of Montgomery County. 324 Md. 376, 597 A. 2d 447 (Md Ct. App. 1991). Retrieved December 27, 2002, from LexisNexis database.

Fischer, L., & Sorenson, G. P. (1996). *School law for counselors, psychologists, and social workers* (3rd ed.). White Plains, NY: Longman.

Gammon v. Edwardsville Community Unit School District, 82 Ill. App. 3d 586 (1980).

Garvey, J., Aleinikoff, A., & Farber, D. (2004). *Modern constitutional theory: A reader* (5th ed.). St. Paul, MN: West Group Publishing.

Gladding, S., Remley, T. P., Jr., & Huber, C. (2001). *Ethical, legal, and professional issues in the practice of marriage and family therapy* (3rd ed.). Upper Saddle River, NJ: Merrill Prentice Hall.

Grant v. Board of Trustees of Valley View School District. No 365-U, 676 N.E.2d 705 (Ill. App. Ct. 1997)

H. L. v. Matheson, 450 U.S. 398 (1981).

Houston-Vega, M. K., Nuehring, E. M., & Daguio, E. R. (1997). *Prudent practice: A guide for managing malpractice risk*. Washington, DC: National Association of Social Workers Press.

Imber, M., & Van Geel, T. (2004). *Education law* (3rd ed.). New York: McGraw Hill.

Lezner v. Shaw and-Gresham School District (1990) 156 Wis. 2d 466; 458 N.W.2d 388; 1990 Wisc. App. LEXIS 357 April 17, 1990.

Moore v. Vanderloo 386 N.W.2d 108 (Iowa 1986).

Parrott, J. (2001, July 9). Are advisors risking lawsuits for misadvising students? *The Mentor: An Academic Advising Journal*. Retrieved January 20, 2002, from www.psu.edu/dus/mentor/

Peter W. v. San Francisco Unified School District, 60 Cal. App. 3d 814, 825 [131 Cal. Rptr. 854] (California 1976).

Portner, J. (2002). Suicide: Many schools fall short on prevention. *Education week*. Retrieved January 20, 2002, from http://www.edweek.org/ew/eprintstory.cfm?slug=32solution.h19

Prosser, W. (1971). *The law of torts*. St. Paul, MN: West.

Raquel R.S. v. Necedah Area Sch. Dist., 2003 WI App 22 (2002).

Reid, K. (2001, May 2). Iowa's high court holds counselors liable. *Education Week*. Retrieved January 20, 2002, from http://www.edweek.org/ew/ewstory.cfm?slug=33guide.h20

Remley, T. P., & Herlihy, B. (2001). *Ethical, legal, and professional issues in counseling*. Upper Saddle River, NJ: Merrill Prentice Hall.

Sain v. Cedar Rapids Community School District, 626 N.W.2d 115 (Iowa 2001).

Scott v. Stevens Point Area Public School District, 650 N.W.2d 560 (Wisconsin 2003).

Simpson, M. (1999). *The suicide of a child is an unthinkable tragedy. But can parents hold school employees legally liable?* Washington, DC: National Education Association. Retrieved January 17, 2005, from http://www.nea.org/neatoday/9902/rights.html

Smith v. The School Board of Orange County Court of Appeal of Florida, 5th District, 642 So. 2d 577; 1994 Fla. August 12, 1994.

Stone, C. (2001). *Legal and ethical issues in working with minors in schools* [Film]. Alexandria, VA: American Counseling Association.

Tribe, L. (2000). *American constitutional law* (3rd ed.). New York: Foundation Press.

Valente, W. (1998). *Law in the schools* (4th ed.). Upper Saddle River, NJ: Merrill: Prentice Hall.

Willis, S. P. (2004). Iowa school counselors had better get it right! *Iowa Law Review, 89*, 1093.

Zirkel, P. (2001). Ill advised. *Phi Delta Kappan, 83*, 98-99.

CHAPTER 5

Obligations to the Courts

IN THIS CHAPTER

Objectives

By the time you have completed this chapter, you should be able to:

- Understand that schools are governmental agencies and how this fact affects legal behavior for educators.
- Discuss how constitution, statutory and case law form the legal foundation on which the public schools are based.
- Understand the difference between privileged communication and confidentiality.
- Explain the difference between case notes and educational records.
- Determine what to do if you receive a subpoena.
- Discuss how to advocate for your students without becoming involved in the court system.

Introduction

Schools are governmental agencies. The legal authority of schools is as diverse as the 50 states that enact laws to govern schools. Even though the United States comprises a union of states under one central government, we have a "unique education system that is governed by laws of fifty states, with component parts amounting to several thousand local school district operating units. Through all of this organization, multiformity, and indeed complexity, run the legal basis on which the entire system is founded" (Alexander & Alexander, 2005, p. 2). State legislation provides the basis for public school law and the courts through litigation interpret the laws. "The combination of constitutions, statutes, and court (or case) law forms the primary legal foundation on which the public schools are based" (Alexander & Alexander, 2005, p. 2).

State legislatures give school boards authority to create their own rules and regulations, and school boards must act in accordance with their own requirements (Imber & Van Geel, 2004). A case in which a school counselor served as the hearing officer for a drug offense resulted in expulsion for the student. However, the courts overturned the recommendation because it did not follow the school board's own policies stating that a first offender could seek drug counseling instead of being expelled (*Camlin v. Beecher Community School District*, 2003).

The courts have traditionally maintained and enforced the concept of separation of the different branches of power when confronted with cases involving education (Alexander & Alexander, 2005; Imber & Van Geel, 2004). Their reluctance is due in part to "an appreciation of the importance in our system of the concept of separation of powers so that each division of government may function freely within the area of its responsibility" (*Ricker v. Board of Education of Millard County School District*, 1964). In short, school districts are not often sued and when they are, the lower courts are reluctant to rule against school districts in many cases.

According to the courts, statutes are the basis for "the most common litigation involving school operation" (Alexander & Alexander, 2005, p. 4). Courts determine the constitutionality of such legislation. If a statute can be interpreted in two ways, one of which will be constitutional, the courts will adopt the constitutional interpretation (*Bonvento v. Board of Public Instruction of Palm Beach County*, 1967; *Hobbs v County of Moore*, 1966).

The United States has court systems at both the federal and the state levels. This book includes court cases involving educators at both levels, although state courts decide most cases (Alexander & Alexander, 2005; Imber & Van Geel, 2004). From highest to lowest, state court systems include the courts of last resort such as the state supreme courts; intermediate appellate courts; courts of general jurisdiction, otherwise known as district, circuit, superior or juvenile; and courts of limited jurisdiction, otherwise known as small claims courts, probate or justice of the peace (Fine, 1999).

The highest court in terms of this body of law is the supreme court of a state, called the Court of Appeals or Supreme Judicial Court in seven states. The states' supreme courts are not considered lower courts even in relation to the Supreme Court of the United States. State supreme courts follow the U.S. Supreme Court's ruling on the meaning of the U.S. Constitution, but the highest court in each state is free to interpret state laws or the state constitution in any way that does not violate principles of federal law (Alexander & Alexander, 2005).

Intermediate appellate courts exist in 38 states to hear appeals from trial court, to review trial court proceedings and to correct errors in the application of law and procedure (Alexander & Alexander, 2005). Courts of general jurisdiction are major courts in which defendants or plaintiffs can appeal to higher courts. About three-fourths of all cases in the limited jurisdiction courts involve traffic offenses (Alexander & Alexander, 2005; Imber & Van Geel, 2004).

In the federal court system, each state has at least one federal district court, with most states having two courts. California, Texas and New York each have four district courts. These federal courts litigate cases involving citizens of several different states and cases involving federal statutes. Appeals go to the district circuit courts of appeals or directly to the U.S. Supreme Court. Beyond the Supreme Court, citizens of the United States have no redress (Alexander & Alexander, 2005; Imber & Van Geel, 2004).

All court cases in this book began at the lower or district court level by a plaintiff or petitioner, one who initiates a court action by filing a complaint with the appropriate court. The court serves a summons on the person or persons named as the defendant(s). The next step is the plea, in which the defendant can respond by a denial, by seeking independent relief or by introducing an affirmative defense (Alexander & Alexander, 2005; Imber & Van Geel, 2004).

Prior to trial, there is a process of discovery in which the attorneys may require an oral or written deposition; written interrogatories requiring written responses to questions; certain documents or materials; a request to submit a listing of facts that are not in dispute; and/or a physical or mental examination of one of the parties of the lawsuit (Alexander & Alexander, 2005; Imber & Van Geel, 2004).

The case may be disposed of before going to trial if the judge dismisses the case or allows a motion for summary judgment if there is no dispute of the facts and a trial is not necessary to establish them. Alternatively, the plaintiff may voluntarily dismiss the case or the parties may reach an out-of-court settlement. The vast majority of civil suits are settled out of court (Alexander & Alexander, 2005; Fischer & Sorenson, 1996). If the case goes to trial, it would be heard by a judge or a jury. The plaintiff bears the burden of proof.

Cases in this book involve school counselors as defendants and witnesses. When a school counselor becomes a defendant in a case, it is often a civil case: a wrong against a student or his or her parents (see Chapter 4 on "Negligence."). A criminal wrong might involve sexual misconduct with a minor student. Some of the most common cases in which a school counselor might become a defendant involve defamation and qualified privilege, abortion or birth control counseling, academic advising, failure to report child abuse, or unauthorized disclosure of information (Fischer and Sorenson, 1996; Stone, 2001).

Court proceedings involving school counselors as witnesses for the court are usually cases of child custody, child abuse or disciplinary action (Stone, 2001). Generally speaking, school counselors are required to testify in a court proceeding. While school counselors have confidentiality requirements, they cannot deny the courts their testimony unless school counselors are given privileged communication in state statutes (Remley, Herman, & Huey, 2003; Stone, 2001).

School counselors should know whether or not they have privilege. In an informal survey, school counselors from 25 states responded as to whether or not their students can render them incapable of testifying about their counseling (or privileged) communications (Stone, 2005). Reviewing the statutes for these 25 states, almost all counselors correctly identified whether or not they had privileged communication. However, counselors from the few states that do have privilege believed their privilege is more extensive than it really is. In most states where statutes give privilege, there are many caveats about when a judge can decide that the needs of the state outweigh the privileged communication.

There is judicial reluctance to extend the privilege to school counselors because of the age of their clients and the setting in which they work (Fischer & Sorenson, 1996). Another problem with privilege is the definition of what constitutes counseling. The court's tendency is to interpret privilege statutes for school counselors very narrowly (Fischer & Sorenson, 1996). For school counselors, counseling takes place everywhere: the playground, the bus loading zone, the hallways. Currently, there are no court cases to give us authoritative guidance on this matter (Fischer & Sorenson, 1996; Stone, 2005).

Intent, a critical component in a court case, may not be enough to secure your privilege. A counselor may intend that an exchange with a student in the cafeteria is counseling, but the judge may or may not rule that privilege applies in the situation. Whereas, if an attorney and client exchange any information anywhere – the subway, sauna, tennis court – every utterance is privilege. For our profession, the interpretation is much more constricted, with nearly every state statute offering exceptions to school counselor-student privilege to be interpreted as the judges see fit (see Kentucky 2A, 2B and 2C, which follows, to see one state's exceptions to privilege).

A CONFIDENTIALITY CODE FOR SCHOOL COUNSELORS

A good example of a confidentiality code can be found in California Education Code § 49602 says:

Any information of a personal nature disclosed by a pupil 12 years of age or older in the process of receiving counseling from a school counselor, as specified in Section 49600, is confidential. Any information of a personal nature disclosed to a school counselor by a parent or guardian of a pupil who is 12 years of age or older and who is in the process of receiving counseling from a school counselor, as specified in Section 49600, is confidential. The information shall not become part of the pupil record, as defined in subdivision (b) of Section 49061, without the written consent of the person who disclosed the confidential information. The information shall not be revealed, released, discussed, or referred to, except as follows:

(a) Discussion with psychotherapists as defined by Section 1010 of the Evidence Code, other health care providers, or the school nurse, for the sole purpose of referring the pupil for treatment.

(b) Reporting of child abuse or neglect. ...

(c) Reporting information to the principal or parents of the pupil when the school counselor has reasonable cause to believe that disclosure is necessary to avert a clear and present danger to the health, safety, or welfare of the pupil or the following other persons living in the school community: administrators, teachers, school staff, parents, pupils, and other school community members.

(d) Reporting information to the principal, other persons inside the school, as necessary, the parents of the pupil, and other persons outside the school when the pupil indicates that a crime, involving the likelihood of personal injury or significant or substantial property losses, will be or has been committed.

(e) Reporting information to one or more persons specified in a written waiver after this written waiver of confidence is read and signed by the pupil and preserved in the pupil's file.

Notwithstanding the provisions of this section, a school counselor shall not disclose information deemed to be confidential ... to the parents of the pupil when the school counselor has reasonable cause to believe that the disclosure would result in a clear and present danger to the health, safety, or welfare of the pupil. ... A school counselor shall disclose ... to law enforcement agencies when ordered to do so by order of a court of law, to aid in the investigation of a crime, or when ordered to testify in any administrative or judicial proceeding. ...

It is the intent of the Legislature that counselors use the privilege of confidentiality under this section to assist the pupil whenever possible to communicate more effectively with parents, school staff, and others.

No person required by this section to keep information discussed during counseling confidential shall incur any civil or criminal liability as a result of keeping that information confidential.

As used in this section, "information of a personal nature" does not include routine objective information related to academic and career counseling. (California Education Code, 2004)

EXAMPLES OF STATE STATUTES REGARDING PRIVILEGED COMMUNICATION

Privileged Communication with Exceptions

Indiana
Indiana has privilege with exceptions: "A school counselor is immune from disclosing privileged or confidential communication made to the counselor as a counselor by a student …" (Ind. Code Ann., 2004a, § 20-6.1-6-15). "[Privilege] is not a ground for excluding evidence in any judicial proceeding resulting from a report of a child who may be a victim of child abuse or neglect or relating to the subject matter of the report or failing to report as required by IC 31-33" (Ind. Code Ann., 2004b, § 31-33).

Kentucky
Kentucky has privilege with exceptions. From the state statute on counselor-client privilege:

A "counselor" includes … A certified school counselor who meets the requirements of the Kentucky Board of Education and who is duly appointed and regularly employed for the purpose of counseling in a public or private school of this state …

(b) General rule of privilege. A client has a privilege to refuse to disclose and to prevent any other person from disclosing confidential communications made for the purpose of counseling the client, between himself, his counselor, and persons present at the direction of the counselor, including members of the client's family. …

(d) Exceptions. There is no privilege under this rule for any relevant communication. … (2) If the judge finds:

(A) That the substance of the communication is relevant to an essential issue in the case;

(B) That there are no available alternate means to obtain the substantial equivalent of the communication; and

(C) That the need for the information outweighs the interest protected by the privilege. The court may receive evidence in camera to make findings under this rule. (Kentucky Revised Statutes, 2004, § 506)

Ohio
Ohio grants school counselors confidentiality excluding the following circumstances: communication indicates that the student or other persons are in danger of child abuse or neglect; the student gives the counselor permission to testify; if the student volunteers to testify, the counselor may feel the need to testify on the same topic; if the student is deceased, the parent or legal guardian gives consent; the court determines that the information is not relevant to the counselor-student relationship; the court determines that the counselor's testimony is pertinent if a student brings action against a school, its administrators or personnel; or the child is in danger of being harmed (Ohio Revised Code, 2003, § 2317.02).

Examples of State Statutes Granting Privileged Communication

Idaho
Idaho seems to leave little doubt that school counselors have privilege. When listing all the professionals who cannot be forced to testify against their clients, Number 6 of the list reads: "Any certificated counselor, psychologist or psychological examiner, duly appointed, regularly employed and designated in such capacity by any public or private school in this state for the purpose of counseling students, shall be immune from disclosing, without the consent of the student, any communication made by any student so counseled or examined in any civil or criminal action to which such student is a party. Such matters so communicated shall be privileged and protected against disclosure" (Idaho Code, 2001, § 9-203).

Iowa
Iowa school counselors who have met the requirements for certification and accreditation standards of Iowa's Department of Education are not allowed to disclose confidential information the student or the student's parents have entrusted to the counselor that enables the counselor to perform his duties (Iowa Code Ann., 2003, § 622.10).

Montana
Montana gives privilege. "A counselor, psychologist, nurse, or teacher employed by any educational institution cannot be examined as to com-

munications made to him in confidence by a duly registered student of such institution. However, this provision shall not apply where consent has been given by the student, if not a minor, or, if he is a minor, by the student and his parent or legal guardian" (Montana Code Ann., 2003, § 26-1-809).

Nevada
Nevada has confidential communication (Nevada Rev. Stat., 1979, § 49.290). However, school counselors cannot testify in any criminal and civil actions to which the student has been connected unless the student gives consent.

North Carolina
In North Carolina, school counselors cannot "testify in any action, suit, or proceeding concerning any information acquired in rendering counseling services to any student..., and which information was necessary to enable him to render counseling services; provided, however, that this section shall not apply where the student in open court waives the privilege conferred" (North Carolina Gen. Stat., 2004, § 8-53.4).

North Dakota
Elementary and secondary school counselors in North Dakota have confidential communication unless the student or counselee requests that the information provided be disclosed (North Dakota Century Code, 2003, § 31-01-06.1).

Oregon
In Oregon, school counselors are listed among those being granted privilege. "Section 40.245, Rule 504-3. School employee-student privilege. . . . (2) A certificated school counselor regularly employed and designated in such capacity by a public school shall not, without the consent of the student, be examined as to any communication made by the student to the counselor in the official capacity of the counselor in any civil action or proceeding or a criminal action or proceeding in which such student is a party concerning the past use, abuse or sale of drugs, controlled substances or alcoholic liquor. Any violation of the privilege provided by this subsection may result in the suspension of certification of the professional school counselor as provided in ORS 342.175, 342.177 and 342.180. However, in the event that the student's condition presents a clear and imminent danger to the student or to others, the counselor shall report this fact to an appropriate responsible authority or take such other emergency measures as the situation demands" (Oregon Rev. Stat., 2003).

South Dakota
South Dakota has privileged communication between students and elementary or secondary school counselors with the following exceptions: privilege is waived in writing by the student; the information was disclosed to the counselor for the purpose of being publicized; the counselor has cause to suspect that the student or other individuals have been abused or their physical or mental health is at risk (South Dakota Code, 2003, § 19-13-21.1, Rule 508.1).

Examples of State Statutes Not Granting Privileged Communication

Arkansas
Arkansas grants privileged communication to licensed professional counselors but not to school counselors. "The confidential relations and communications between a licensed counselor and a client, a licensed associate counselor and a client, a licensed marriage and family therapist and a client, or between a licensed associate marriage and family therapist and a client are placed upon the same basis as those between an attorney and a client" (Arkansas Code, 2004, § 17-27-311).

Wyoming
Wyoming's statutes allow privileged communication for licensed professional counselors, marriage and family therapists, social workers, and chemical dependency specialists. However, this does not apply to school counselors (Wyoming Code, 2004, § 33-38-113).

If your state is not mentioned above and you would like to see how it addresses the issue of privileged communications, review your state statutes or visit the Web site http://nccanch.acf.hhs.gov/general/legal/statutes/immunity.pdf.

Ethical Standards Addressed in This Chapter

Professionalism means knowing your professional associations' codes and adhering to them. Those ethical standards from American School Counselor Association that are most germane include the following:

- The professional school counselor keeps information confidential unless disclosure is required to prevent clear and imminent danger to the student or others or when legal requirements demand that confidential information be revealed. Counselors will consult with appropriate professionals when in doubt as to the validity of an exception. (A.2.b)

- The professional school counselor requests of the court that disclosure not be required when the release of confidential information may potentially harm a student or the counseling relationship. (A.2.d)
- The professional school counselor protects the confidentiality of students' records and releases personal data in accordance with prescribed laws and school policies. Student information stored and transmitted electronically is treated with the same care as traditional student records. (A.2.e)
- The professional school counselor keeps sole-possession records separate from students' educational records in keeping with state laws. (A.8.b)
- The professional school counselor recognizes the limits of sole-possession records and understands these records are a memory aid for the creator and in absence of privilege communication may be subpoenaed and may become educational records when they (1) are shared with others in verbal or written form, (2) include information other than professional opinion or personal observations and/or (3) are made accessible to others. (A.8.c)
- The professional school counselor establishes a reasonable timeline for purging sole-possession records or case notes. Suggested guidelines include shredding sole-possession records when the student transitions to the next level, transfers to another school or graduates. Careful discretion and deliberation should be applied before destroying sole-possession records that may be needed by a court of law such as notes on child abuse, suicide, sexual harassment or violence. (A.8.d)

The full text of American Counseling Association ethical codes and ASCA ethical codes can be found at these Web sites: ACA at http://www.counseling.org and ASCA at www.schoolcounselor.org.

Getting Started: What Would You Do?

The following case is answered for you at the end of this chapter by practicing school counselors. Before you read their responses, formulate in your own mind how you would approach this ethical dilemma.

COUNSELORS, CUSTODY ISSUES AND THE COURTS

You have been working with a student whose parents are going through a bitter divorce. The student tells you how much she wants to live with her mother while the father continues to paint a picture of the mother as overindulgent, not able to set boundaries for their daughter, encouraging their daughter's sexual relationship with her boyfriend, and allowing the boyfriend to stay overnight. The back-and-forth accusations between the daughter and father are endless. You have rarely heard from the mother and the few times that you have, you tend to agree that the father's picture might be accurate. You receive a subpoena from the father's attorney to appear for a deposition in a custody hearing. Legally, must you give a deposition? Are there any ethical considerations that you need to make in this situation?

Working Through Case Studies

LICENSED WITH PRIVILEGE PRACTICING IN A PROFESSION WITHOUT PRIVILEGE

You are a licensed counselor practicing as a school counselor. You live in a state that grants privileged communication for licensed counselors but not for school counselors. You are called to testify. If the student in question does not give you permission to testify, can you invoke privileged communication and therefore not be required to appear in court?

Points to Consider

Some school counselors across the nation hold dual licensure; they are licensed counselors and they also are certified school counselors. State statutes may tell licensed counselors that their communications with school-aged clients are privileged because they are licensed, even though the school counselors they work with do not have privilege. I believe that the role in which you are functioning defines the rules by which you must practice, but a court case is needed to settle the issue. To date, it does not appear that a judge has addressed any licensed school counselor's bid to invoke privilege while practicing in a profession (school counseling) that did not grant privilege.

Here is one lawyer's opinion: "I would think a judge would not let a school counselor fall back on privilege as they are acting as a school counselor and not as a licensed counselor with a private client. If I were a judge in a hairy custody case and my whole decision rested on the school counselor, I would not want to let them off the hook because I was unlucky enough to get the one school counselor who is also licensed. It is not fair to the justice system … that some get off the hook and some do not. The legislature should make these rules so it is fair to all school counselors. If one school counselor gets privileged communication, they all should in that state. If the legislature wants to let a school counselor off the hook, it is up to them, because it is a policy decision in the big picture" (A. L. Colvin, Esq., personal communication, December 2004).

Here is a school counselor's opinion: "I believe that the role in which you are functioning defines the rules by which you must practice – that is the law. The law considers 'intent' when considering the truth of the matter. This also pertains to oral contracts and the intent of the legislators when a bill is passed" (J. Freiden, NCSC, LPC, personal communication, January 13, 2005).

STUDENT TRUST VERSUS COURT APPEARANCE

You have been the primary advocate and confidant for a student who has been in and out of foster homes all his life, and in the three years you have known him, Hansen has been in three miserable foster homes. Hansen has a difficult time trusting adults; basically communicates only when necessary; and is guarded, closed and suspicious. You have painstakingly built a bond with Hansen, although it is a very fragile bond. One of the foster families Hansen lived with for eight months is being investigated for receiving and selling stolen property, and you receive a subpoena from the prosecution to give testimony about your confidential conversations with Hansen. The reason for your testimony is for the courts to learn all they can about what Hansen saw and heard while living in this home in order to aid the prosecution as they build their case. You think that Hansen, who has already given a deposition, was probably closed and guarded in his responses and the attorneys are hoping you learned more from him about his time in this home. What are your legal responsibilities to the court? What are your ethical responsibilities to Hansen?

Points to Consider

As explained in earlier discussion in this chapter, school counselors are required to give their testimony to the courts unless their communications are considered privileged according to state statute. However, ethically, we can try to protect our students' confidences and stay out of court. Consult your state statutes and school board attorney to see if you have a legal obligation to breach confidentiality when subpoenaed by the courts. Consult with the attorneys in the case to see if one is willing to issue a motion to quash the subpoena. A motion to quash makes the subpoena null and void, and therefore you would not have to testify. Inform the attorney that you do not have any information to help the case (if this is true).

Explain that your obligations are to your student. Cite your ethical codes, which support you in safeguarding your student's confidences and advise you to stay out of court if possible. Advocate. Explain that the relationship is too fragile and too much at risk if once more you, like all the other adults in Hansen's life, cannot be trusted to stand with him and protect his confidence. If the situation is such that you need to go the extra mile, then perhaps you can seek research on abandonment issues, foster care children, and other children in Hansen's situation. Use whatever means you can – letters, phone calls or other – to draw attention to the fact that you cannot be called on to breach your student's confidence, but if possible attend court with him in a supportive role.

If your efforts fail, ask the judge to help you protect your trusting relationship with the student by using only notes that are pertinent, sealing documents and excusing you from the court proceedings, or request an informal conference with only the lawyers and the court in chambers. If all else fails, you must testify unless your student has privilege under state statute, rendering you incapable of testifying about him or her.

COURT ORDER VERSUS SUBPOENA

The prosecution's attorney has subpoenaed you. Is this different from receiving a court order from a judge?

Points to Consider

A court issues a court order requiring a person to do a specified act, such as producing material or appearing in court (Nagy, 2000). If a court orders a school counselor to provide the court with information, that person must provide the necessary documents or oral information unless the counselor is protected by a privileged communication statute in that state. The government has the right to obtain a person's information by court order.

A subpoena duces tecum (Latin meaning "under penalty you shall bring with you"), is a court order issued by a clerk of court, justice of the peace, notary public or lawyer, usually signed by a lawyer. It requires the recipient to perform a specified act, such as appearing in court to answer questions about something he or she has witnessed or heard, or producing records as evidence (Nagy, 2000). Although both documents require a response from the school counselor, legal counsel may be more successful with a motion to quash a lawyer-signed subpoena than a motion to reverse a court order. Always seek help from your school board attorney before responding to a court order or lawyer-signed subpoena. There are penalties if you fail to respond to a subpoena or court order, so try to submit a motion to quash (A. L. Colvin, Esq., personal communication, 2005; Alexander & Alexander, 2005).

PRIVILEGED COMMUNICATION VERSUS CONFIDENTIALITY

You explain to Shirin's mother that you are not able to go to court and testify because Shirin has privileged communication given to her in state statute. What does this mean?

Points to Consider

Depending on the states in which Hansen and Shirin reside, it could be that their state's statutes extend privilege to them as students, which would render their school counselor incapable of testifying in court about their communications. Although all school counselors have an ethical responsibility for confidentiality, their relationships with students are rarely privileged in legal terms. In most states, school counselors do not have privileged communication, which is given in state statutes to the clients of certain professionals such as lawyers and psychiatrists. Privileged communication renders the counselor incapable of testifying to information related in confidence. Check your state statutes. The school counselor's ethical responsibility to keep confidential almost all communications with students is complicated because of the school setting.

What should be your first step when you receive a subpoena for your testimony or your case notes? As discussed in the Hansen case, try to get the legal counsel for your school district, the attorney who issued the subpoena, or the opposing attorney to issue a motion to quash a subpoena. Generally speaking and supported by your ethical codes, you do not want your records or your testimony in court. Your loyalty is to your students and the confidentiality you owe them. Advocate, advocate, advocate to protect your case notes and to be excused from testifying.

You are probably thinking that there are occasions such as child abuse situations in which you will want to testify and share your records. Absolutely; but exercise caution before entering the legal arena on behalf of students. School counselors are often asked to endorse one parent over another in custody battles. Ask yourself, "Have I ever spent hours, days, maybe even years with someone and they turned out not to be the person I thought they were?" If you answered "yes" to this, could it be that we rarely have the entire picture as to which parent is a better fit for a student? Could there be more to the story than we are able to learn from the student, teacher, or our own interactions with the parents?

Some of the most heart-wrenching calls I have received as ASCA Ethics Chair are from parents involved in heated custody battles who felt wronged because their child's counselor sided with the other parent in the form of a letter or testimony. We will continue to enter the legal arena as our judgment dictates, but a sobering dose of caution may help us reevaluate some of our involvement. We want to protect students' privacy to the extent possible. However, if all attempts to avoid relinquishing your records or your testimony fail, then by all means cooperate.

CASE NOTES AND EDUCATION RECORDS

You have been seeing Stephen off and on for the first six months of the school year. You have received a request from Stephen's mother for copies of your case notes. Are you legally required to provide her with your case notes?

Points to Consider
As introduced in Chapter 3, "Family Education Rights and Privacy Act," not all the information collected and maintained by schools and school employees about students is subject to the access and disclosure require-

ments under FERPA (1974). One of the five categories exempt from the definition of "education records" under FERPA is records made by teachers, supervisors, counselors, administrators and other school personnel that "are kept in the sole possession of the maker of the record and are not accessible or revealed to any other person except a temporary substitute for the maker of the record." FERPA means that school counselors' case notes – unlike case notes for a mental heath counselor in a private or agency setting – can become education records unless they meet very specific criteria.

FERPA says that school counselors' case notes are "sole-possession records" and not education records – which parents are entitled to see – if the records meet very specific criteria. They must:

- Serve as a memory aid
- Not be accessible or shared in either verbal or written form
- Be a private note created solely by the individual possessing it, and
- Include only observations and professional opinions.

Parents have rights to education records; therefore, if our case notes do not meet the criteria above, then we are legally required to respect the spirit and intent of FERPA and provide these case notes as education records to the requesting parent. The general belief that unless shared and accessible, case notes remain sole-possession records, applies to our fellow agency, rehabilitation or community mental health counseling colleagues. Counselors in noneducational settings do not have to filter what they write through the lens of FERPA, as their records will not cross the line into education records. However, application is more complex for school counselors. FERPA requirements have far-reaching influence in our setting. We must write case notes, recording only observations and professional opinions if we desire to meet the spirit of sole-possession records. Think about the last student who came to you for a personal or emotional issue. Try to write a case note that does not record details but rather just your professional opinion and your observations. Meeting the definition of sole possession records is very difficult to do!

School counselors do not usually keep prolific notes, as this is not realistic in a school setting. Often case notes record simply the student's name, time and a few details to jog our memory. However, when we do write detailed notes – as in the case of a child-abuse situation, a student who is self-mutilating, a student who has suicidal ideations – we write with great care because we know our notes can be subpoenaed in most states, and parents can access the case notes if they record other than observations and professional opinion. Therefore, we take great care to write professionally and with caution as our notes can be read by others if they cross over the line from sole-possession records to education records.

The fact that it is hard to meet the criteria for sole-possession records does not mean that we do not write anything down. However, we must constantly remind ourselves that it can be read in a court of law (if your students do not have privileged communication) and that parents can request it. Do write down what you must remember about your student, but not with the assurance that it will never be read by others. Even if you manage to meet the criteria of sole-possession records, for most of us these records can still be subpoenaed. Never respond to a subpoena until you have tried to get it quashed through your school board attorney, the attorney who ordered the subpoena or the opposing attorney. We do not want our records or our testimony in court! Our loyalty is to our students and the confidentiality we owe them. We want to protect their privacy to the extent possible. However, if all attempts to avoid relinquishing your records to the court fail, you must submit them for the court.

Check your state statutes carefully. With 50 states and 50 state legislatures it is impossible to say conclusively that your notes will be presented as evidence. One state example presented in this chapter is California's. California Education Code § 49602 (2004) says, "Any information of a personal nature disclosed by a pupil 12 years of age or older in the process of receiving counseling from a school counselor, as specified in Section 49600, is confidential. ... The information shall not become part of the pupil record. ... The counselor shall disclose ... to law enforcement agencies when ordered to do so by order of a court of law, to aid in the investigation of a crime, or when ordered to testify in any administrative or judicial proceeding. ..." Thus, California has a generous code for school counselors to be able to work confidentially with students; however, like most states, California will not protect testimony or records if a court requests them.

In a Position to Know: School Counselors Speak

The case presented at the beginning of the chapter is revisited here and answered by practicing counselors. Compare their responses with your approach.

COUNSELORS, CUSTODY ISSUES, AND THE COURTS

You have been working with a student whose parents are going through a bitter divorce. The student tells you how much she wants to live with her mother while the father continues to paint a picture of the mother as overindulgent, not able to set boundaries for their daughter, encouraging their daughter's sexual relationship with her boyfriend, and allowing the boyfriend to stay overnight. The back-and-forth accusations between the daughter and father are endless. You have rarely heard from the mother and the few times that you have, you tend to agree that the father's picture might be accurate. You receive a subpoena from the father's attorney to appear for a deposition in a custody hearing. Legally, must you give a deposition? Are there any ethical considerations that you need to make in this situation?

Response From a Guidance Director

In my state if the student is underage and the parents are allowing sexual relationships, then I would have to make a report to the Department of Social Services. In my state, I would be in quite a pickle about having to explain why I did not file a report of what the father had told me. When in court, I would answer questions with facts and not opinion: attendance, grades, discipline, how many times I had seen the student and so on. If I were asked to evaluate either parent's parenting skills, I would only state I am not in the best position to evaluate parenting and here is how many times I have had contact with each of them. However, I do not have a confidentiality arrangement with the dad and could add his comments about the sex going on in the home. I would expect and encourage the courts to retrieve information from the student and explain my confidentiality loyalty.

ASCA North Atlantic Vice President Janice M. Tkaczyk, Massachusetts (personal communication, January 26, 2005)

Response From a High School Counselor

The student is my client. I do not believe I have a choice in being deposed. I would consult the school district attorney (or a personal attorney) about the deposition. Ethically, I believe my focus needs to be on the "best interests" of my student. This poses a moral dilemma, not necessarily an ethical dilemma. The mother's lack of supervision or permissiveness is not an area about which I can make a judgment with limited information. If I do not have firsthand knowledge of the issues outlined by the father, I would not disclose any information.

ASCA Past President for 2002-03, Brenda Melton, Texas (personal communication, January 26, 2005)

Response From a Middle School Counselor
I certainly want to protect the child, yet we rarely have all the information to know for sure what is best. The rapport and working relationship with the student is a critical consideration in any deposition and school counselors must do whatever they can to protect the integrity of their position. To be swayed by one parent and placed in the middle is not where the school counselor wants to be. Picking sides is not a win-win situation.
ASCA Governing Board Member Kevin Quinn, Rhode Island (personal communication, January 26, 2005)

Response From a Middle School Counselor
When in a divorce situation, I am quite honest with both parents that it is not my role to be taking sides with either parent, that I am the advocate for the student and his/her needs. I respectfully decline to write up an opinion but I will give an update on how the student is doing under a particular arrangement at school
Fran Meffen, M.S., M.Ed., NHSCA Advocacy Chair, New Hampshire (personal communication, January 26, 2005)

Response From an Elementary School Counselor
If you are subpoenaed and your state does not have laws that protect you from testifying, then you have no choice. I would be very careful to give only the facts. Remember that the father wants you to think that the mother is not the best choice for the child. The father may be very clever and only paint an undesirable picture that is believable, but may not necessarily be true.
Pat Estes, Georgia (personal communication, January 26, 2005)

Response From a Mental Health Counselor
When asked to write a recommendation to the court on where her child should live, I respectfully reply that the only letter I would write would include information on my diagnosis, dates of sessions, and therapeutic recommendations (including whether or not the parent followed through on them). I give a copy of the letter to both parents. I am employed by a mental health agency, not the courts; therefore, it is not my position to

give recommendations on where a child should live. I would consult legal counsel and try to get out of appearing in court. If I were ordered to appear, I would give only information pertaining to my direct work with the child, and not get into opinions on where the child should live. I might encourage the involvement of child advocates such as a guardian ad litem.

Krylyn Peters, Arizona (personal communication, January 26, 2005)

Making Connections

1. Discuss the federal and state court systems and your understanding of the two court systems.

2. Determine if your state extends privileged communication to students in schools. How does the statute read? If your students do not have privileged communication in statute, is there any language that encourages you to protect their confidences?

3. Explain when your counseling notes have crossed the line over to educational records. Why is recording only observations and professional opinion so hard to achieve?

4. Read and discuss the responses in the section titled "In a Position to Know: School Counselors Speak." Which response do you particularly agree with and why? Which response do you disagree with and why?

Key Terms

State legislature
Separation of power
Federal court
State court
Court of Appeals
Process of discovery
Deposition
Testimony
Written interrogatories

Plaintiff
Defendant
Witnesses
Privileged communication
Subpoena
Court order
Duces tecum
Case notes
Guardian ad litem

References

Alexander, K., & Alexander, D. (2005). *American public school law* (6th ed). Belmont, CA: Thomson West.

American School Counselor Association. (2004). *Ethical standards for school counselors.* Alexandria, VA: Authors.

Arkansas Code Archive § 17-27-311 (2004).

Bonvento v. Board of Public Instruction of Palm Beach County, 194 S. 2d 605 (Fla. 1967).

California Education Code § 49602 (2004).

Camlin v. Beecher Community School District, App. 3d 1013; 791 N.E.2d 127 (2003).

Family Educational Rights and Privacy Act, 20 U.S.C. § 1232g (1974).

Fine, T. M. (1999). How the U.S. court system functions. *Issues of Democracy*, 4, 6-11.

Fischer, L., & Sorenson, P. (1996). *School law for counselors, psychologists, and social workers.* White Plains, NY: Longman.

Hobbs v. County of Moore, 267 N.C.665, 149 S.E. 2d 1 (1966).

Idaho Code § 9-203 (2001).

Ind. Code Ann. § 20-6.1-6-15 (2004a).

Ind. Code Ann. § 31-33 (2004b).

Imber, M., & Van Geel, T. (2004). *Education law* (3rd ed.). Mahway, NJ: Earlbaum.

Iowa Code Ann. § 622.10 (2003).

Kentucky Revised Statutes § 506 (2004).

Montana Code Ann. § 26-1-809 (2003).

Nagy, T. (2000). *Ethics in plain English: An illustrative casebook for psychologists.* Washington, DC: American Psychological Association.

Nevada Rev. Stat. § 49.290 (1979).

North Carolina Gen. Stat. § 8-53.4 (2004).

North Dakota Century Code § 31-01-06.1 (2003).

Ohio Revised Code § 2317.02 (2003).

Oregon Rev. Stat. § 40.245, Rule 504-3 (2003).

Remley, T. P., Herman, M. A., Huey W. C. (2003). *Ethical and legal issues in school counseling.* Alexandria, VA: American School Counseling Association.

Ricker v. Board of Education of Millard County School District, 16 Utah 2d 106, 396 P.2d 416 (1964).

South Dakota Code § 19-13-21.1, Rule 508.1 (2003).

Stone, C. (Speaker). (2001). *Legal and ethical issues in working with minors in schools* [Film]. Alexandria, VA: American Counseling Association.

Stone, C. (2005). Students' self-direction and autonomy: Educating versus directing. *ASCA School Counselor*, 42(3), 6-7.

Wyoming Mental Health Professions Practice Act, Wyoming Code § 33-38-113 (2004).

CHAPTER 6

Child Abuse

IN THIS CHAPTER

Objectives

By the time you have completed this chapter, you should be able to:

- Identify the signs and symptoms of child abuse.
- Understand both short-term and long-term effects of abuse on students.
- Discuss why suspicion of abuse is enough to establish duty to report.
- Understand school counselors' legal and ethical obligations in child abuse reporting.
- Understand good faith reporting and how it protects school counselors.

Introduction

According to the National Child Abuse and Neglect Data System, an estimated 1,400 children died in 2002 as a result of abuse or neglect. One or both parents were involved in close to 80 percent of all cases (National Clearinghouse on Child Abuse and Neglect Information, 2004). The American Academy of Pediatrics reports that about one in 20 children is physically abused each year (American Academy of Pediatrics, 1999).

Most researchers agree that child abuse and neglect are severely underreported. A 10-year study reviewing the medical examiner's reports in North Carolina revealed that the state's record system underreported the number of deaths due to battering or abuse by almost 60 percent (American Medical Association, 1999). The meaning of these statistics is clear: Child abuse is not uncommon. Each year, thousands of these youngsters come through the halls of America's schools and interact with other students, teachers and school counselors. This chapter will help the school counseling professional recognize signs and symptoms of child abuse or neglect and understand the legal and ethical dimensions of this often-hidden problem.

Child abuse and neglect are defined in both state and federal law, and the standard of what constitutes abuse varies from state to state (NCCANCH, 2003c). Professionals can determine what constitutes abuse or neglect in their own states by visiting the State Statutes Search at http://nccanch.acf.hhs.gov/general/legal/statutes/search/.

Anyone who suspects child abuse or neglect of any kind can report it by calling the police, by contacting the Childhelp USA National Child Abuse Hotline at 1-800-4-A-CHILD, or the local child abuse hotline. However, counselors, as well as other educators, are mandated in all states to report suspected abuse under penalty of criminal charges. School counselors are mandated reporters required by law to report the reasonable suspicion of abuse, even in the absence of hard evidence. Mandated reporters are immune from legal proceedings brought by parents or guardians who have been erroneously reported to Child Protective Services. You can access state-specific information about child abuse reporters, policies and hotline numbers at http://nccanch.acf.hhs.gov/general/statespecific/index.cfm. There you will find not only extensive information about specific state guidelines but also about the level of incidence for child abuse and neglect.

SIGNS OF ABUSE

Abuse comes in many different forms: physical abuse, sexual abuse and child neglect. Men and women who are working or plan to work in schools should be prepared to recognize the signs of child abuse or neglect. Appearance of a single sign is not typically indicative of child abuse. Rather, when these signs occur repeatedly and in combination, an alert professional may consider child abuse as a possible reason. There may be abuse or neglect when a student:

- Exhibits sudden changes in behavior or school performance
- Comes early or stays late at school activities, is reluctant to go home, or seems frightened of his or her parents
- Is absent frequently
- Steals or begs for food or money
- Uses drugs or alcohol
- Does not want to participate in gym or other physical activities
- Reports bedwetting or nightmares
- Has a sudden change in appetite
- Shows strange, sophisticated or unusual sexual knowledge or behavior
- Runs away from home
- Shows extremes in behavior, appearing overly compliant or demanding, extremely passive or aggressive
- Behaves in an inappropriately adult or infantile manner
- Has attempted suicide
- Is not clean or has consistent body odor
- Is not dressed appropriately for the weather

- Has physical or medical problems that have been ignored by his or her parents
- Has not been given routine medical or dental care, immunizations or eyeglasses
- Has bruises, burns, bites or broken bones that cannot be explained
- Has marks or fading bruises after an absence from school
- Reports injury by a parent or other caregiver
- Indicates that there is no caregiver at home
- Has difficulty sitting or walking
- Contracts a venereal disease or is pregnant, especially if under 14 years of age
- Has learning problems that cannot be linked to physical or psychological causes
- Is anxious, as if waiting for something bad to happen
- Is withdrawn, passive or overly compliant
- Seems to fear adults
- Is emotionally or developmentally delayed
- Does not report an attachment to his or her parents.

(Adapted from NCCANCH, 2003b)

Ethical Standards Addressed in This Chapter

Professionalism means knowing your professional associations' codes and adhering to them. Those ethical standards from American School Counselor Association that are most germane include the following:

- The professional school counselor adheres to laws, local guidelines and ethical standards of practice when assisting parents/guardians experiencing family difficulties that interfere with the student's effectiveness and welfare. (B.1.b)
- The professional school counselor is sensitive to diversity among families and recognizes that all parents/guardians, custodial and noncustodial, are vested with certain rights and responsibilities for the welfare of their children by virtue of their role and according to law. (B.1.d)

The full text of American Counseling Association ethical codes and ASCA ethical codes can be found at these Web sites: ACA at http://www.counseling.org and ASCA at www.schoolcounselor.org.

ASCA Position on Child Abuse and Neglect Prevention

ASCA's position paper titled Professional School Counselor and Child Abuse and Neglect Prevention position statement begins, "It is the professional school counselor's legal, ethical and moral responsibility to report suspected cases of child abuse/neglect to the proper authorities" (ASCA, 2003, p.1).

ASCA recognizes that it is the absolute responsibility of professional school counselors to report suspected cases of child abuse or neglect to the proper authorities. Professional school counselors can take responsible action if they recognize and understand the problem, know reporting procedures, and participate in available child abuse information programs. School counselors are instrumental in early detection of abuse. The association also recognizes that abuse of children is not limited to the home, and that corporal punishment by school authorities can be considered child abuse.

Professional school counselors commit themselves to providing strategies to help break the cycle of child abuse. School counselors can help children and adults cope with abusive behavior, facilitate behavioral changes and develop positive interpersonal relationships, which may reinforce appropriate parenting skills. Professional school counselors coordinate team efforts on behalf of the child, provide support to staff and other school personnel, work to reestablish trust, provide follow-up counseling or refer to ongoing counseling services outside the school community, provide developmental workshops or support groups enhancing parenting skills, and coordinate or provide programs and in-services designed to help prevent child abuse.

As school counselors, we are mandated legally and ethically (ASCA, 2004) to report child abuse. Statutes even go so far as to lay out penalties for those who, however misguided or misinformed, do not act accordingly. But, as noted earlier, child abuse can be notoriously insidious and cannot always be definitively identified. What really constitutes child abuse? What's the difference between "bad parenting" and abuse?

The ethical dilemma lies in deciding. Some cases are simple; the evidence is irrefutable and conclusive. Physical and sexual abuse can fall into this category. See it, hear about it and report it; simple! Other cases fall into a gray area, where determining what is neglect, mental or emotional harm, or threat almost always involves making judgments about degrees. These are occasions to weigh the facts and specific considerations, deciding what is a preponderance of evidence and what extenuating circumstances to consider. In matters of family and the sanctity of the home, we need to give due process of thought, acknowledging that our individual perceptions and personal beliefs will influence choices. Being a mandatory reporter requires judgment. Being directed by law to report means being aware and alert to the potential of abuse, then deciding whether it is present. There are no easy answers.

School counselors must be willing to identify and also acknowledge the signs of abuse and be brave enough to take action, knowing that there is tremendous support for them in the law and their ethical codes. School counselors can also admit that there is fear associated with reporting abuse, but are reminded that adult feelings of fear are magnified greatly in abused children who have no control over their situation. These are our most vulnerable citizens, and our mandate is to use good judgment and courage to care for them.

State statutes vary slightly in language, but the meaning is generally the same and reads similarly. Educators and counselors are mandatory child abuse reporters, which means they:

- Have an absolute duty to report
- Do not have to be certain – suspicion is enough to establish a duty
- Have a duty that is not discretionary; it is inextricably clear
- Have an obligation to report within 48 hours
- Are protected, since good faith reporting is assumed
- Do not have to give their names as part of the school report
- Understand that there is not a statute of limitations on child abuse reporting.

Getting Started: What Would You Do?

The following case is answered for you at the end of this chapter by a practicing school counselor. Before you read her response, formulate in your own mind how you would approach this ethical dilemma.

CHILD PROTECTIVE SERVICES AND GOING THE EXTRA MILE

For the third time in a year, you need to call the Child Protective Services about a second-grader whose mother has once again beaten her so badly she has black and blue marks up and down her legs. Last time, Child Protective Services went to the home early in the morning, and the child came home at 3:30 p.m. to find her mother screaming obscenities at her and wishing her dead for "tattling to the counselor" about what goes in the privacy of their home. You also reported this incident to Child Protective Services. Five quiet months have gone by and you find yourself once again calling Child Protective Services. You try to convince Child Protective Services that they have to go out after 5 p.m. when the father will be home, or call the father to come home and meet them so that the mother will not be left alone with the child to hurl verbal abuses or worse. The father appears to be a calming, rational force in the family. The Child Protective Services worker thanks you for your suggestion, but says that they are not able to take these special requests as they cannot always guarantee that they can follow through with visits at certain times or with certain family members. What more, if anything, can you do?

Working Through Case Studies

PERSONAL JUDGMENT IN REPORTING ABUSE

You work in a school in which the principal uses his own judgment about whether or not to call Child Protective Services. The principal decides if the case is a possible child abuse situation or if "over-discipline" has occurred. There are many times when black eyes and bruised cheeks go unreported because the principal knows the child's parents and has asked that they not be reported. The reasons he gives for not reporting vary: the parents just got carried away; the child seems fine and is not really hurt; we are just beginning to get the parents to trust us and a call will destroy all that; or, these parents will uproot their child and go to another school if we report, and we know the child is better off in this school. The principal says he can do far more good by preserving and building relationships with families by simply calling and discussing the situation with parents and explaining that they must not continue to bruise their child. The principal works hard to help the children in this very troubled community, and the school has a reputation of being an oasis in a community fraught with social ills to include a high incidence of problems including child abuse.

The teachers almost always inform both you and the principal when they see signs of possible abuse. The principal screens the cases and directs you to call in Child Protective Services when he decides it is appropriate. Is there a legal or ethical dilemma for you in these situations?

Points to Consider

Without question, school counselors are ethically, morally and legally responsible to report suspected child abuse. Some states and school districts have policies requiring that a child abuse report is funneled through a designee in the school, which could be the principal, but educators can't excuse their obligation to see that abuse is reported if they see signs of child abuse. In this situation, there exist signs of child abuse that continue to remain unreported because of the principal's approach to handling child abuse. Legally and ethically, a school counselor is required to report this abuse, even if it goes against individual school practice. Politically, this is fraught with land mines, because the principal may view your calls as interference and insubordination.

The principal is not a bad man nor is he intentionally trying to harm his students. He believes that he is trying to work within the standards of his community. He also believes that if he reported every suspected case of child abuse, he would be fueling the breakup of a mother and father or disrespecting family structure. He hesitates getting the authorities involved because he wants to present the school as a trustworthy, inviting place for parents.

It is necessary to talk to the principal about the legal duty to report so that you protect him, yourself and the teachers from liability. Going against the principal's decision in such a situation is likely to cause turmoil between the school counselor and the principal; however, the reasons to report far outweigh reasons not to report. The school counselor should assure the principal that it is possible to work with families by explaining why the report was made and by offering help and support to find resources. Talking about the proactive programs to combat family violence and child abuse with families and administrators will educate adults and prevent some of these problems before they start. If the principal can continue to extend kindness and support, be sympathetic to the frustrations of parenting, and explain to parents that this is not about punishment, it may satisfy his desire to maintain a trusting and inviting school for parents.

However, the fact remains that school counselors cannot abdicate their responsibilities in situations like the one described above. Even if the principal or other educators do not believe a call to Child Protective Services is needed, if reasonable suspicion is present, the school counselor is legally and ethically bound to report the suspected abuse or neglect. Remember, you do not need indisputable evidence of abuse.

UNCERTIFIED SCHOOL COUNSELORS AND CHILD ABUSE REPORTING

You are not yet certified in your state to be a school counselor. You are a teacher hired this year on a teacher contract but placed in a school counseling position. You are not certain of the child abuse laws or any other law that governs schools, and you have two more years in your program. Is there a legal or ethical dilemma for you in this situation?

Points to Consider

Principals and guidance supervisors increasingly face the unfortunate option of having to hire an uncertified school counselor or leaving a position unfilled for months, or in some cases, years. Educators are well aware that hiring an out-of-field or uncertified person leaves the school district more vulnerable in the event of a breach of ethics or law. However, the shortage of educators makes the practice commonplace in some parts of the United States and, rather than having a counseling vacancy, many school districts want their students to have the benefits of a counseling program. When a school district hires an uncertified school counselor, both the counselor and the school district must ensure that the counselor knows his or her affirmative duty to report child abuse.

If you take a position for which you are not certified, it is in your best interest and that of the school district to do all you can to educate yourself about the nature and function of schools, critical information such as the law for mandatory reporting of child abuse, as well as school board policy and practice. In other words, there will be no excuses if you do not know the law about child abuse reporting, and your school district is more vulnerable if an uncertified school counselor commits an offense.

WHEN REPORTING DOES NOT YIELD RESULTS

A middle school student comes to school with severely bruised arms, legs and a black eye. The student freely tells you that her parents beat her for sneaking out of the house last Saturday night. After the beating, she heard her parents discussing the possibility of school officials calling in an abuse report to Child Protective Services and therefore they decided to go on the offense. Her parents called the police and reported her for running away. The police came to the house and took pictures of her bruises, telling her parents that they did not have to worry about charges because it would be viewed as over-discipline. You call Child Protective Services, who send a caseworker to the school. The caseworker seems very sympathetic and takes the student home to meet with the parents. The next day the student reports to you that the caseworker completely turned on her and told the parents that she should have to earn everything, including the clothes she wears and the door on her bedroom. The student says she completely sided with the parents and treated the student like a criminal. What would you do?

Points to Consider

Black eyes and bruises down arms and legs are clear signs of abuse, according to the National Clearinghouse on Child Abuse and Neglect Information (2003b). You can follow up with Child Protective Services to see whether or not the case was labeled abuse. It may well be that the caseworker and parents reached an agreement in which future incidents would be handled with lost privileges and the need to earn the privileges back. Just because the student is not satisfied with the resolution of the case does not mean that the case was not handled properly. If you have doubts you can call to follow up.

Keeping a close watch on the student can help allay your fears and if the abuse happens again, speak to a supervisor in Child Protective Services to discuss your concerns. Stress that you want it on record that you are frightened for this child. Explain to the supervisor that you are taking careful notes because you are afraid your notes may be needed one day in the event this child is severely hurt. Putting pressure on others to act is appropriate when you are concerned and must rely on Child Protective Services to make a difference for the student's safety.

ANGRY PARENTS AND YOUR CHILD ABUSE REPORT

You recently reported a case to Child Protective Services, and the case was deemed unfounded and closed. The parents easily figured out that it was you who called, and they are calling to take issue with you on what you and their child have been discussing, telling the principal that they do not want you ever again working with their child. Can the parents forbid you to work with their child?

Points to Consider

Child Protective Services does not tell parents who reported the abuse, but parents can often surmise who the reporter was from details they are given or by simply asking their child whom they talked to at school. This often places the reporting counselor in a difficult position. The school counselor can refuse to be grilled by the parents; however, some counselors are able to use the opportunity to try to collaborate and help parents develop better approaches in working with their children.

If the parents are in conflict with you over reporting, working with their child can be complicated. In many school districts, parents can refuse counseling services for their child even if the student still wants to come for counseling. Just as the math teacher and English teacher can do their jobs without parental permission, generally speaking, so can school counselors. However, since counseling involves the personal, social and emotional arena, we consider it best practice to have parental permission for individual counseling. When parents expressly state that they do not want counseling for their child, we should rarely ignore their wishes. You might find it beneficial to try to reason with the parents; if the child needs help, implore them to allow someone else to help, perhaps by transferring the student to another counselor in the school. We do not want to give up easily in an effort to get a student the help he or she needs. Our advocacy for the student can be met in other ways besides personally delivering the services.

If you still believe that the child is in danger and the parents are trying to hide their abusive behavior, you are still involved and required by law to call Child Protective Services.

LIABILITY IN CHILD ABUSE REPORTING

You reported a case of child abuse brought to your attention by a teacher. The teacher noticed a horrible slash mark across the back of a child's neck and, upon inspection, the teacher saw that it extended far down the child's back. The mark closely resembled a belt mark. You report the incident to the Child Abuse Registry. The subsequent investigation by Protective Child Services reveals a fall from a piece of playground equipment, witnessed by the child's soccer coach and team members. The parents deduce that the report came from the school and specifically from you. The parents are livid and are threatening to sue you. Can you be sued?

Points to Consider

Good faith reporting is assumed when a professional reports child abuse. A mere suspicion of abuse is all that is necessary when reporting child abuse. By reporting the slash mark, the school counselor acted legally and ethically. If you had not made a report and it was determined that abuse actually did occur, then legal action could be taken against you. By reporting a suspicion, the school counselor becomes immune from all liability. Every state and U.S. territory provides some form of immunity from liability for persons who in good faith report suspected instances of abuse or neglect under the reporting laws. Immunity statutes protect reporters from civil or criminal liability that they might otherwise incur (NCCANCH, 2003a).

CHILD ABUSE FROM THE PAST

You are a high school counselor. One of your students confides in you that five years ago she was the victim of sexual abuse by her mother's boyfriend. Four years ago the perpetrator left the home and moved to another state. She tells you that she never told anyone, not even her mother. She begs you not to tell anyone. What are your obligations?

Points to Consider

The statute of limitations of child abuse in most states is five to 10 years. However, for some states like New Jersey, there is no statute of limitations (Aronson, 2002). The legal determination of statute of limitations, however, is not part of the duty to report to which counselors must adhere. If a situation of abuse is reported, the professional must contact the authorities, who will then pursue the matter and make the necessary legal determinations. In your advocacy role, you can support this student through any subsequent legal proceedings and help her in any way possible, but you are not able to honor her request "not to tell anyone."

DOMESTIC VIOLENCE AND CHILD ABUSE

You are an elementary school counselor and a teacher sends a third-grade student to your office. She is concerned because for the past few days the student has been having trouble staying awake in class and constantly gazes off into space. After you talk with the third-grader and express your concern, the student informs you that for the past two nights while trying to fall asleep, she has listened to her mom and stepfather argue. Her eyes fill with tears as she tells you that the yelling and sounds of things breaking keep her awake all night. Is this considered child abuse? Should you report it?

Points to Consider

Although we can argue that seeing or hearing abuse can result in detrimental psychological effects, the statutes for reporting these types of incidences are far less clear than for other child abuse situations. It is unclear whether hearing parental fighting is considered abuse, because laws pertaining to situations like this fail to exist in most states. Since the majority of states do not have laws concerning reporting situations when children witness or hear abuse, an ethical school counselor would contact the state department of child protection to find out about his or her state laws and consult his or her school attorney or director of guidance (Fontes, 2000).

New York is a state that does not consider viewing domestic violence as child abuse in every situation. Case workers from New York's Statewide Hotline for reporting abuse explains that in New York domestic violence would constitute child abuse only if the child was in imminent danger. The case of *Nicholson v. Williams* (2001) challenged the practice of New York City's Administration for Children's Services of removing the children of battered mothers solely on the basis that the children saw their mothers being beaten by husbands or boyfriends. Judge Weinstein ruled that the practice is unconstitutional and ordered it stopped.

The expert witnesses in the case testified that observing domestic violence is "sometimes, but not always, harmful to children. Even when the child is harmed by witnessing domestic violence, removing the child from the non-offending parent is more harmful. Indeed, one expert testified that a removal under such circumstances 'is tantamount to pouring salt on an open wound'" (*Nicholson v. Williams*, 2001). Another witness testified, "When a child is separated from a mother because of domestic violence, the separation is even more traumatic, because the child 'is terrified that a parent might not be OK, may be injured, may be vulnerable. .... They feel that they should somehow be responsible for the parent and if they are not with the parent, then it's their fault'" (*Nicholson v. Williams,* 2001).

Making a simple phone call to the child abuse hotline can tell you if this is a reportable child abuse offense in your state, or if there is another resource you can take advantage of in seeking help for your student. Domestic shelters can also provide you with resource information to seek help and support for the children of domestic violence.

Charlotte Watson, executive director of the New York State Office for the Prevention of Domestic Violence, gives us some facts regarding child abuse and domestic violence that can be viewed by visiting http://www.opdv.state.ny.us/coordination/model_policy/frames.html. Watson says that wife battering may be the single most important context for child abuse. According to the New York State Office of Children and Family Services, domestic violence is a factor in 45 percent of all foster care placements. In New York City, the Child Fatality Review panel reported that partner abuse was present in 70 percent of households in which a child homicide occurred. Half of all men who are physically violent with their female partners are also physically violent with their children. Fully 90 percent of the children of abusers witness their fathers battering their mothers or witness the aftermath of these assaults. Children who are direct targets of abuse and witnesses to domestic violence often exhibit evidence of somatic, behavioral or emotional problems (Model Domestic Violence Policy for Counties, n.d.)

Separation from an abusive partner often does not end the abuse, nor does it necessarily mitigate the detrimental effects on children. Custody and visitation orders that are entered without adequate regard to the history of abuse can pose a serious threat to both the abused mother and her children. Further, more than half of the estimated 350,000 child abductions that occur annually happen in the context of domestic violence. Forty percent of these abductions occur after the separation and divorce of the parents. Nearly one-third of these children suffer mild to severe emotional damage as a result of the abduction (Model Domestic Violence Policy for Counties, n.d.).

Whether your state considers viewing domestic violence as abuse or not, you will want to do all you can to support these students and to find resources for them and their families. Special teacher placement, attention, and freedom from bullying are just some of the ways you can provide these children with a safe haven in the 35 hours a week they are in school.

NEGLECT AND CHILD ABUSE REPORTING

As a middle school counselor, you begin to express concern for a student who seems to be a "loner." You notice that the student appears to be underweight and about half the time comes to school wearing filthy clothing, with hair that is lifeless and dirty. You speak to his teacher about your concerns, and she tells you that the student is withdrawn, rarely speaks except when absolutely necessary, and keeps a fearful, furtive look on his face. You decide to arrange a conference with the student and his parents. When the parents get to your office, you notice a strong smell of alcohol on their breath. Their eyes, mannerisms and slurred speech convince you that they are under the influence of alcohol. What do you do?

Points to Consider

This case highlights the "grayness" that often occurs in deciding to report suspected child neglect. An ethical school counselor would read deeper into the statutes and guidelines to learn what constitutes abuse in the areas of neglect, emotional harm and threat of harm to gain greater perspective of the situation.

- *Neglect*: Lack of care that risks or causes harm to a child, including lack of food, clothing, supervision or medical attention.
- *Mental injury or emotional harm*: Harm to a child's ability to think, reason or have feelings, such as cruel acts or statements, intimidation, rejection and indifference.
- *Threat of harm*: Activities, conditions or persons that place a child at risk of abuse. Threats, domestic violence and drug or alcohol abuse fall into this category.

These are some fairly subjective conditions and descriptions of potential areas of abuse. Consider these scenarios: Is it a lack of food and clothing, or a lack of income? What level of drug and alcohol use interferes with child-care to a degree that constitutes child abuse? Who can judge intimidation and indifference and not move to a very personal and subjective part of themselves? Proceed with caution. Good protocol in this situation might include discussing your concerns with the school principal and the guidance director. Consulting with colleagues might help illuminate actions you should never wrong to call the abuse hotline and discuss your concerns with one of the supervisors or caseworkers to get another opinion. Err on the side of caution; it is better to have an angry parent than a child in danger who escapes our attention. We can all cite horrific cases where someone should have noticed a child abuse or neglect situation that went undetected until it was too late.

SECONDHAND INFORMATION

Two girls come to you saying that their parents told them to come talk to you about their friend Shania. The girls tell you that they think Shania is being sexually molested by her stepfather. The girls are sketchy and confused about why they believe their friend is being abused, and they just keep saying that Shania says "things" but they cannot recall any particulars of the conversations. What will be your next step?

Points to Consider

School counselors often receive possible child abuse reports through hearsay or secondhand information. Authorities such as the police and child protection workers caution educators against investigating child abuse reports because we may inadvertently ask leading questions of the student, thus hindering the investigation or subsequent trial of alleged perpetrators. However, the courts support us to ask questions of the abused child and others such as Shania's teacher, who may be in a position to help us determine if we have a child abuse report. In *Picarella v. Terrizzi* (1995) the court concluded that a student's constitutional rights were not violated when school officials questioned the student about suspected abuse (LaMorte, 2001; *Picarella v. Terrizzi*, 1995). Likewise in *Landstrom v. Illinois* (1990) school officials who had a student remove her dress and underwear to examine her buttocks were supported by the courts. Know your state statutes to see if your state has granted mandated reporters immunity from liability in these cases of more intrusive investigation. The best rule of thumb in Shania's case and other possible abuse cases is to refrain from asking too many questions, avoid intrusive investigating and let the authorities determine whether abuse has occurred.

Consulting with the school principal or guidance supervisor is a good step. It is also appropriate to decide not to investigate or consult and to make the call to Child Protective Services. If the girls seem credible and you feel there is reasonable suspicion, then that is enough to generate a call to Child Protective Services. If the girls do not appear to be credible and you do not feel there is reasonable suspicion, it is prudent to ask questions of key people such as Shania or her teacher to make certain you are not overlooking something.

CHILD ABUSE REPORTS AND RELATIONSHIPS WITH PARENTS

Benjamin, who is in fourth grade, is continuously in trouble with his teacher for defiant behavior. You have been working with Benjamin and his mother and have been making good progress. Lately, Benjamin's mother is less defensive and appears to be relaxing her guard and cooperating fully with you. You have painstakingly established a very good relationship with Benjamin's mother involving mutual respect. One day Benjamin comes to school with ugly red welts on his arms and face. His mother voluntarily comes in to tell you that she lost control the night before and hit him with a belt. How would an ethical school counselor respond?

Points to Consider

As difficult as it may be to do so, you must make a report to Child Protective Services. As school counselors, we are not permitted to take matters into our own hands. We cannot solicit a promise from Benjamin's mother that this will never happen again and not report the situation. We have a black-and-white mandate with no room for negotiating with parents. An option would be to tell Benjamin's mother that you need to make the call to Child Protective Services, or to call Benjamin's mother after calling Child Protective Services, in order to try to keep the lines of communication open. It is also understandable if a counselor chooses not to say anything to Benjamin's mother about making a report. Individual counselors can decide how they would choose to try to preserve the relationship, but ugly red welts on a child require a report to Child Protective Services.

KNOWN TEACHER-ON-STUDENT SEXUAL ABUSE

You coach tennis in the high school where you are a counselor. You have heard rumors that the volleyball coach is having an affair with one of her students. After an unscheduled tennis practice with two of your students, you enter the coaches' office and hear the frantic rustling of clothes and hushed whispers. After five minutes, this coach and student emerge from behind closed doors, she mumbles something about looking for equipment and they hurry out. You are certain that your unscheduled appearance in the coaches' office has interrupted a sexual encounter. Now what do you do?

Points to Consider

The case of *Doe v. Rains Independent School District* (1994) involved a situation in which a schoolteacher was involved in a sexual relationship with a student, and another teacher had knowledge of the relationship but waited several months before making a report. Dana White was a teacher in a Texas school. A student, Sarah Doe, told White about her relationship with a teacher at a neighboring school, which was hidden under the guise of babysitting for his children. White did not report the incident right away because of her promise of confidentiality to Sarah. She continued to talk with Sarah and with other school officials, but did not report Sarah's abuse to proper authorities until November 1992.

Once Sarah Doe's parents learned the facts, they sued Dana White for depriving Sarah of rights granted to her by Texas state law and by the federal constitution. The Texas law she allegedly violated was that teachers are required to report child abuse within 48 hours. The court found that White did not have supervisory control over the other teacher in question. Therefore, they found no causal connection to Sarah's constitutional injury and that her delay in reporting was not "action under color of state law" (*Doe v. Rains Independent School District*, 1994).

As a school counselor, you do not want to find yourself party to a lawsuit involving nonreport of sexual abuse. Even if the court finds in your favor, you will have suffered immense stress, strain and emotional toll, not to mention the realization of harm caused a child.

CHILD ABUSE IN A COUNSELING SESSION

Your colleague appears to be too familiar with students, and from what you are told by students, he has been walking a very narrow line with some of his questions. Today a girl tells you that he asked her about her menstrual periods and her sexual relationship with her boyfriend. You are stunned. Is this child abuse?

Points to Consider

The differential in power between school counselors and students is considerable, and therefore constitutes great potential for abuse. Although school counselors have great influence over their vulnerable minor students, they rarely abuse this power. Occasionally, we find a school counselor who abuses his or her position of trust, and although it may or may not be accepted as a reportable offense by Child Protective Services, it is grounds for dismissal.

A 28-year Maryland high school counselor is not the first school counselor to be dismissed because of inappropriate sexual comments to students. A county judge upheld the counselor's dismissal for alleged sexual comments made to a female student during a counseling session. Circuit Court Judge David Bruce went on to suggest that school counselors should consider asking a third party to attend student interviews when sensitive topics are being discussed. Judge Bruce said that the counselor went far beyond acceptable limits by asking the junior about her sex life with her freshman boyfriend, whom the student complained "treated [her] like crap." Judge Bruce noted that the counselor had a legal obligation to determine if the girl was being abused, but the counselor stepped far beyond the limits when he asked her how many times she and her boyfriend had sex, which sex acts she liked, whether certain sex acts hurt her, and whether she knew any gay or lesbian students in the school.

The girl reported the incident to her friend, who in turn told her mother, who called social services. The social services investigators dismissed the girl's complaint but referred the case to the board of education. In 2003, both the local and state boards voted to dismiss the counselor. The counselor's attorney argued that this was the student's word against his client's, but Judge Bruce said the county judge heard the witnesses and found the girl more credible. The counselor does not face legal charges in the matter, and he prevailed in his legal battle to be allowed to receive his retirement, but the school system is appealing the ruling (Capital-Gazette Communications, 2004).

SCHOOL COUNSELOR COMMITS CHILD ABUSE

What if a school counselor's conduct is not necessarily criminal but teeters on the precipice, as in the case of the school counselor who was charged with the criminal offense of indecent liberties with a child?

Points to Consider

A fifth-grade girl, A.U., was referred to school counselor A.S. because she was struggling academically and her parents had not responded to deficiency notices. A.S. met with A.U. five times to motivate her to complete her homework each day, and after determining that she was not receiving much attention from her busy parents, he tried to show his personal concern for her progress. He permitted her to sit on his knee while they talked; he hugged her, and when she threw her arms around his neck and cried he stroked her back, arms and legs. On one occasion, she complained of a lump on her hip, and A.S. felt the lump and discovered that it was not tender. A.U. testified that he felt her hip both inside and outside her pants. A.S. admitted on the witness stand that he violated one of the cardinal rules of counseling, in that he had become emotionally involved with A.U.'s problem more as a parent than a counselor, which he later regretted. He denied that he had any sexual contact with her.

A number of teachers and former students of school counselor A.S. testified that he had an excellent reputation for honesty and integrity. The school superintendent did not support school counselor A.S., testifying that his conduct was not proper and created an unhealthy dependence between student and counselor. An expert in the field of school counseling testified that physical encounters with students, such as allowing a child to sit on the counselor's lap, touching the student's leg and back, tickling and becoming emotionally involved, are not professionally accepted counseling practices.

The board of education dismissed school counselor A.S. for taking indecent liberties with a student, using highly improper counseling techniques to the detriment of the students, and immoral and unprofessional conduct resulting in irreparable loss of confidence in his ability to perform his duties as a teacher and counselor. The hearing officer did not agree with the board, finding student A.U. not credible and school counselor A.S. extremely credible. The hearing officer concluded that the boards of education failed to sustain each charge by a preponderance of the evidence.

On appeal, the appellate court examined the entire record and focused on the credibility of the witnesses: the hearing officer who did not believe the child, numerous persons who testified without contradiction to school counselor A.S.'s excellent lifelong reputation, and several witnesses who testified that the student was known to tell stories. The appellate court reversed the judgment of the circuit court, affirmed the decision of the hearing officer, and held that the board of education for the Tonica schools did not have good cause for dismissing the school counselor. While A.S.'s conduct was unethical and unprofessional, the court did not consider it a criminal activity (*Board of Education of Tonica Community High School District v. Adelbert E. Sickley*, 1985).

In a Position to Know:
A School Counselor Speaks

The case presented at the beginning of the chapter is revisited here and answered by a school counselor. Compare her response with your approach.

CHILD PROTECTIVE SERVICES AND GOING THE EXTRA MILE

For the third time in a year, you need to call the Child Protective Services about a second-grader whose mother has once again beaten her so badly she has black and blue marks up and down her legs. Last time, Child Protective Services went to the home early in the morning, and the child came home at 3:30 p.m. to find her mother screaming obscenities at her and wishing her dead for "tattling to the counselor" about what goes in the privacy of their home. You also reported this incident to Child Protective Services. Five quiet months have gone by and you find yourself once again calling Child Protective Services. You try to convince Child Protective Services that they have to go out after 5 p.m. when the father will be home, or call the father to come home and meet them so that the mother will not be left alone with the child to hurl verbal abuses or worse. The father appears to be a calming, rational force in the family. The Child Protective Services worker thanks you for your suggestion, but says that they are not able to take these special requests as they cannot always guarantee that they can follow through with visits at certain times or with certain family members. What more, if anything, can you do?

Response From a School Counselor

When any person suspects children are being abused or neglected, school counselors and others have been mandated to report child abuse/neglect to a constituted authority, primarily the agency in the state providing Child Protective Services and law enforcement. However, it appears that someone in Child Protective Services is not taking responsible steps to protect the child from harm or that the existing services are unable to meet the needs of the child and family.

Preventing and treating child abuse/neglect is a multidisciplinary concern and often cannot be left to any one agency. In addition to Child Protective Services, there must be collaboration among law enforcement, the courts, mental health agencies, physicians (especially pediatricians), schools, day-care centers, medical facilities and public health agencies to prevent, discover and treat abuse/neglect. An essential resource for school counselors is their individual state's code concerning the statutory obligations related to child abuse/neglect. Also, Child Protective Services should have a printed policy describing their duties, powers and responsibilities.

The history in this case demonstrates that after reports have been made and the parent is confronted, the child suffers harm and is at risk of more serious harm once again. Therefore, safety plans are needed which may include removing the child from the home, as this case is ongoing.

As a professional school counselor, you have other avenues to take advantage of at this point. It would be appropriate to inform the school's administrator of the situation, making him or her aware of your interventions on behalf of this child. According to the Ethical Standards, Section D.2., parts a and b, the school counselor can extend collaboration with individuals and agencies in the best interest of this student (ASCA, 2004). There are other workers to contact about this child at Child Protective

Services. If these contacts do not respond to your report, contact the agency's director. If there is no response with that contact, the local law enforcement should then be contacted about this case since the child is at risk of serious harm. Many schools have a school resource officer at the school during the day who may provide contact information, thus starting the collaboration of a multidisciplinary concern. Prevention of future abuse/neglect is the goal for this child.

Angie Stansell, LPC, NCC, NBSC, a 7-12 school counselor at Hatton High School in Town Creek, Ala., and a member of ASCA's Ethics Committee

Making Connections

1. If after you make a child abuse report the perpetrator shows up at your office door the next day wanting to take issue with you, what will you do? This is not a person whom you fear, but someone who is angry and confused about why you would consider their "discipline" as child abuse.

2. You need to make a child abuse report and your principal instead wants to call the parents in and talk to them about better approaches to discipline. Write up how you would make your principal feel heard and supported, and yet at the same time meet your statutory obligations.

3. Call Child Protective Services in your area and inquire whether they consider domestic violence to be child abuse for your state. Gather resources that they suggest might help if you have a student in this situation.

4. Visit the State Statutes Search at http://nccanch.acf.hhs.gov/general/legal/statutes/search/ and write a summary of the information about child abuse and reporting that apply to your state. What constitutes abuse? Who are the mandated reporters?

5. Although a Child Protective Services investigation did not yield any evidence of abuse, you are still uncomfortable about the way Jacob comes to school. He is unkempt and never eats lunch. His parents refuse to allow him to get free lunch and it appears they do not give him lunch money. The other students shun him and he has been the target of bullying at the school. Besides contacting Child Protective Services again if necessary, what other strategies might you employ to assist Jacob and his family?

6. Some states have designated Child Protective Services reporters. The history department chairman is the designated Child Protective Services reporter in your building. You have noticed that his reporting is often delayed beyond the 48-hour deadline and he has even dismissed one of your colleague's concerns regarding a potential case of abuse as being "completely ridiculous." He is also the track coach and the family in question includes one of his track stars. What can you do? What should you do?

Key Terms

Child abuse
Child neglect
Mandated reporter
Reasonable suspicion
Child Protective Services

Immune from liability
Domestic violence
Emotional harm
Threat of harm

References

American Academy of Pediatrics. (1999). Child abuse and neglect. Excerpted from *Caring for baby and young child: Birth to Age 5* (Bantam, 1999). Retrieved February 11, 2005, from http://www.medem.com/ MedLB/article_detaillb.cfm?article_ID=ZZZ3S3DRUDC&sub_cat=355

American Medical Association. (1999). *JAMA patient page: Protecting our children from child abuse.* Retrieved February 11, 2005, from http://www.medem.com/medlb/article_detaillb.cfm?article_ID=ZZZDP-BQXMAC&sub_cat=355

American School Counselor Association. (2003). *The professional school counselor and child abuse and neglect prevention.* Alexandria, VA: Author.

American School Counselor Association. (2004). *Ethical standards for school counselors.* Alexandria, VA: Author.

Aronson, B. (March 2002). *Why statutes of limitations for child abuse should be extended, as Pennsylvania legislators have proposed.* Retrieved February 13, 2005, from http://writ.news.findlaw.com/aronson/ 20020321.html

Board of Education of Tonica Community High School District V. Adelbert E. Sickley, 479 N.E.2d 1142 (Ill. 1985).

Capital-Gazette Communications, Inc. (2004, October 19). Annapolis, MD. Retrieved on February 16, 2005, from http://hometownannapolis.com/vault

Doe v. Rains Independent School District 865 F. Supp. 375 (E.D. Tex 1994).

Fontes, L. A. (2000). Children exposed to marital violence: How school counselors can help. *Professional School Counseling*, 3(4), 231.

LaMorte, M. W. (2001). *School law*. Boston: Allyn & Bacon.

Landstrom v. Illinois Department of Children and Family Services, 892 F.2d 670 (7th Cir. 1990).

Model Domestic Violence Policy for Counties. (n.d.) Retrieved on February 24, 2005, from http://www.opdv.state.ny.us/coordination/ model_policy/frames.html

National Clearinghouse on Child Abuse and Neglect Information. (2003a). *2003 child abuse and neglect state statute series ready reference reporting laws: Immunity for reporters*. Retrieved February 12, 2005, from http://nccanch.acf.hhs.gov/general/legal/statutes/immunity.pdf

National Clearinghouse on Child Abuse and Neglect Information (DHHS). (2003b). *Recognizing child abuse and neglect: Signs and symptoms*. Retrieved February 12, 2005, from http://nccanch.acf.hhs.gov/ pubs/factsheets/signs.cfm

National Clearinghouse on Child Abuse and Neglect Information (2003c). State statutes series 2003, *Definitions of child abuse and neglect*. Retrieved February 12, 2005, from http://nccanch.acf.hhs.gov/ general/legal/statutes/define.cfm

National Clearinghouse on Child Abuse and Neglect Information. (2004). *Child abuse and neglect fatalities: Statistics and interventions*. Retrieved February 12, 2005, from http://nccanch.acf.hhs.gov/pubs/factsheets/ fatality.cfm

Nicholson v. Williams, 00-CV2229, U.S. District Court, Eastern District of New York (2001). Retrieved January 13, 2005, from http://www.nccpr.org/index_files/page0007.html

Picarella v. Terrizzi, 893 F. Supp. 1292 (Pa. 1995).

CHAPTER 7

Individual and Group Counseling and Classroom Guidance

IN THIS CHAPTER

Objectives

By the time you have completed this chapter, you should be able to:

- Describe the meaning and limits of confidentiality in classroom guidance and individual and group counseling.
- Define the process of informed consent.
- Apply the American School Counselor Association (2004) ethical standards for individual and group counseling.
- Understand the responsibility of group leadership for small groups.

Introduction

The legal and ethical complexities of working with minors in schools require that school counselors remain vigilant about the rights and responsibilities of students and their parents, as well as the implications of these rights on their work (American Counseling Association, 2005; ASCA, 2004; Imber & Van Geel, 2004). The numerous responsibilities school counselors have in a setting designed to deliver academic instruction further complicate the legal and ethical realm of school counseling (Baker & Gerler, 2004; Gibson & Mitchell, 2003; Sink, 2005; Stone, 2001). These complications are acutely present in both individual and group counseling (Smead, 1995; Thompson, Rudolph, & Henderson, 2004; Vernon, 2004). There is additional concern in group counseling, where confidentiality cannot be guaranteed and sensitive information about the private world of students and their families is often discussed (Corey, 2004; Greenberg, 2003).

Confidentiality, found in Standard A.2 of the American School Counselor Association Ethical Standards, means that the professional school counselor discloses terms of counseling at or before entering the counseling relationship or at the beginning of counseling sessions. The purpose of informed consent is to give the counselee the purposes, goals, techniques and rules of procedure under which he or she may receive counseling. The counselor explains the meaning of confidentiality in developmentally appropriate terms and helps the student understand that school counselors will try to keep confidences, except when the student is a danger to self or others, or a court orders the counselor to disclose information.

The complications of confidentiality are discussed in every chapter of this book, especially in the section "Introduction to Legal and Ethical Issues" in Chapter 1, so details here are not necessary. However, to recap in brief, confidentiality is difficult in school settings because of the school counselor's competing interests and obligations that extend beyond the students to parents, administrators and teachers. Working with clients who are minors poses special considerations with parents, but never more so than in a setting designed for academic instruction rather than counseling.

In some instances, parents may demand and obtain information that their child is discussing with the school counselor. In *Parents v. Williamsport Area School District* (1991) a psychologist could not use his professional confidentiality as a basis for refusing to reveal to parents what was said in an individual counseling session recorded in individual case notes. So this tells us that parents probably have a right to their children's information, especially information that is value laden and is revealed to a school counselor in a setting designed for academic instruction.

Other court cases have supported the school counselor's confidentiality to the extent possible; however, the courts tell us to be ready to defend our behavior and to show we are competent to address sensitive subjects with a student in isolation from his or her parents. Generally speaking, school counselors should feel free to discuss relevant but controversial issues with students such as drug and alcohol abuse, pregnancy, abortion and birth control. We should carefully consider developmental and chronological levels, parents' rights, *in loco parentis* status, the legal status of minors, and the courts' stance that parents have the right to be the guiding voice in their children's lives in value-laden issues.

This chapter gives us an opportunity to revisit and highlight some of the basic principles of legal and ethical issues for individual and group counseling. In this chapter we will discuss confidentiality, informed consent, appropriateness of group topics for a school setting, screening of potential group members, and unrealistic skill expectations.

Ethical Standards Addressed in This Chapter

Professionalism means knowing your professional associations' codes and adhering to them. Those ethical standards from ASCA that are most germane include the following:

- The professional school counselor informs students of the purposes, goals, techniques and rules of procedure under which they may receive counseling at or before the time when the counseling relationship is entered. Disclosure notice includes the limits of confidentiality such as the possible necessity for consulting with other professionals, privileged communication, and legal or authoritative restraints. The meaning and limits of confidentiality are defined in developmentally appropriate terms to students. (A.2.a)

■ The professional school counselor protects the confidentiality of information received in the counseling relationship as specified by federal and state laws, written policies and applicable ethical standards. Such information is only to be revealed to others with the informed consent of the student, consistent with the counselor's ethical obligation. (A.2.f)

■ The professional school counselor makes referrals when necessary or appropriate to outside resources. Appropriate referrals may necessitate informing both parents/guardians and students of applicable resources and making proper plans for transitions with minimal interruption of services. Students retain the right to discontinue the counseling relationship at any time. (A.5.a)

■ The professional school counselor screens prospective group members and maintains an awareness of participants' needs and goals in relation to the goals of the group. The counselor takes reasonable precautions to protect members from physical and psychological harm resulting from interaction within the group. (A.6.a)

■ The professional school counselor notifies parents/guardians and staff of group participation if the counselor deems it appropriate and if consistent with school board policy or practice. (A.6.b)

■ The professional school counselor establishes clear expectations in the group setting and clearly states that confidentiality in group counseling cannot be guaranteed. Given the developmental and chronological ages of minors in schools, the counselor recognizes the tenuous nature of confidentiality for minors renders some topics inappropriate for group work in a school setting. (A.6.c)

■ The professional school counselor follows up with group members and documents proceedings as appropriate. (A.6.d)

■ The professional school counselor respects the rights and responsibilities of parents/guardians for their children and endeavors to establish, as appropriate, a collaborative relationship with parents/guardians to facilitate the student's maximum development. (B.1.a)

■ The professional school counselor informs parents/guardians of the counselor's role with emphasis on the confidential nature of the counseling relationship between the counselor and student. (B.2.a)

■ The professional school counselor recognizes that working with minors in a school setting may require counselors to collaborate with students' parents/guardians. (B.2.b)

The full text of ACA ethical codes and ASCA ethical codes can be found at these Web sites: ACA at http://www.counseling.org and ASCA at www.schoolcounselor.org.

Getting Started: What Would You Do?

The following two cases are answered for you at the end of this chapter by two counselor educators. Before you read their responses, formulate in your own mind how you would approach these ethical dilemmas.

SMALL GROUP COUNSELING AND SCREENING POTENTIAL MEMBERS

You develop a small group in response to complaints from seventh-grade teachers who say some students are having difficulty getting along with their peers and are interrupting class lessons. The teachers also say they believe the behavior is affecting the students' grades. You establish a set of goals for the group that includes learning ways to get along with others while improving grades. The teachers recommend eight students for the group; the principal requests you also include two boys who are repeatedly in trouble for fighting. This brings your group to 10 students. After you secure parental permission, you conduct your first meeting to discuss the ground rules, confidentiality and goals for the group. By the third session, bickering escalates. The two boys who are repeatedly in trouble are not benefiting from the group and are fueling the group's negativity by making threatening comments to the other members. Are there ethical issues with the small group?

CONTRACTS TO PREVENT SELF-HARM

You are a high school counselor. Melanie, a 17-year-old female student you have seen periodically since she enrolled in high school and with whom you have a good relationship, discloses to you that she no longer wants to live. As part of your session with her you remind her of your obligation to act to help protect students who are at risk of harming themselves. Melanie sits with you in your office as you call her mother and waits in your office until her mother comes to discuss the problem. Together, you make plans to get Melanie specialized outside help. School administrators ask that the outside professional submit an evaluation before Melanie returns to school. Melanie comes back to school with a letter from a mental health professional saying she has agreed not to harm herself; she also brings a copy of her suicide prevention contract. Names of people are listed on the contract that the student has agreed to call should she feel herself slipping and wanting to harm herself. Two of those listed are fellow 17-year-old students in your school. How will you want to proceed in this case?

Working Through Case Studies

PARENTAL PERMISSION FOR SMALL GROUPS

You are conducting a group for children who have been unable or unwilling to make friends in school. These five students are so isolated from their peers that it is affecting their attendance, class participation, academic success, and from all appearances, their happiness. Do you need to get written or oral parental permission before beginning this group?

Points to Consider

According to the Ethical Standards for School Counselors (ASCA, 2004) "the professional school counselor respects the inherent rights and responsibilities of parents for their children and endeavors to establish, as appropriate, a collaborative relationship with parents to facilitate the counselee's maximum development" (B.1.a). School counselors may find that by communicating the purpose and goals of the small group programs, they strengthen partnerships with parents. It is an appropriate, ethically sound practice to gain written parental permission for a student to participate in a small group (ASCA, 2004).

Another point to consider about group work and parental permission is that the school counselor cannot guarantee confidentiality of information exchanged in groups, regardless of what students agree to (ASCA, 2004). Because school counselors want to build, not erode, credibility and maintain a strong working relationship with parents, when they seek parental permission they facilitate trust and cooperation with parents.

School counseling, as part of the school curriculum, generally allows counselors to meet with children without parent permission, particularly when the welfare and protection of children are at stake (for example, risk of harm). School counselors may find that some districts have local policies regarding how often a child can see a counselor before a parent must be notified. Small groups are part of the school guidance curriculum (ASCA, 2003) and as such may entitle school counselors to meet with students without parental permission. However, fostering a solid relationship with parents ultimately benefits the school counseling program; thus, we consider parental permission as an ethical practice benefiting parents, students and the program.

The Association for Specialists in Group Work's Best Practice Guidelines (1998) also address the need to obtain proper consent for work with minors. One guideline states: "Group Workers obtain the appropriate consent forms for work with minors and other dependent group members." See http://www.asgw.org/best.htm for the complete document.

A review of these ethical codes tells us to involve the family, act in the best interests of students, work collaboratively with parents, adhere to laws and local guidelines, and obtain consent when working with minors.

CONFIDENTIALITY IN GROUP COUNSELING

You are a middle school counselor. A mother asks you to work with her daughter who, for three years, was a victim of incest. The perpetrator has been through the legal system, is no longer in the home, and until recently provided financial support for the victim's counseling. You are already working with another incest survivor and even though a third student has not sought your help, you know she is not receiving counseling for the sexual abuse she suffered at the hands of a neighbor. You decide it is in the best interest of all three girls to bring them together for group counseling sessions. At the first meeting you spend a great deal of time on confidentiality and its limits. The students sign a contract promising never to reveal anything said in the group. You are comfortable that the students understand the imperative to keep all revelations confidential. Are there any ethical dilemmas in this situation?

Points to Consider

Working with minors in groups requires that school counselors understand the reality that whatever is said in a group will be repeated. School counselors risk the emotional safety of students when they expect that developmentally maturing students will respect confidentiality. The ASCA codes (2004) specifically state that confidentiality cannot be guaranteed in a group. A school counselor "establishes clear expectations in the group setting and clearly states that confidentiality in group counseling cannot be guaranteed. Given the developmental and chronological ages of minors in schools, the counselor recognizes the tenuous nature of confidentiality for minors renders some topics inappropriate for group work in a school setting" (ASCA, 2004, A.6.c.).

Since there is no guarantee of confidentiality in groups, even adult groups, best practice dictates that you avoid putting young people together in groups where highly sensitive and personal material may be discussed. Minors often change friends and loyalties, and with this fluid behavior there is the danger of a student wanting attention, seeking revenge, or just acting thoughtlessly, without malice in revealing another student's personal pain. For every group that school counselors form, regardless if the topic is as innocuous as School Success Skills or as value-laden as Children of Alcoholics, Children in Divorce Situations, or Victims of Date Rape, it is imperative to remember confidentiality will be breached. School counselors must continually ask if the potential emotional cost to students and their families is worth any gains from having a group. Competence to help must also be considered.

GROUP WORK WITH DISCIPLINE REFERRALS

You are a middle school counselor. Your principal asks you to conduct a small group with five students accused of sexual harassment. The principal is very responsive to issues of bullying and harassment, and believes these five students have the potential to change their behavior and provide testimonials to other students about the harm sexual harassment does to victims. Is it appropriate to conduct groups designed to correct a discipline issue? If so, what are some things you may want to consider before starting the group?

Points to Consider

Smead (1995) states, "Counseling is a voluntary effort to improve oneself. Change and personal growth cannot be legislated" (p. 14). She further explains that "involuntary group members need to know that they have the same rights (and responsibilities) as voluntary members, except the right to attend" (p. 14).

There are two key considerations in this case. One is the reference to the students as "accused" of sexual harassment. The risk is that if the student is innocent, then wrong accusations would further complicate the situation. The second consideration is that the school counselor may be viewed as the arm of administration and tied to disciplinary actions.

If you conduct the group, you will want to adhere to ethical practice and provide informed consent and delineate the limits of confidentiality (ASCA, 2004). Informed consent has major implications in this case. Is the counselor in this situation running a group in which a student may later regret participating? Is a student really competent to give informed consent to participate in this group? Competence, voluntariness and knowledge are necessary elements if students are to give us informed consent to participate in a group. An adolescent may developmentally be unable to understand the ramifications of discussing painful personal information in the presence of other students. Are these middle schoolers able to comprehend that they will be discussing a sensitive topic, and that their private revelations may well be repeated in the halls and locker rooms? What happens when a student participates in an incest group and the next year his or her revelations are fodder for school gossip? It is highly suspect that a middle schooler's developmental level is sufficient to constitute informed consent.

If you do conduct the group, you must stress that students should not reveal the name or any identifying information about their alleged victims. It is very important to explain at the beginning of each group meeting how critical confidentiality is in all groups, but especially for one in which other people – innocent victims – are peripherally involved. Participation should be voluntary. Be honest about the principal's belief that the students can make positive change, and stress that the purpose of the group is to raise awareness of the serious emotional toll sexual harassment exacts on their victim. This discussion should help the students decide if they want to participate. Stressing that they must come prepared to work and to take ownership of their behavior can set the stage for real work.

DUTY TO WARN AND INDIVIDUAL COUNSELING

You are convinced that Katie is suffering from an eating disorder. You bring her in for a counseling session and learn that she is very cautious and closed. You think it will be many sessions before she is likely to be willing to confide in you. You discuss her appearance and behavior with two of her teachers whose judgment you respect, and they agree that an eating disorder is a serious likelihood. Of course, you have no medical proof but you are worried. You finally decide to confront her and Katie denies it. What do you do?

Points to Consider

Like suicide, an eating disorder meets the criteria of clear imminent danger. We can't ignore the problem in hopes someone else will address it. Above all, we can't assume Katie's parents even know what an eating disorder is. We aren't medical personnel; however, the ethical counselor will confront the student. This confrontation is very hard as a person's weight and eating habits are considered private and personal. Generally speaking, students believe we should not involve ourselves in something as personal as their body image (Stone, 2004).

The nature of the condition means denial is almost always part of the problem. The ethical school counselor will insist that the student involve his or her parents as too much hangs in the balance. If parents become angry and complain to the principal, it is a minor hurt compared to ignoring the possibility that the student is ill and going unsupported.

Bardick, Bernes, McCulloch, Witko, Spriddle, and Roest (2004) give an excellent overview of the problem and suggestions for school counselors in their article. They stress making "honest, objective statements defining the behaviors of concern followed by insistence on obtaining the opinion of a trained professional" (p. 170). Telling students that you care about them but you believe they are not fine and need help is the brave thing to do. Make a statement if you believe you have a child with a problem. Even if their parents are also in denial, you have forced them to discuss the situation and you hope you have planted some seeds so they will consider the possibility that their child is not well.

Can you be charged with negligence for not acting? Probably not, especially with anorexia; unlike bulimia, where you can observe purging, anorexia is harder to determine. This situation is really less about avoiding a lawsuit and more about not being afraid to offend someone by refusing to look the other way when you think someone is ill.

INDIVIDUAL COUNSELING AS ENTRAPMENT

You have been asked by a parent to find out if his daughter is using alcohol. This father says his daughter was found stealing wine from the grocery store, but she says she was put up to it by an older neighborhood child who wanted the wine for himself and that she had no intentions of drinking any. The father asks you to gain his child's trust so he can learn if she is in danger of becoming alcohol dependent. He says alcoholism runs in his family and he is afraid for his daughter, who seems easily led. How would you handle this situation? Are there any ethical issues to consider?

Points to Consider

There are a number of connections to ethical standards of confidentiality in this case and one important point to keep in mind is that "the counselor has a primary obligation to the student" (ASCA, A.1.a.) and that individual counseling is not a tool parents can use to acquire evidence on their children.

One effective way to approach this situation is to be forthcoming with the student about the parent's fear, which allows the school counselor to avoid being trapped into deception. The counselor can then work on opening the line of communication between father and daughter. If the student admits she is consuming alcoholic beverages, the school counselor should try to convince the student to tell her father the truth. The school counselor can then provide the student and father with contact information for an outside agency that deals with alcohol use and abuse. It is important the counselor not be deceitful when working with the student and parent, but take the opportunity to help the two confront the issue. The counselor does not want to lose the trust that has been built or risk losing the trust of other students who might side with the girl. Neither does the counselor want to jeopardize the collaborative relationship with the father.

EATING DISORDERS

There are six students in your school for whom teachers have expressed varying degrees of concern regarding professed or suspected eating disorders. You are planning to establish a group for these students. Are there any legal or ethical concerns with running a group on eating disorders in a school?

Points to Consider

Group work occurring in this situation is fraught with legal and ethical considerations. However, this situation gives school counselors a good opportunity to revisit and highlight some of the basic principles of counseling in the complex setting of schools. In the context of a brief reaction to this scenario we will address two issues: the appropriateness of group topics for a school setting, and unrealistic skill expectations.

Topics for group counseling in schools require careful consideration, as many topics cannot be addressed properly in a setting designed for academic instruction. Can school counselors adequately address such difficult therapeutic issues as eating disorders, whose victims are known to be resistant to change even with inpatient help? Smead (1995) indicated that "group work is more suited for children whose psychological needs are equally balanced" (p. 49). School counselors can tackle the issue of body image and nutrition in classroom guidance lessons for the benefit of all students, but there are some topics that can't be adequately addressed in schools.

It is unrealistic for members of the school and larger community to expect that school counselors should have all the skills and knowledge necessary for group work when topics involve serious clinical issues that many of our students face (Kaffenberger & Seligman, 2003).

> Children and adolescents who are diagnosed with eating disorders will need to have long-term medical and mental health interventions. However, professional school counselors can assist these students in schools, support the efforts of their mental health therapists, and help parents find resources for themselves and their families. (Kaffenberger & Seligman, p. 270)

Because children come to school for academics, this case immediately sets up possible conflict between students' rights to privacy and parents' rights to decide what they want their children exposed to in the personal counseling arena (ASCA, 2004). School counselors' primary objective is to support all students to be successful learners (ASCA, 2003; Education Trust, n.d.; Erford, House, & Martin, 2003). While students with serious emotional issues often cannot learn if their needs are not met, it is unfair and unrealistic for the school and wider community to expect that the school counselor can be in charge of the complete mental health needs of students.

School counselors are becoming managers of resources (Education Trust, n.d.), reaching beyond the walls of their school to reposition mental health support into their schools or to develop a mechanism for helping students find support outside. Competence is not the issue. It isn't that school counselors are less talented or less competent than their colleagues in agency or community settings; it is that the needs are bigger than we are. The mental health needs of our youth simply are beyond the scope of what we can address in the schools, and must become the responsibility of the larger community.

SAFETY IN CLASSROOM GUIDANCE

You have been delivering a series of classroom guidance lessons on school success skills. Your most recent lesson in a fourth-grade class takes a turn toward the unexpected. When you ask the students about barriers they have overcome this school year, one student raises his hand and graphically describes how his father murdered his mother, then took his own life. The class seems shaken, so you spend an extra 15 minutes discussing how to overcome barriers to learning. What is your reaction to this situation? Are there any ethical issues to be considered? Does informed consent play a role?

Points to Consider

While in the classroom setting, the emotional safety of all students is primary (ASCA, 2004). This means that the counselor must know when and how to skillfully intervene without dismissing the student's feelings, making him feel unheard or devalued, or displaying to the entire class that the student is being cut off. By speaking with the student immediately after the classroom session, the counselor can connect with him directly and begin to plan for an individual meeting. At that time, the counselor can seek outside resources for the student if he is not already getting assistance and can help the student understand the ramifications of revealing his issue to classmates.

To protect the rest of the children in the classroom, the counselor can use the opportunity to skillfully talk to the students about what they heard and offer services to anyone who might want to talk. Collaboration with the teacher is essential in this situation, and the counselor should prepare to speak individually with any student upset by the graphic details revealed in class. Proactive counselors will notify parents about what transpired in the class and be ready to assist them with tips on how to support their children.

Students can frequently ask the unanticipated. Predicting questions and spotting potential land mines is part of the overall preparation counselors undertake before providing a counseling lesson. The following newspaper article describes the events of a similar classroom guidance lesson, the actions of a school counselor, and subsequently the school district's reaction. (Names were removed for privacy.)

October 24, 2003
School forming death talk protocol
By Tom Carr

A panel of school officials wants to avoid a repeat of a recent incident in which a student graphically described his parents' murder-suicide to his sixth-grade classmates. The Middle School principal and three school counselors are setting a protocol to follow whenever discussing the deaths of a student's immediate family members.

Meanwhile, counselor Linda B., who school officials said asked the boy if he wanted to share his story with classmates, was suspended for two days during an investigation, the superintendent R.F. said. The board then took "appropriate remedial action," he said, though he would not be more specific. The counselor since has returned to work.

The panel's efforts were spurred by a student's talk in Carole R.'s sixth-grade class on Oct. 6 regarding his parents' deaths downstate in September. The boy moved to the area to live with relatives and enrolled in classes here. Both R. and B. declined to be interviewed, Principal J. said. Several parents, including J.C., whose 11-year-old daughter was in the class, told the school board and administrators of the incident. "My first impression was that it should've been brought to the parents' attention before they talked about it in the classroom,"

J.C. said. "So now, instead of one kid that needs counseling, you've got a whole classroom of kids that need counseling."
(The Traverse City (Mich.) Record-Eagle, 2003).

In a Position to Know: Counselor Educators Speak

The cases presented at the beginning of the chapter are revisited here and answered. Read the two counselor educators' opinions carefully to see what you can learn. Compare their answers with your own approach.

SMALL GROUP COUNSELING AND SCREENING POTENTIAL MEMBERS

You develop a small group in response to complaints from seventh-grade teachers who say some students are having difficulty getting along with their peers and are interrupting class lessons. The teachers also say they believe the behavior is affecting the students' grades. You establish a set of goals for the group that includes learning ways to get along with others while improving grades. The teachers recommend eight students for the group; the principal requests you also include two boys who are repeatedly in trouble for fighting. This brings your group to 10 students. After you secure parental permission, you conduct your first meeting to discuss the ground rules, confidentiality and goals for the group. By the third session, bickering escalates. The two boys who are repeatedly in trouble are not benefiting from the group and are fueling the group's negativity by making threatening comments to the other members. Are there ethical issues with the small group?

Response From a Counselor Educator
The school counselor's intent for this small group is commendable and the group goals are worthy. Despite the well-intended actions of the school counselor, there are ethical issues related to this case.

Ethical guidelines call for appropriate screening of potential members. "The professional school counselor screens prospective group members and maintains an awareness of participants' needs and goals in relation to the goals of the group. The counselor takes reasonable precautions to protect members from physical and psychological harm resulting from interaction within the group" (ASCA, 2004, A.6.a).

School counselors are the front-line professionals responsible for creating an experience that ultimately fulfills the goals of the group and the goals of each member. Screening prospective group members is an essential ethical practice. In this case, the school counselor relied on teacher referrals and complied with the principal's request. Group membership was based on others' perceptions of students who might benefit from the small group experience, rather than the professional school counselor adhering to best practices (ASGW, 1998) and following ethical practices for group leaders (ASCA, 2004). In this case study, the counselor did not meet with group members until the first session; thus, assessing the suitability of each student for the group and formulating individual goals with each student did not happen. Therefore, the degree of commitment and investment of each student to the group experience and fellow members of the group is at best questionable.

Smead (1995) described a number of helpful ways to screen students for their appropriateness to participate in small groups. Typically, the more preferred method of screening is an individual interview. Individual meetings may be dismissed because of time constraints, but school counselors need to remember that screening is an ethical practice for conducting small groups in schools and will contribute to the effectiveness of the group experience. Smead suggested individual meetings (a) afford the group leader the opportunity to discuss the "purpose and goals of the group" (p. 287); (b) confirm the student's willingness to participate; (c) check for "compatibility" (p. 287) with other group members; and (d) check that the student is indeed interested in and committed to participating in the group. In the case presented, students were drafted as members of the group and only in the first meeting can we assume that expectations were discussed.

A second issue related to screening is the selection of members and the number of members for a group. Typically, a group size for middle school would range from six to eight members. This group had 10 members, all of whom were in the group because of unacceptable and aggressive behaviors. Because of the homogeneity of the group, the potential for appropriate modeling behaviors between group members significantly decreased. The size and composition of this group would potentially pose challenges for any group leader.

The school counselor did follow ethical practices of notifying the students' parents or guardians for consent to participate. The school counselor, however, omitted an important step in the informed consent process. By not screening the students, the counselor did not inform or seek consent from the students themselves for participation. Young adolescence is such a pivotal developmental period. Students at this age seek adult approval but they also search to develop identity and autonomy (Kaplan, 2004; Stevenson, 2002). For ethical practice, informed consent should be done with both students and parents or guardians.

In this case, following ethical practices might have increased the odds for a successful group experience for students. Unfortunately, this case had a number of pitfalls. One, appropriate screening of the students referred to the group did not occur. Two, the composition of the group was potentially too homogeneous (too many like-behaviors and not enough students to model appropriate behaviors) and contained too many students. Three, there was no indication that students voluntarily joined this group, or had an opportunity to express their thoughts and feelings about participation.

This case was described as "some students" having "difficulty getting along." Before leaping into a small group based on referrals, the school counselor would want to review and try to determine more objectively, "how many students" are indeed "not getting along." It would be good practice to first review the data on grades and the discipline referrals for seventh grade. What do the grades show? What are the grades of students in the different subjects? Breaking down or disaggregating the data could prove more enlightening and supplement teacher comments. If the curriculum is designed by separate subjects, look to see which students in which classes have low grades. What about discipline referrals? Where do most discipline referrals occur and who are the students being referred? A host of questions can be explored around data.

Rather than singling out "some students" for small groups, the school counselor might find it beneficial to conduct classroom lessons, using the same goals developed for the small group counseling. One can assume that the "interruptions," as described by the teachers, affect every seventh-grader. It is reasonable then to believe that every student could benefit from developing an understanding about relationships and skills for resolving conflicts. By delivering classroom lessons on peer relationships and skills for better working relationships, the counselor is not only addressing an immediate issue within the seventh grade, but contributing to the learning climate of the seventh-grade classrooms, and equally important, educating students in a topic that will be beneficial for adult life.

Group work for the two boys "repeatedly in trouble for fighting" is not appropriate for the boys or potentially for other members in the group because of the risk of physical harm to others. The school counselor may find a collaborative consultation more helpful for changing behaviors. For example, developing a behavioral contract with each boy that enlists support from parents, teachers and the principal may be more likely to change the negative behaviors.

Small group work is a complex and difficult process that has the potential for effectively helping students in schools. It is the responsibility of school counselors to be informed and knowledgeable of the ethical, legal and professional standards of group work. Developing knowledge and skills for leading groups with children and adolescents is a continual process that calls for professional development, supervision and practice.

Rebecca A. Schumacher, Ed.D., counselor educator at the University of North Florida

CONTRACTS TO PREVENT SELF-HARM

You are a high school counselor. Melanie, a 17-year-old female student you have seen periodically since she enrolled in high school and with whom you have a good relationship, discloses to you that she no longer wants to live. As part of your session with her you remind her of your obligation to act to help protect students who are at risk of harming themselves. Melanie sits with you in your office as you call her mother and waits in your office until her mother comes to discuss the problem. Together, you make plans to get Melanie specialized outside help. School administrators ask that the outside professional submit an evaluation before Melanie returns to school. Melanie comes back to school with a letter from a mental health professional saying she has agreed not to harm herself; she also brings a copy of her suicide prevention contract. Names of people are listed on the contract that the student has agreed to call should she feel herself slipping and wanting to harm herself. Two of those listed are fellow 17-year-old students in your school. How will you want to proceed in this case?

Response From a Counselor Educator

If a signed release of information does not already exist, the counselor will want to request that a parent give signed permission for the counselor and the outside mental health professional to talk about the case. This collaboration will help the school counselor know how she or he and possibly other school staff can best support the student while the mental health professional continues to work with the student.

The issue of emergency contacts is a significant one. At least one of the contacts needs to be a 24-hour emergency services agency staffed with trained professionals. Melanie's parents also need to know what behaviors should trigger an emergency call.

The fact that two minor students are among the names of persons whom the student has agreed to call should she feel herself slipping and wanting to harm herself should also be addressed with the outside mental health professional. The school counselor will want to know how to support these two students and how comfortable they are being in such a heavy role. If the two students did not volunteer to be a part of this significant responsibility, then hopefully the mental health agency counselor can either help the friends become comfortable with this role or help Melanie identify adults or others who can help her. The friends will need instructions and training in how to respond to a call for help from Melanie. Melanie's friends need to know when to notify the mental health professional. The friends' parents will need to be aware of the responsibility and possible concerns and stress they may have because they are included on the list to call. All of this will be handled by the agency counselor, but as the school counselor you will be able to advocate for the protection of both Melanie and her contact friends.

This case has a number of "hot-button" issues. Suicide has become an increasing focus of concern of those of us who work with adolescents. The responsibility put on two minor friends is also an issue. Consulting with the outside professional or other knowledgeable counseling colleagues about suicide is important.

The fact that the student and the two fellow 17-year-old students are minors may become a legal as well as an ethical issue. Seventeen-year-old students need to be empowered as well as protected. The school counselor's primary responsibility is to students, but the counselor also has a duty to work with parents in the best interest of the students.

The ASCA Ethical Standards for School Counselors provides an excellent base for considering appropriate action. Consulting with other mental health professionals can also be very helpful. Our primary concern as professional school counselors must be the welfare of students — in this case, both the student at risk and the two friends who may feel overwhelmed and ill-prepared to act if their friend calls.

Pat Partin, Ed.D., is a counselor educator at Gardner-Webb University in North Carolina

Making Connections

1. You are a middle school counselor. You are considering running a small group for children of alcoholics. Are there any ethical issues you should consider regarding this topic?

2. You are an elementary school counselor. You are considering running a small group for children whose parents are going through a divorce. Are there any ethical considerations you must consider?

3. You would like to enlist a group of parent volunteers to help you follow through on a behavior management program for a group of seven students who are having difficulty finishing their work every day. The volunteers will stop by five classrooms and check to see if the participants have finished their work and if so, bring them to the school counselor's office to put stickers on their charts. Are there any legal or ethical issues you must consider before involving parent volunteers in this behavior management program?

4. When is it best practice to get parental permission for individual and group counseling?

5. If a parent wants to know what is being said by his or her child in the individual counseling session with you, must you share? What are some techniques for making the parent feel included without breaching a child's confidence?

Key Terms

Parental permission

Clear imminent danger

Classroom guidance

Group counseling sessions

Confidentiality in group counseling

Informed consent

Screening members

References

American Counseling Association. (2005). *Code of ethics and standards of practice.* Alexandria, VA: Author.

American School Counselor Association. (2003). *The ASCA national model: A framework for school counseling programs.* Alexandria, VA: Author.

American School Counselor Association. (2004). *Ethical standards for school counselors.* Alexandria, VA: Author.

Association for Specialists in Group Work. (1998). Best practice guidelines. *Journal for Specialists in Group Work, 23,* 237-244.

Baker, S. B., & Gerler, E. R. (2004). *School counseling for the twenty-first century* (4th ed.). Upper Saddle River, NJ: Merrill Prentice Hall.

Bardick, A., Bernes, K., McCulloch, A., Witko, K., Spriddle, J., & Roest, A. (2004). Eating disorder intervention, prevention, and treatment. *Professional School Counselor, 8*(2), 168-175.

Carr, T. (2003, October 24). School forming death talk protocol. *Traverse City* (Mich.) *Record-Eagle*, pp. 1-2.

Corey, G. (2004). *Theory and practice of group counseling* (6th ed.). Pacific Grove, CA: Brooks/Cole.

Education Trust. (n.d.) *Transforming school counseling initiative.* Retrieved January 25, 2005, from http://www2.edtrust.org/EdTrust/Transforming+School+Counseling/Counseling+tsci.htm

Erford, B. T., House, R., & Martin, P. (2003). *Transforming the school counseling profession.* In B. T. Erford (Ed.), Transforming the school counseling profession (pp.1-20). Upper Saddle River, NJ: Merrill Prentice Hall.

Gibson, R. L., & Mitchell, M. H. (2003). *Introduction to counseling and guidance* (6th ed.). Upper Saddle River, NJ: Merrill Prentice Hall.

Greenberg, K. R. (2003). *Group counseling in K-12 schools: A handbook for school counselors.* Boston: Allyn & Bacon.

Imber, M., & Van Geel, T. (2004). *Education law* (3rd ed.). Mahway, NJ: Erlbaum.

Kaffenberger, C. J., & Seligman, L. (2003). Helping students with mental and emotional disorders. In B. T. Erford (Ed.), *Transforming the school counseling profession* (pp. 249-283). Upper Saddle River, NJ: Merrill Prentice Hall.

Kaplan, P. (2004). *Adolescence.* Boston: Houghton Mifflin.

Parents against child abuse in school v. Williamsport Area School District, 594 A.2d 796 (Pa. Commw. Ct. 1991).

Sink, C. A. (Ed.). (2005). *Contemporary school counseling: Theory, research, and practice.* Boston: Lahaska Press, Houghton Mifflin.

Smead, R. (1995). *Skills and techniques for group work with children and adolescents.* Champaign, IL: Research Press.

Stevenson, C. (2002). *Teaching ten to fourteen year olds* (3rd ed.). White Plains, NY: Longman.

Stone, C. (Speaker). (2001). *Legal and ethical issues in working with minors in schools* [Film]. Alexandria, VA: American Counseling Association.

Stone, C. (2004). [Survey of school counselors attending legal and ethical workshops: September 2000 to January 2005]. Unpublished raw data.

Thompson, C. L., Rudolph, L. B., & Henderson, D. (2004). *Counseling children* (6th ed.). Pacific Grove, CA: Brooks/Cole.

Vernon, A. (2004). *Counseling children and adolescents* (3rd ed.). Denver, CO: Love Publisher.

CHAPTER 8

Sexually Active Students

IN THIS CHAPTER

Objectives

By the time you have completed this chapter, you should be able to:

- Discuss the complications of confidentiality regarding sexually active students.
- Define your own values regarding sexually active students.
- Recognize when and if your values interfere with your ability to work effectively with students.
- Understand how the school setting complicates efforts to respect confidentiality.
- Understand parents' rights to be the guiding voice in their children's lives in value-laden issues.
- Discuss the prevalence of sexual activity among teens.

Introduction

This chapter deals with the highly sensitive and value-laden issue of sexually active students. Students are becoming sexually active at ever younger ages and the consequences of sexual activity can place school counselors in vulnerable positions with students and parents. Through a series of case studies, we will examine the difficulties of working with minors in this very sensitive area.

School counselors regularly face ethical dilemmas of confidentiality for which there are few definitive answers. The American School Counselor Association (2004) provides guidelines for ethical behavior, but it is ultimately the school counselor's responsibility to negotiate the rights and privileges of students and parents with regard to disclosing information to parents (Stone, 2001). Parents' legal rights to guide their children, community standards, a counselor's own personal values, school board policy, and the school setting all contribute to the complex nature of working with sexually active students. We must always make the difficult decisions involving value-laden issues against the backdrop of parental rights, and that may affect our judgment as to what constitutes danger to self or others.

Court decisions give us some guidance in issues involving abortion counseling. However, the answers to complex questions involving sexually active students elude us. Concrete black-and-white answers are not possible in absence of clear-cut school board policies. Of all the topics we tackle as school counselors, sexually active students pose the most nail-biting, tense moments with regard to confidentiality. The school counselor's best defense is to seek supervision and consultation with other professionals who are in a position to understand how prevailing community standards, school board rules and other context-specific issues affect the world in which school counselors operate. School counselors can take comfort that they will never stand alone legally and ethically if they seek guidance from supervisors and fellow professionals.

Students are sexually active. In 2004, Princeton Survey Research Associates International conducted a national poll commissioned by NBC News and *People* Magazine in which they questioned 13- to 16-year-olds about their sexual behavior. Almost three in 10 reported that they were sexually active, defined as intimate in a sexual way such as touching someone's genitals, oral sex or intercourse. The majority of teens (68 percent) responded that it is very important to be in love before having sexual intercourse (Princeton Survey, 2004).

Three-quarters of teens classified oral sex as sex but less than half said touching someone's genitals is sex (45 percent). Oral sex is not seen as being as consequential as sexual intercourse for 43 percent of respondents. More than half (54 percent) of the respondents believe that teens who engage only in oral sex are still virgins. Responding teens do not think 13- to 14-year-olds should have oral sex (87 percent), nor should 15- to 16-year-olds (70 percent); however, the number dropped to 35 percent for 17- to 18-year-olds (Princeton Survey, 2004).

One in 10 teens have had oral sex. In rank order, the reasons are:

- The other person wanted to (75 percent)
- Met the right person (71 percent)
- Wanted to satisfy a sexual desire (70 percent)
- Didn't have to worry about pregnancy (68 percent)
- Was curious (64 percent)
- Wanted to remain a virgin (49 percent).

The majority understand that STDs can be spread through oral sex (89 percent), but only 30 percent use protection when they have oral sex and only two in three use protection during sexual intercourse (Princeton Survey, 2004).

Casual relationships (friends with "benefits") are not uncommon among sexually active students and involve both oral sex (78 percent) and sexual intercourse (79 percent), and the reasons are to satisfy a sexual desire (67 percent) and avoid the complications of a serious relationship (48 percent). You can read the complete study at http://msnbcmedia.msn.com/i/msnbc/Sections/TVNews/Dateline%20NBC/NBCTeenTopline.pdf.

Ethical Standards Addressed in This Chapter

Professionalism means knowing your professional associations' codes and adhering to them. Those ethical standards from ASCA that are most germane include the following:

- The professional counselor informs students of the purposes, goals, techniques and rules of procedure under which they may receive counseling at or before the time when the counseling relationship is entered. Disclosure notice includes the limits of confidentiality such as the possible necessity for consulting with other professionals, privileged communication, and legal or authoritative restraints. The meaning and limits of confidentiality are defined in developmentally appropriate terms to students. (A.2.a)
- The professional counselor keeps information confidential unless disclosure is required to prevent clear and imminent danger to the student or others or when legal requirements demand that confidential information be revealed. Counselors will consult with appropriate professionals when in doubt as to the validity of an exception. (A.2.b)
- The professional counselor informs parents/guardians or appropriate authorities when the student's condition indicates a clear and imminent danger to the student or others. This is to be done after careful deliberation and, where possible, after consultation with other counseling professionals. (A.7.a)

The full text of American Counseling Association ethical codes and ASCA ethical codes can be found at these Web sites: ACA at http://www.counseling.org and ASCA at www.schoolcounselor.org

Getting Started: What Would You Do?

DEVELOPMENTALLY DELAYED, PREGNANT STUDENTS

The following case is discussed for you at the end of this chapter by a counselor educator. Before you read her response, formulate in your own mind how you would approach this ethical dilemma.

Sharon is slightly developmentally delayed. Chronologically Sharon is 14, but developmentally she is more like an 11- or 12-year-old. Sharon is pregnant and her mother is aware of the pregnancy. Sharon has long been a concern of everyone in the school. She is unkempt, unclean, explosive and violent. Her developmental problems mean she is always out of sync with her age group. Her peers avoid her because they are afraid of her. You are horrified that she will now be responsible for a baby. Sharon is not capable of taking care of herself and you fear for the safety of her child. She tells you she is going to have her baby because this will bring the father of the baby back to her. Sharon says her mother will help her raise the baby. She talks excitedly and animatedly about how she has "always wanted a baby." She explains that her cousin who is also 14 has a baby and is doing quite well and that everyone comes up to the baby and makes a big deal over her. What is your reaction to this situation? What steps would you take in this case?

Working Through Case Studies

NOTIFYING PARENTS WHEN THEIR CHILD IS SEXUALLY ACTIVE

You are a middle school counselor in a high-poverty rural area in which teen-age pregnancy is common. Fourteen-year-old Jessica comes to you distraught over a fight she has had with her boyfriend, Michael. In the course of the counseling session, the student reveals she and Michael are sexually active and she is terrified of getting pregnant. You encourage Jessica to seek help from her parents or a close relative, but she says that is out of the question. Jessica refuses to meet with the school nurse, explaining that she trusts only you. You are convinced that without your help, Jessica will never visit a clinic. You make an appointment for her, and with Jessica's approval, call Michael's mother to take her to the clinic. She refuses and you agree to transport her to the clinic. Can you transport a student to a clinic for the purpose of receiving birth control? Are you required to call the parents of students who are engaged in unprotected sex?

Points to Consider

Taking Jessica to get birth control risks potential repercussions from her mother, and in many communities in America, you would be overstepping your authority. Transporting a student to get any kind of medical attention is risky with parental permission but it is out of the question without parental involvement in most parts of the country.

You should also consider the parents' position and how Jessica's mother might react if she found out you had contacted Michael's mother. Your actions could affect the relationship between the mothers, their children and you. As a professional counselor, you have the responsibility to work with Jessica and help her figure out a way to involve her mother. As you continue to counsel Jessica, keep in mind what the policies are regarding sexual activity in your school district. In a few school districts a counselor may be mandated to inform parents when a child talks about sexual activity in a session.

Know your state law. Certain states have laws concerning the right of minors to consent to specific health services, such as pregnancy testing, HIV testing and counseling. If Jessica lives in one of those states she may be able to visit the clinic herself.

At 14, how prepared is Jessica to understand the potential repercussions of having sex, either unprotected or protected? Find out what she thinks about how her decisions will affect her future. Help her think through the issues through a sequential problem-solving approach. Generally speaking, best practice is to encourage this student to involve her parents. Easier said than done, but in a 2004 survey, 40 percent of teens said they talked with their parents about sex (Princeton Survey, 2004). Is this a girl who has a strong handle on what she is doing, or does her age belie her maturity? In general, the younger the child, the more rights are vested in the parents. This applies to mental maturity as well as physical maturity.

The astute counselor avoids having to scramble in a crisis by being prepared. Know the multicultural makeup of your school and community
and the prevailing opinions of minors and pregnancy. Know the resources
in the community that can help students with the issues surrounding their
sexual activity.

Essential to establishing a network of support is developing relationships
with the school principal and staff members, including teachers, school
nurse, cafeteria workers, janitors and secretaries. Such a network is one of
the secrets of being an investigative reporter in the world of journalism –
cultivating sources on the front lines – and you too can benefit from
knowing the people who see and hear everything. Let them know from
the beginning that you will do everything in your power to protect their
confidences so they feel free to share information with you.

The following are recommendations for the school counselor when counseling students in the area of sexuality or abortion:

■ *Know your school board policy.*
School counselors can sometimes find guidance in school board policy
and must adhere to the stated policy. School counselors behaving as advocates work appropriately to change policies that they believe have an
adverse impact on students.

■ *Consider developmental issues when making decisions.*
When working with minors on value-laden issues, it is especially important to consider their chronological and developmental levels in order to
determine whether you need to make an intervention, and if so, how
extensively. School counselors promote the autonomy and independence
of a minor and carefully consider how much they need to support a student to make his or her own decisions without interference or breach of
confidentiality. Primary to the counselor's decision making is the seriousness of a minor's behavior in the framework of his or her developmental
milestones and the minor's history of making informed decisions (Stone,
2001).

■ *Consider the impact of the school setting and parental rights.*
Parental rights are more complicated when a minor is in a school setting
since parents send minors to school for academics, not for personal counseling. Therefore, when a minor seeks counseling in a value-laden area
such as abortion, which may infringe on the parents' religious beliefs or
rights to be the guiding voice in their children's lives, the counselor must

give consideration to the wishes of parents. The onus is not on the school counselor to know the religious beliefs of every student and his or her family. However, if a student confides that religion is at issue or if the counselor learns this from another source, then it is appropriate that you consider this information as you determine how to proceed with the student.

■ *Consider diversity issues.*
Each decision for ethical dilemmas must be made in context and must consider a minor's ethnicity, gender, race and sexual identity.

■ *Consult with a supervisor or respected colleague.*
It is ethical, lawful and beneficial to inform and consult with supervisors and colleagues. As you do so, examine with your colleague the good and bad consequences of each course of action, striving to minimize the risk to the student while respecting the inherent rights of parents. After you implement a course of action, you will need to process the results to strengthen the probability that the student will make appropriate decisions in the future.

■ *Know yourself and your values.*
School counselors will want to understand their own values in sensitive areas such as abortion and understand the impact of those values on their ability to act in the best interest of their students. Professionals know they cannot leave their values out of their work, but they use caution when their values might inappropriately interfere with promoting a student's autonomy. School counselors will want to refer students to a colleague when they can no longer be effective.

■ *Avoid involvement in a student's medical care.*
Referring students to birth control clinics should be avoided and a school counselor should never agree to take students for any kind of medical procedure, especially a procedure as controversial as abortion (Stone, 2004).

PREGNANT STUDENTS AND CONFIDENTIALITY

Your assistant principal comes to you and asks you for a list of all students in the school that you know are pregnant. He explains that he wants to notify these students about an alternative school for pregnant and parenting teens and encourage them to go there. Do you have any concerns about this request? Must you comply with this request?

Points to Consider

In a 2002 California court case, *Holt v. Bellflower Unified School District*, school counselor Mary Beth Holt filed suit against the district for wrongful termination and other complaints after she refused to disclose the names of pregnant students at her high school. Holt was not rehired but the district did not give a reason for refusing to rehire her.

The assistant principal at her school ordered Holt to disclose the names of students who were pregnant so that they could be transferred to another school specifically designed to handle the circumstances of pregnant students. The vice principal told Holt the reason for the request was that the school board did not want pregnant girls on the school campus, and they had adopted a policy of transferring pregnant students out of the regular school program. Testimony showed that the alternative school was considered inferior to the home school. Holt explained that the information was confidential, having been disclosed during private counseling sessions protected under California statute for school counselors and confidentiality. Holt contacted the department of education to inform them of the situation. Her employers at Bellflower then informed her that they would not continue her employment the following year, and she was told there was "no cause" for her firing.

Holt sued the school district, the principal and vice principal, and each member of the Bellflower Board of Education. On appeal it was revealed that the Bellflower Unified School District did not initially plead their case in the complaint or before the court regarding their "need to know" so students could be encouraged to participate in the Cal-Safe program. Therefore, the appeals court found that the case brought by Holt was not heard accurately and the school counselor was allowed to proceed further with her complaint, meaning the case went back to the lower court to be heard again. The results of the lower court's decision are not published and may have been settled.

In some cases it may be possible to avoid conflict with your administration by telling them that you will consult with the students and seek their permission to be included on a list to the administration. It would also be ethical to tell administration that you will make certain these students know transferring is not mandatory but optional, and depending on the context of the situation, give your opinion on the academic program provided by the alternative school. Holt's willingness to put her students above the system is admirable. However, we must remember that we have taken employment in a system designed for academic instruction and the rules are different than in a system designed exclusively for counseling. The bottom line is that confidentiality is much harder to respect because of competing interests in a school setting.

This is an example of a no-win situation unless the scholl counselor can figure out how to respect students' autonomy, such as getting their permission to have their names on the list, while also letting the administrators know we are listening to their requests. Holt appears to be a student-centered counselor and it is always unfortunate to lose good people because a compromise could not be reached, or worse, was never even considered.

ABORTION COUNSELING

Regina is 16 years old and pregnant. She comes to you, her school counselor, seeking help as she considers an abortion. Regina tells you she really needs to talk over her options with an adult who is "outside of her family." Can you discuss with Regina her pregnancy and her consideration of an abortion? Does this scenario automatically trigger for you the need to call and inform Regina's parents about her pregnancy?

Points to Consider

To avoid ambiguity when counseling students – and to delineate the limits of your pledge to preserve confidentiality – you must give students the opportunity for informed consent, letting them know that when you believe they are in danger you may need to contact their parents.

A school counselor has a strong ethical responsibility to Regina at a time when she may be most vulnerable. The counselor's choice of words, body language and tone carry enormous weight as Regina decides what to do about her pregnancy. If possible, encourage Regina to tell her parents or a close relative, explaining how discussing her problem with loved ones can benefit her.

Assist Regina in exploring her options without imposing your own views and giving her advice. Generally speaking, if a student is not developmentally delayed, it is best practice to let the student supply the options along with good and bad consequences of each. If you supply the options you may inadvertently nudge her toward one decision over another. Maybe abortion is not one of her considerations, and if you list this along with other options, you may be planting a thought that the student might not have considered.

The legal and ethical complications of working with minors in schools pose daily dilemmas, never more so than with value-laden issues such as abortion, which involves a family's religious beliefs, values about sexual conduct, parental rights to be the guiding voice in their children's lives, and other rights. Respecting students' confidences requires school counselors to balance the rights of minors with the rights of their parents (Isaacs & Stone, 2001; Kaplan, 1996). Legal rulings combined with the Ethical Standards for School Counselors (ASCA, 2004) offer suggestions and guidance in the complexities of confidentiality. However, it is ultimately the school counselor's responsibility to determine an appropriate response for individual students who put their trust in the security of the counseling relationship.

School counselors need to be advocates and sources of strength for the individual students who come to them for help in dealing with issues such as sexual activity and abortion. Under what circumstances would a counselor be held liable for giving abortion advice?

In *Arnold v. Board of Education of Escambia County* (1989), Jane and John, two high school students, filed suit along with their parents against the School District of Escambia County, Ala., alleging that the school counselor, Kay Rose, and the assistant principal, Melvin Powell, coerced and assisted Jane in getting an abortion. Further, they complained that Powell had paid someone $20 to drive Jane to the abortion clinic and that Powell and Rose hired Jane and John to perform menial tasks to earn money for the abortion. John, the father of the baby, and Jane claimed that their constitutional rights, including free exercise of religion, were violated and that they were coerced into involuntary servitude. The parents claimed that Rose and Powell violated their privacy rights when the parents were not informed that Jane was pregnant and when school officials urged the students not to tell them. The trial court dismissed the suit and plaintiffs appealed (*Arnold v. Board of Education of Escambia County*, 1989; Zirkel, 2001).

The U.S. 11th Circuit Court of Appeals partially reversed the decision of the trial court and found Jane's privacy claim and both students' religious claim worthy of further consideration by the courts. In other words, if Jane and John's religion prohibited abortion, and Rose and Powell coerced Jane and John to proceed with Jane's abortion, then their constitutionally protected right of freedom of religion might have been violated. Further, Jane's constitutionally protected right to choose to carry or abort a pregnancy had been violated if she was coerced into having an abortion. Jane's parents claimed that their privacy rights were violated when the school counselor and assistant principal coerced Jane into having an abortion and urged her and John to refrain from discussing their options with a parent. The case was remanded back to the lower court for a trial to take place (Zirkel, 2001).

In fact finding, the trial court found that Jane had visited a physician who confirmed she was pregnant and provided her with abortion information upon her request. John and Jane told Rose that they did not want their parents to know about the pregnancy since they were not supposed to be seeing each other, and that Jane had left home because she was being abused by her stepfather. Rose presented various alternatives but the students rejected all of them except abortion. Rose repeatedly urged Jane and John to consult with their parents. She reported the alleged abuse by the stepfather to the Department of Human Resources, who sent a representative to meet with Jane. The representative urged Jane to consult with her mother and offered alternatives such as foster care and adoption. When Jane rejected all alternatives, the representative assisted Jane in trying to obtain financial assistance and Medicaid. Jane and John said they felt Rose pressured them to have an abortion when Rose fired questions at them about future care for the baby.

During the process of discovery, Jane admitted that Rose's questions were good, that she alone made the decision to have an abortion, and that she was not coerced by Rose or Powell. John admitted that he had chosen not to tell his mother. The trial court concluded that the students were not deprived of their free will, had chosen to obtain an abortion, had chosen not to tell their parents, and that there was no coercion on the part of school officials (*Arnold v. Board of Education of Escambia County*, 1989; Zirkel, 1991; Zirkel, 2001).

After the Arnold ruling, the question remains: may counselors be held liable for giving abortion advice to pregnant minors? Counselors in the course of fulfilling their job responsibilities may assist students with value-laden issues such as abortion if they are competent to give such advice and if they proceed in a professional manner. School counselors must consider that their responsibilities extend beyond the student to parents and guardians and take great care in abortion counseling. Fischer and Sorenson (1996) stated:

If an immature, emotionally fragile young girl procures an abortion with the help of a counselor, under circumstances where reasonably competent counselors would have notified the parents or would have advised against the abortion, liability for psychological or physical suffering may follow. The specific facts and circumstances must always be considered. (p. 60)

Complicated, value-laden counseling requires that the school counselor assess the developmental age of the student and the ability of the student to make informed, sound decisions. School counselors must continually ask themselves what the reasonably competent professional would do under similar circumstances. Consider if Jane Doe had been 13 years old. Would Rose have responded differently? Stadler's (1990) test of universality is a good gauge because the test asks the professional to consider the advice they would give to a colleague who is in the throes of a similar ethical dilemma. If the school counselor would advise a colleague to take a different path, then this suggests the counselor should further examine the proposed action. Perhaps the counselor is planning an action that is too conservative, too risky, or outside the bounds of what the reasonably competent professional would do.

Can school boards adopt policies forbidding school counselors to engage in any discussions with their students about contraception, abortion or sexual activity? School boards can (and some do) adopt policies forbidding counselors to address certain topics or instructing them to immediately call parents if such topics are brought up by their students. However, in the absence of a school board policy expressly forbidding counselors to discuss abortion, school counselors can discuss the topic with students. School counselors must be ready to argue that they behaved as the reasonably competent professional would have. Coercion or imposing one's values on a minor student would not be appropriate actions of a reasonable and professional school counselor (Stone, 2004).

SCHOOL COUNSELORS' VALUES

You are vehemently opposed to abortion. How will this affect your response and behavior with Regina in the case described above? How will you know when you can address a value-laden issue with a student and when your own values will require that you refer this student to someone else?

Points to Consider

A counselor who is vehemently opposed to abortion ethically would not want to work with a minor in the throes of an abortion decision. The ethical and responsible course of action would be to refer Regina to another counselor if at all possible. Sometimes an outside agency or a school nurse would be a good choice. School nurses can provide medical advice but – a word of caution – not necessarily emotional support, so your work may not be done just because you referred a student to the school nurse.

The counselor who is vehemently opposed may not voice his or her opposition to abortion, but values are revealed in voice tone, a raised eyebrow at certain junctures in the counseling session, a heavy sigh, a diverted glance – all of which inadvertently impose the counselor's values on a vulnerable student. The influence a counselor can have on a pregnant minor cannot be understated. Not only do counselors have authority over students; students may suffer from inexperience, lack of awareness of their rights, lack of confidence in their own feelings and beliefs, and emotions related to the pregnancy they may be experiencing – all can be compounded, resulting in a state of vulnerability for the client.

AIDING A STUDENT IN GETTING AN ABORTION

You have an exceptional rapport with one of your counselees, whom you also coach in swimming. She finds herself pregnant, distraught and unwilling to involve her parents, and turns to you for help. You believe your relationship is such that you can support this student in acquiring the abortion she desperately wants. You take steps to give her and her boyfriend all the necessary information they will need to have this procedure in a neighboring state, since your state requires parental consent. You are convinced you have done the right thing. Have you? Have you jeopardized your job?

Points to Consider

A couple in the Hatboro-Horsham School District in Pennsylvania sued their daughter's high school counselor after it was revealed that the counselor advised her to obtain an abortion, a violation of Pennsylvania state law (Family Education, n.d.). The school counselor allegedly advised the young woman to get the abortion, helped her to get out of school for the procedure, cashed the checks written by her boyfriend for the abortion and created a map to the abortion clinic in the neighboring state of New

Jersey. Pennsylvania state law requires the consent of a parent or guardian before a minor can undergo an abortion procedure, but New Jersey state law does not include this regulation.

The parents' suit centers on their rights, protected under the 14th Amendment, that they be the guiding force in matters of family life and the upbringing of children (U.S. Constitution, n.d.). The parents also named the Hatboro-Horsham School District as codefendant in the suit, and the parents sought to prevent the school district from counseling students about abortion or assisting students to obtain medical procedures or information without parental consent.

School counselors' work is influenced by community standards as well as local and state laws. State laws on contraceptive services and abortions, while not directly dictating how we behave, certainly influence our approach. If we are in a state that allows students to make medical decisions about their reproductive lives, then we find our work with minors different than in a state or community that believes parents should decide if a child takes birth control or has an abortion.

STATES' STANCE ON PARENTAL CONSENT OR NOTIFICATION FOR MINORS' ABORTION

Consent Laws Not In Effect	Notice Laws Not In Effect	States Requiring Consent	States Requiring Notice	States With No Laws
Alaska	Florida	Alabama	Arkansas	Connecticut
California	Illinois	Arizona	Colorado	Hawaii
New Mexico	Montana	Idaho	Delaware	New York
Oklahoma	Nevada	Indiana	Georgia	Oregon
	New Hampshire	Kentucky	Iowa	Vermont
	New Jersey	Louisiana	Kansas	Washington
		Maine	Maryland	Washington, D.C.
		Massachusetts	Minnesota	
		Michigan	Nebraska	
		Missouri	Ohio	
		North Carolina	South Dakota	
		North Dakota	Texas	
		Pennsylvania	Utah	
		Rhode Island	West Virginia	
		South Carolina		
		Tennessee		
		Virginia		
		Wisconsin		
		Wyoming		

- Twenty-one states and the District of Columbia grant all minors the authority to consent to contraceptive services. Eleven other states grant most minors this authority.
- Thirty-four states and the District of Columbia authorize a pregnant minor to obtain prenatal care and delivery services without parental consent or notification.
- All 50 states and the District of Columbia give minors the authority to consent to the diagnosis and treatment of sexually transmitted infections (Alan Guttmacher Institute, 2005).

To view the entire report and read additional critical details, visit the Planned Parenthood site at http://www.plannedparenthood.org/pp2/portal/files/portal/medicalinfo/abortion/fact-parental-consent.xml.

Judicial bypass is a process by which minors can get state approval to have an abortion without parental cmnsent or notification in states requiring parental involvement. Although highly variable among the states (Planned Parenthood Federation of America, Inc., 2004), the common factor is that minors seeking judicial bypass must demonstrate the maturity to make the decision to have an abortion without parental notification. The minor must show that she understands the health risks involved in getting an abortion, that she understands and has considered the alternatives to abortion that are available, and finally, that she is aware of the psychological and emotional consequences that may occur as a result of the abortion, including how the abortion may affect her family relationships in the future (American Lawyer Newspapers Group, Inc., 2000.)

RAPE, STATUTORY RAPE AND CHILD ABUSE

A 15-year-old student tells you that she lives at home with her parents and 21-year-old boyfriend. A 14-year-old tells you he is having sex with his 14-year-old girlfriend. A 17-year-old student and a 14-year-old are having sexual relations. A 15-year-old tells you about a night of drinking and drugs and waking up without her clothes. She says others reported to her that four or five boys had sex with her while she was unconscious. A student confides that her mother's live-in boyfriend has been spying on her while she undresses and tries to rub up against her in what he pretends to be just a playful act. Do any of these situations involve a crime that you must report?

Points to Consider

These issues are applicable to several chapters in this book because they describe criminal activity and child abuse as well as legal sexual activity. The answer for all the scenarios except the one involving the mother's boyfriend is that it depends on the state. Each state defines the "age of consent" or the age minors can legally engage in sexual activity.

Sometimes it is the age differential between partners – three or more years for minors – that makes sexual relationships a crime, such as the 14-year-old and the 17-year-old having sexual relations. In some states it is illegal for two minors to have sexual relationships. Depending on the state, adults 18 or older having a sexual relationship with a minor of certain ages is statutory rape, and the age of both victim and perpetrator are variable depending on the state. Even when parents are aware and approve such a union, it is still considered statutory rape if one party is an adult and the minor is under a certain age. Some educators believe that if parents know, then it is not our place to report sexual relations that are not legal. However, law enforcement agencies and Child Protective Services do not necessarily agree.

Child abuse is occurring in the case with the mother's boyfriend, because the perpetrator is in a custodial or caretaker role such as a parent, relative, adult living in the home, babysitter, school counselor, pastor or coach (National Clearinghouse on Child Abuse and Neglect Information, 2004).

School counselors are being drawn into an increased emphasis nationwide on reporting statutory rape. Encouraged by congressional action, state legislators in the mid-1990s began strengthening and enforcing statutory rape laws in an effort to lower teen-age pregnancy rates and welfare costs. Significant numbers of teen-age pregnancies are caused by men more than four years older than their partners, spurring states to enforce statutory laws (Findholt & Robrecht, 2002).

There is considerable variance in the lawful age of consent, which defines whether or not statutory rape has been committed. Age of consent varies from 14 to 17 and by a differential of three or more years (Mitchell & Rogers, 2003). To find how your state statutes describe age of consent, go to the Web site http://www.law.cornell.edu/statutes.html#state.

In order to determine if a situation you know about is statutory rape, seek help from the legal counsel of your school board or call the Child Protective Services or sheriff or police headquarters. Visit the Mandatory

Reporting of Child Abuse and Neglect (http://www.smith-lawfirm.com/ mandatory_reporting.htm) site.

The following newspaper article is an example of what can happen to a counselor who has even limited information that a student may have been the victim of statutory rape. (Names removed for privacy.) The message for us is to report possible statutory rape cases even if we think the autorities may not consider the reports as viable.

Sept. 5, 2003
School Worker Said To Be Negligent
By Jennifer Thomas

PALATKA - The case of a Putnam County School District guidance counselor who was suspended without pay on Aug. 25 is linked to a fifth-grade girl who was impregnated by a 19-year-old Palatka man, sources say. The Putnam County Sheriff's Office listed JW, a Browning-Pearce Elementary School guidance counselor, as a witness in a May 15 incident report.

On Aug. 25, the school board approved School Superintendent David Buckles' request to suspend JW without pay for failure to report a potential abuse situation. Her case has been forwarded to the state Department of Education/Education Practices Commission for review, as required by law. JW has requested an administrative hearing.

On April 19, the mother of the girl reported the pregnancy case to the Palatka Police Department, which launched an investigation, according to the PPD report. The mother reported that her daughter had had sex with the 19-year-old male twice in December 2002 and January, it read. On April 23, she reported that her daughter was eight weeks pregnant.

Although the sheriff's report read that the PPD closed the case because of a lack of cooperation from the girl's mother, Palatka Police Chief Gary Getchell said Thursday his agency is still investigating the case.

The suspect denied impregnating the girl, according to the PPD report. "To my knowledge, speaking to the officer that is investigating it, it is very difficult to secure cooperation from the mother and daughter," Getchell said.

Browning-Pearce Principal D.D. reported the girl's pregnancy to the abuse registry after first learning about it on May 7, and was advised it was accepted, the report read. D.D. later called the sheriff's office on May 14 when she had not heard a response, the report read.

The sheriff's office contacted a state Department of Children and Families investigator who said the registry never forwarded the abuse complaint to his office. After looking into the matter at the sheriff's office request, the investigator said the registry acknowledged the complaint, but the registry never called him back regarding why the case was sent to his office.

According to the sheriff's report, the girl told JW that she was pregnant between March 25-28, that her mother had taken her to a clinic where she underwent an abortion and that the father was a 19-year-old man.

Robert L. McLeod II, a St. Augustine attorney representing JW, said, however, that JW was unaware of the pregnancy issue. McLeod said the girl was sent to JW's office on a disciplinary notice and a teacher advised her before she met with the girl that there were rumors that the girl was pregnant. He said she questioned the girl who denied that she was pregnant. After leaving JW's office, the girl gave JW an indication that the rumors could be fact.

McLeod said JW left several messages with the girl's mother, but she never responded to the calls. "Ms. JW's position was and always has been that the whole reason why she was talking to this child did not have anything to do with those issues," he said.

He said the actions that JW – who has received exemplary ratings in her job – took at the time seemed appropriate. "There is no question that the referral to guidance had nothing to do with any alleged pregnancy. I mean, that's not even a part of the school board's complaint or issue," McLeod said. "There has not been nor has there been a complaint of abuse, a rape or anything like that."

Buckles voiced concern that the system had "failed the child." "You just want to ensure that those things don't happen to children," Buckles said. He added that the DCF had also "dropped the ball" in the case.

Tom Barnes, spokesman for DCF in Gainesville, said DCF only deals with child protection issues, which involve the abuse of a child in the care of a caretaker. He said a statutory rape – cases in which adults reportedly have sex with a minor – would be something DCF or the abuse registry would refer to a law enforcement agency for a criminal investigation.

Barnes said the registry usually informs the caller if it is a case in which it cannot get involved. Otherwise, DCF would look at whether the child's caretaker acted responsibly in the situation.
The Palatka (Fla.) Daily News, 2003

SAFE HAVEN LAW

In an effort to protect newborns from being discarded, as in recent cases of babies being found in dumpsters and public restrooms, most states have passed laws that allow birth mothers to leave their newborns at hospitals, fire stations, police stations and other select safe havens for abandoned babies. The understanding is that no questions will be asked and the mother is relinquishing any legal rights to the child. Your sister works with social services and continually tells you about the incidence in your community of abandoned babies left in harm's way. You want to advertise the state law on bulletin boards throughout your school in an effort to protect the unborn. Your principal will not allow any reference to this law displayed in the school. Her concern is that this law sends the message to students that they can be irresponsible, have unprotected sex and then fix an unwanted pregnancy by abandoning their "problem." The principal says that the only involvement your school will have in the subject of teen-age sexual relations is to promote and implement the district's abstinence-based curriculum. What do you do?

Points to Consider

Many states have enacted or are actively considering new "safe haven" laws to prevent such tragic abandonment. These laws allow a woman to leave her baby at a hospital, medical clinic, police or fire station anonymously, mostly with no questions or no legal repercussions. Women in 44 states now have the option to leave their child at a hospital or fire station, in some cases within three days of the newborn's birth. Identified with bracelets, the mother also has the opportunity to reclaim a child within two weeks of dropping off the infant (Aguilar, 2004).

Research, delicate diplomacy and probably a collection of compromises could help the school counselor who wants this law to be known to his or her students. Abstinence-based curriculum versus comprehensive sex education deeply divides both scientific and religious communities. Even when limited by district's policy, the school counselor has the responsibility to work with the administration and community to develop programs that are in the best interest of students, as explained in the ASCA's ethics codes D.1 and D.2 (2004). Gather information from local and national organizations (such as Planned Parenthood and the Centers for Disease Control and Prevention) that provide statistics concerning teen-age pregnancy and the practice of abandoning unwanted children. Maybe you can invite a local nurse, emergency medical technician or firefighter to share a success story in which a child was saved because of the safe haven law.

Explain to your principal that the idea of such laws is not to encourage teen-age pregnancy or irresponsibility, but to protect the life of a newborn in the event of a mistake. If the idea of public service posters detailing the safe haven law is out of the question, perhaps the principal would be more amenable to classroom talks or an assembly. Establishing a think tank composed of health care workers, district officials, educators, parents, and counselors might be a way to spearhead ideas on how to educate teens about sex while preserving the spirit of district policy.

In a Position to Know: A Counselor Educator Speaks

The case presented at the beginning of the chapter is revisited here and answered by a counselor educator. Compare her answer with your own approach.

DEVELOPMENTALLY DELAYED, PREGNANT STUDENTS

Sharon is slightly developmentally delayed. Chronologically Sharon is 14 but developmentally she is more like an 11- or 12-year-old. Sharon is pregnant and her mother is aware of the pregnancy. Sharon has long been a concern of everyone in the school. She is unkempt, unclean, explosive and violent. Her developmental problems mean she is always out of sync with her age group. Her peers avoid her because they are afraid of her. You are horrified that she will now be responsible for a baby. Sharon is not capable of taking care of herself and you fear for the safety of her child. She tells you she is going to have her baby because this will bring the father of the baby back to her. Sharon says her mother will help her raise the baby. She talks excitedly and animatedly about how she has "always wanted a baby." She explains that her cousin who is also 14 has a baby and is doing quite well an that everyone comes up to the baby and makes a big deal over her. What is your reaction to this situation? What steps would you take in this case?

Response From a Counselor Educator

Legal, ethical and clinical issues related to teen-age pregnancy are problematic for school counselors. Sharon's case is particularly challenging because of her chronological age compounded by her developmental delay. Furthermore, a school counselor would be likely to have concerns about how Sharon's violent tendencies might create an unsafe environment for the baby and how Sharon will care for a baby if she doesn't physically care for herself very well.

A primary consideration for school counselors whenever they are working with pregnant minors is school counselors' ethical duty to remain aware of their own values and ascertain the values of the students they serve. It is often difficult to separate one's values from the clinical, legal and ethical issues involved in these cases; however, the Ethical Standards for School Counselors (ASCA, 2004) clearly state that a school counselor respects "the student's values and beliefs and does not impose the counselor's personal values" (A.1.c.). The standards clarify that a school counselor's primary obligation is to the student and that each student is to be treated with respect (A.1.a.). A school counselor is also expected to address the personal and social needs of students and encourage maximum student development (A.1.b.). Thus, even though a school counselor may be horrified that Sharon will be responsible for a baby, the counselor has an ethical duty to address the issues presented by the student's pregnancy and act in the student's best interest without making value judgments.

Ethical guidelines provide a framework for the clinical implications of this case. The fact that Sharon's mother knows about the pregnancy and is willing to help raise the child eliminates the dilemma of whether or not to breach confidentiality and tell a parent about the student's pregnancy. Yet, the parental rights of Sharon's mother still need to be considered. The Ethical Standards for School Counselors (ASCA, 2004) explain that professional school counselors respect the rights of parents (B.1.a.). School counselors are also advised to develop a collaborative relationship with parents, when it is appropriate (B.1.a.). In Sharon's case, discussing the pregnancy, the reality of raising a child, and options such as adoption with Sharon and her mother may be an appropriate course of action. As previously indicated, such an intervention should be approached with care and consideration of the values of the student and her mother.

If the school counselor decides to meet with Sharon and her mother, the school counselor may want to express concerns about Sharon's view of parenthood. Sharon, like many teen-agers, appears to have an idealized view of what caring for a baby will be like. Her references to the attentio her cousin gets support the notion that Sharon has little idea of what caring for a baby really involves. Furthermore, her idea that the pregnancy will bring the baby's father back to her is a common belief among pregnant teen-agers that usually isn't borne out.

Several other issues could be addressed in a conversation with Sharon and her mother. Clinically, a school counselor may want to explore whether Sharon's unkempt appearance could be indicative of depression. Her lack of grooming could also be linked to an inability to take care of herself. Her violent tendencies could put the baby at risk. Sharon's age and developmental delay will make caring for a child very difficult. Involving Sharon's mother may help Sharon and her mother make a wise decision about whether keeping the baby is in Sharon's and her baby's best interests. If Sharon and her mother decide Sharon should keep her baby, discussing these types of issues could help Sharon and her mother create a plan for caring for both Sharon and the baby.

Group counseling is another option for Sharon. Many schools are implementing groups for teen-age parents. Attending such a group could help Sharon become better aware of the realities of raising a child. Group settings also provide additional support from peers who are struggling with the harsh realities of teen-age parenthood.

From a legal standpoint, the school counselor is expected to act as a reasonable school counselor would act under the circumstances. Sharon's mother is aware of Sharon's pregnancy and has agreed to help take care of the child. Thus, in this situation, respecting a student's ethical right to privacy while balancing parents' legal rights is probably not as challenging an issue. However, school counselors need to remain cognizant of their legal duty to report suspected child abuse. Accordingly, a school counselor needs to determine whether Sharon's unkempt appearance is indicative of neglect. Furthermore, if Sharon keeps her baby and the school counselor suspects that the baby is being neglected or abused, the school counselor would be legally required to report that suspected abuse as well.

Stone (2002) provides guidelines for school counselors who are counseling students in situations like Sharon's. Stone suggests that school counselors look to school board policy for guidance, consider the student's developmental level when providing interventions, and remain cognizant of parental rights and values. Stone also recommends consulting with a colleague or supervisor when faced with issues related to a student's pregnancy. Finally, Stone cautions school counselors to avoid involving themselves in a student's medical care.

Sharon's case presents yet another example of the legal, ethical and clinical complexities of working with minors in school settings. Attending workshops and other continuing education opportunities on legal, ethical and clinical issues is vitally important in remaining competent, practicing in an ethical manner, and minimizing legal liability. And, because school counselors face such challenging issues in a litigious society, school counselors are wise to maintain professional liability insurance.

Mary Hermann, J.D., Ph.D., counselor educator at Mississippi State University

Making Connections

1. Do you believe you have an obligation to tell a parent that his or her child is pregnant if the child refuses to involve her parents?

2. Under what circumstances if any would you help a pregnant student get medical care of any kind?

3. How do your state statutes read regarding minors and abortion?

4. How do the standards of your state and community impact your behavior regarding pregnant students?

5. How do your state statutes read regarding age of consent? What are the implications of your state's age of consent laws for you as a school counselor?

Key Terms

Developmentally delayed
Sexually active students
Abortion
Judicial bypass
Value-laden counseling

Safe haven law
Age of consent
Statutory rape

References

Alan Guttmacher Institute. (2005). *Report on sexual and reproductive health rights*. Retrieved February 21, 2005, from http://www.agi-usa.org/

Aguilar, E. (2004, July 22). Two babies abandoned in PA. *The Stanford Daily*. Retrieved February 19, 2005, from http://daily.stanford.edu/daily/servlet/tempo?page=content&id=14480&repository=0001_article

American Lawyer Newspapers Group, Inc. (2000). Justices divided on interpretation of parental notification law. *Texas Lawyer*, p. 15.

American School Counselor Association. (2004). *Ethical standards for school counselors*. Alexandria, VA: Author.

Arnold v. Board of Education of Escambia County, 880 F. 2d 305 (Alabama 1989).

Constitution of the United States of America. (n.d.). *Fourteenth Amendment—Rights guaranteed: Privileges and immunities of citizenship, due process, and equal protection*. Retrieved on February 19, 2005, from http://www.gpoaccess.gov/constitution/html/amdt14.html

Family Education. (n.d.). *Group sues Pennsylvania school over abortion*. Retrieved February 19, 2005, from http://www.familyeducation.com/article/0,1120,1-8846,00.html

Findholt, N., & Robrecht, L. (2002). Legal and ethical considerations in research with sexually active adolescents: The requirement to report statutory rape. *Perspectives on Sexual and Reproductive Health*. Retrieved February 20, 2005, from http://www.guttmacher.org

Fischer, L., & Sorenson, P. (1996). *School law for counselors, psychologists, and social workers*. White Plains, NY: Longman.

Holt v. Bellflower Unified School District, Court of Appeal of California, Second Appellate District, Division Eight 2002 Cal. App. Unpub. Lexis 6135, June 28, 2002.

Isaacs, M., & Stone, C. (2001). Confidentiality with minors: Mental health counselor's attitudes toward breaching or preserving confidentiality. *Journal of Mental Health Counseling, 23*(4), 342-356.

Kaplan, L. (1996). Outrageous or legitimate concerns: What some parents are saying about school counseling. *The School Counselor, 43,* 165-170.

Legal Information Institute. (n.d.). Marriage laws of the fifty states, District of Columbia and Puerto Rico. Retrieved March 19, 2005, from http://www.law.cornell.edu/statutes.html#state

Mitchell, C., & Rogers, R. (2003). Rape, statutory rape, and child abuse: Legal distinctions and counselor duties. *Professional School Counselor: Special Issue on Legal and Ethical Issues in School Counselor, 6* (1).

National Clearinghouse on Child Abuse and Neglect Information. (2005). *What is child abuse and neglect?* Retrieved January 12, 2005, from http://nccanch.acf.hhs.gov/

Planned Parenthood Federation of America, Inc. (2004, August). *Teenagers, abortion, and government intrusion laws.* New York, NY: Author.

Princeton Survey Research Associates International (2004). NBC News/PEOPLE Magazine: *National survey of young teens' sexual attitudes and behaviors.* Retrieved February 19, 2005 from http://msnbcmedia.msn.com/i/msnbc/Sections/TVNews/Dateline%20NBC/NBCTeenTopline.pdf

Smith, S. K. (2003). *Mandatory reporting of child abuse and neglect.* Retrieved January 15, 2005, from http://www.smith-lawfirm.com/mandatory_reporting.htm

Stadler, H. A. (1990). Confidentiality. In B. Herlihy & I. B. Golden (Eds.), *AACD ethical standards-casebook* (4th ed; pp.102-110). Alexandria, VA: American Association for Counseling and Development.

Stone, C. (Speaker). (2001). *Legal and ethical issues in working with minors in schools* [Film]. Alexandria, VA: American Counseling Association.

Stone, C. (2002). Negligence in academic advising and abortion counseling: Courts rulings and implications. *Professional School Counselor: Special Issue on Legal and Ethical Issues in School Counselor, 6* (1).

Stone, C. (2004). Legal and ethical dilemmas in abortion counseling. *ASCA School Counselor, 41*(3), 8-9.

Thomas, J. (2003, September 5). School worker said to be negligent. *The Palatka* (Fla.) *Daily News.*

Zirkel, P. (1991). End of story. *Phi Delta Kappan, 72,* 640-642.

Zirkel, P. (2001). A pregnant pause? *Phi Delta Kappan, 82,* 557-558.

Sexual Harassment

IN THIS CHAPTER:

Objectives

By the time you have completed this chapter, you should be able to:

- Discuss the legal implications of ignoring sexual harassment.
- Explain the emotional cost to victims of sexual harassment.
- Strategize ways to protect victims of sexual harassment from being victimized twice.
- Talk about the role of the U.S. Department of Education Office for Civil Rights in sexual harassment.
- Understand the elements of a sexual harassment policy and how a policy can be put into practice.

Introduction

In their role as advocates for students, school counselors empower and serve as anchors and sources of strength for individual students in dealing with issues of sexual harassment in schools. School counselors promote a safe and respectful school climate for all students by providing students with the knowledge and support they need.

As leaders within school settings, school counselors can raise awareness among students and fellow educators as to the problem of sexual harassment. Part of the problem is that many students do not tell a school official that they have been victimized, further complicating support for victims (Harris/Scholastic Research, 2001). According to Stone (2004), "Students have described being ignored, disbelieved, blamed, and sometimes punished when they report instances of harassment to teachers and other adults" (p. 2).

School counselors must take into account the legal and ethical complications of working with minors in schools, especially with regard to sexual harassment issues. Through the multitude of roles they play in school settings, school counselors primarily serve students. As advocates and human behavior specialists, school counselors serve as a source of strength in confronting and dealing with sexual harassment. They also raise awareness as to the prevalence of sexual harassment and assist their colleagues in formulating school plans for prevention and intervention.

School counselors must balance the confidentiality issues that respect the rights of minors, the rights of parents and the need to protect students from further abuse. Sources such as codes of ethical behavior of the American School Counselor Association and the American Counseling Association, as well as legal decisions of court cases, provide the framework with regard to the parameters of confidentiality issues. The school counselor ultimately has the responsibility to determine an appropriate response within a trusting, secure counseling relationship when confronted with an individual student suffering sexual harassment.

Generally speaking, there are two types of sexual harassment in schools. *Hostile environment* involves student-on-student harassment in which a student feels the environment is not a safe place. *Quid pro quo* generally involves teacher-on-student sexual harassment, in which a teacher gives a better grade or a favor in exchange for a sexual act.

School counselors engage in a variety of strategies to encourage victims to report sexual harassment, and once they do, to make certain they are properly supported to lessen the emotional costs of harassment or their chances of being victimized by the system.

The purpose of this chapter is to explore through case study the legal and ethical implications of deliberate indifference to sexual harassment, the emotional cost to youth, and the financial cost to school districts if we do not act on students' behalf.

The whole issue of sexual harassment has been the focus of much discourse within the context of social and educational policy. Understanding what constitutes sexual harassment and who defines it are matters for debate. Males and females often look at sexual harassment in different ways. Students engage in sexual harassment without understanding the pain they cause.

Recent court rulings have further clarified the legal definition of sexual harassment and resulted in legislation that aids counselors in advocating against student-on-student harassment. Sex discrimination, especially with regard to the influence of gender in educational opportunities, was outlawed by Title IX, enacted by Congress in 1972 (Title IX of the Educational Amendments of 1972). In Title IX the U.S. Department of Education Office for Civil Rights sees sexual harassment within a school setting to be harassment that is "sufficiently severe, persistent, or pervasive that it adversely affects a student's education or creates a hostile or abusive educational environment and the conduct must be sexual in nature" (U.S. Department of Education Office for Civil Rights, 1997b, p. 12036).

Regardless of which group is defining sexual harassment, three elements are present: the behavior is sexual in nature or at least related to the gender of the person; the behavior occurs in an unequal relationship where one person has more power over another (physical, psychological, authoritative, or other); and the behavior is unsolicited or unwelcome (Hyde & Soronen, 2004).

In 2001, the American Association of University Women repeated its well-known 1993 study titled "Hostile Hallways," which brought to public awareness the level of sexual harassment in America's schools (Harris/Scholastic Research, 2001). When asked in 2001 to define sexual harassment, nearly all 2,064 students responded that it is physical and nonphysical behavior, words, gestures, jokes and looks. As in the 1993 study, the 2001 survey found that four out of five students have experienced some form of sexual harassment in school (Harris/Scholastic Research, 2001).

Fourteen percent of the participants in the survey said there was a lot of sexual harassment in their schools, representing little change over the past 10 years. Students reported the worst offenses happen when someone pulls off their clothing, spreads sexual rumors about them, or calls them gay or lesbian (Harris/Scholastic Research, 2001).

The biggest change between the 1993 and 2001 surveys was the awareness of a sexual harassment policy. Fewer than three in 10 students in 1993 reported their school districts had policies, but now seven in 10 say their school districts have policies and almost four in 10 say their school districts advertise the policies in written material (Harris/Scholastic Research, 2001).

Students are reluctant to report sexual harassment to adults in their schools. Only four out of 10 respondents said they would complain to a school adult if they were sexually harassed. With 80 percent of students experiencing sexual harassment and fewer than 40 percent of that number reporting the harassment to an adult at school, there has been progress but advocacy continues to be important (Harris/Scholastic Research, 2001).

Court rulings have given school counselors support for raising awareness and making positive change for victims of sexual harassment. One important court case, the U.S. Supreme Court decision in *Davis v. Monroe County Board of Education* (1999), established sexual harassment as a violation of Title IX. The Supreme Court demands advocacy against known sexual harassment (*Davis v. Monroe County Board of Education*, 1999; U.S. Department of Education, Office for Civil Rights, 1997b; Yell & Katsiyannis, 2000).

In the Davis case a fifth-grade girl and her mother, Mrs. Davis, repeatedly complained to teachers and the principal for five months regarding sexual abuse behaviors by another student, G.F., but they received no relief of any kind (Sullivan & Zirkel, 1999). In desperation, Mrs. Davis filed a complaint with the Monroe County, Ga., Sheriff's Department and G.F. pled guilty to sexual battery. Mrs. Davis' subsequent lawsuit under Title IX's prohibition of sex discrimination in schools ended with a Supreme Court decision in her favor (*Davis v. Monroe County Board of Education*, 1999; Hyde & Soronen, 2004).

Justice Sandra Day O'Connor emphasized a relatively stringent standard of proof for plaintiffs. Liability may be imposed if the harassment is so severe, pervasive and objectively offensive that it deprives a student of an equal educational opportunity (Yell & Katsiyannis, 2000). Additionally, school officials must know of and be deliberately indifferent to the sexual harassment (*Davis v. Monroe County Board of Education*, 1999; Hyde & Soronen, 2004). The Davis case decidedly supports school counselors in exercising their leadership and advocacy role to help students victimized by their peers.

Following the Franklin case, Sullivan and Zirkel (1999) examined 21 cases, in which they found that there was a statutory basis in Title IX for a claim of student-on-student sexual harassment in 20 of those cases. Indeed, as overall awareness of sexual harassment has increased, schools have determined that sexual harassment between peers is a pervasive problem (Stone, 2004).

Teacher-on-student sexual harassment also takes place in America's schools. The U.S. Supreme Court decision in *Franklin v. Gwinnett County Public Schools* (1992) established a legal precedent in that it drew a parallel between teacher-on-student sexual harassment and supervisor-to-subordinate harassment in the workplace (Zirkel, 2001/2002).

Ethical Standards Addressed in This Chapter

Professionalism means knowing your professional associations' codes and adhering to them. Those ethical standards from American School Counselor Association (ASCA, 2004) that are most germane include the following:

- The professional school counselor supports and protects the educational program against any infringement not in students' best interest. (D.1.a)
- The professional school counselor informs appropriate officials in accordance with school policy of conditions that may be potentially disruptive or damaging to the school's mission, personnel and property while honoring the confidentiality between the student and counselor. (D.1.b)
- The professional school counselor assists in developing: (1) curricular and environmental conditions appropriate for the school and community, (2) educational procedures and programs to meet students' developmental needs and (3) a systematic evaluation process for comprehensive, developmental, standards-based school counseling programs, services and personnel. The counselor is guided by the findings of the evaluation data in planning programs and services. (D.1.g)

The full text of ACA ethical codes and ASCA ethical codes can be found at these Web sites: ACA at http://www.counseling.org and ASCA at www.schoolcounselor.org.

Getting Started: What Would You Do?

The following case is discussed for you at the end of this chapter by a counselor educator. Before you read his response, formulate in your own mind how you would approach this ethical dilemma.

CYBERSEXUAL HARASSMENT

Using computers at both the school and her home, Ashley has been sending Kenneth provocative pictures of herself and long love letters, not seeming to care that he has asked her to leave him alone. Ashley has e-mailed her communications to Kenneth and to friends, who have also sent them to other friends. She is instant-messaging people as to every move

Kenneth makes, what he wears, and what his after-school activities are each day. All this attention across electronic media feels very creepy to Kenneth. Ashley has made such an issue of her "love" for him that Kenneth feels he has become the object of ridicule. Despite his embarrassment, he feels frustrated that he does not seem to have any recourse with Ashley and must simply endure, continuing to tell her that he is not interested. Is this harassment? Could this be sexual harassment? Could Ashley be breaking any laws or school board policies? What recourse, if any, does Kenneth have?

Working Through Case Studies

SEXUAL HARASSMENT AND CONFIDENTIALITY

Subjected daily to sexually suggestive remarks by a group of boys in the hallway near her economics class, 14-year-old Kathryn has started to come late to class to avoid the boys' taunts and jeers. Kathryn's economics teacher, Ms. Lopez, unaware of the situation, has sent Kathryn to the office for tardy slips but it has not changed her behavior. Now Kathryn is in danger of being suspended. Ms. Lopez, sensing that something unusual is happening to her conscientious-student-turned-truant, asks you, the school counselor, to talk with Kathryn. You begin to learn the extent of Kathryn's attempt to protect herself when she starts to confide about the harassment. Kathryn describes her embarrassment and her attempts at coping by "laughing it off," "avoiding them," "taunting back" (which she said only made her feel more dirty) or "dressing in really baggy clothes." She begs you not to tell anyone, saying, "it [the harassment] will only get worse." Must you report the sexual harassment to the administration of your school? Can you keep Kathryn's identity confidential? Can the school administration keep Kathryn's identity confidential when confronting the perpetrators?

Points to Consider

Kathryn fits the profile of the harassed student: She blames and doubts herself, uses avoidance techniques, and wants to be free of the harassment but endures it rather than risk becoming known as an informant or having the boys take their revenge on her for reporting them. Once regarded as harmless, flirtatious or playful, sexual harassment is now widely understood to be destructive, illegal and damaging.

Must you report the sexual harassment to the administration of your school? Absolutely. School counselors are required by law to report sexual harassment to school officials. "A school has actual notice of sexual harassment if an agent or responsible employee of the school receives notification" (U.S. Department of Education, Office for Civil Rights, 1997b, p. 12037). Once Kathryn confides that she is being harassed, this constitutes "notice," triggering the school counselor's legal requirement to report the harassment and the school's responsibility to take corrective action.

Can you keep Kathryn's identity confidential? The Office for Civil Rights – the arm of the federal government that requires compliance with anti-discrimination policy and practice for school districts – promotes protecting confidentiality. OCR understands that breaching a student's confidences will often discourage reporting harassment, already identified as a problem for many students in our schools (Harris/Scholastic Research, 2001). If your school has a procedure or policy in place in which the victim is identified on the report, then your advocacy role can spark a change in this practice. Reporting is critical; identifying the victim in a report is not critical.

The school counselor will need to educate Kathryn about the legal requirement to report the sexual harassment, and if appropriate, encourage Kathryn to allow her identity to be known to support addressing it. However, the Office for Civil Rights does not require that educators breach confidentiality just to ensure that the perpetrators are disciplined; rather, it requires that educators address the harassment, which can take many forms. What OCR advocates as best practice should be carefully considered.

Can the school administration keep Regina's identity confidential when confronting the perpetrators? Several factors complicate the question of maintaining confidentiality of the sexually harassed student. These factors include the rights of the victim to confidentiality and the due process rights of the accused to face his ora her accusers. Maintaining the anonymity of the victim very often interferes with the investigation. School administrators and school counselors in an effort to "remedy the harassment and take steps to prevent further harassment" (USDOE/OCR, 1997b, p. 12037) must struggle with whether or not to reveal the victim's identity.

OCR promotes the protection of a victim's identity during the investigation and discipline of the perpetrator. Sometimes discipline and investigation of the perpetrator must be forfeited to protect the victim's identity. However, schools can address harassment in more global ways, such as an assembly or a classroom presentation. A strategy to have an adult catch students in the act could reduce suspicion that someone told on the perpetrator. As a last resort, you may have to reveal the identity of the sexual harassment victim. In the hypothetical case of Kathryn, there isn't a compelling reason for revealing her identity.

TEACHER IGNORING HARASSMENT

Kayla, a seventh-grader, comes to see you about her discomfort with two boys from her mathematics class. Kayla explains that these boys are handing her nude pictures to pass to a boy who sits on the other side of her. She has asked them to stop, and she refuses to pass the pictures, but they always lean over her desk and pass them in such a way to make certain she sees them. Kayla tells you she reported this to the teacher who told her "not to make a big deal out of it," nor has the teacher made any attempts to stop the practice. Kayla seeks your help. Is Kayla being sexually harassed?

Points to Consider

What constitutes a hostile environment with regard to sexual harassment within a school setting? A hostile environment exists if "the school knows or should have known of sexual harassment, and the school fails to take immediate and appropriate corrective action" (USDOE/OCR, 1997b, p. 12049). A hostile environment occurs if conduct of a sexual nature is "sufficiently severe, persistent, or pervasive to limit a student's ability to participate in or benefit from the education program or to create a hostile or abusive educational environment" (USDOE/OCR, 1997b, p. 12041).

Unfortunately, the reality is that school officials historically have not pursued investigation of sexual harassment complaints. Sullivan and Zirkel (1999) analyzed 21 cases of sexual harassment involving students and were "startled by the number of people the victims of harassment notified without obtaining suitable resolution. School districts in the cases to date would have difficulty escaping liability due to the number of staff the target notified" (p. 618). The rule of thumb when it comes to litigation is that liability increases when an entity has knowledge of harm and does not take concrete action to protect the person in their care from this harm. School districts are no exception. The imperative to act that comes from the Supreme Court supports the advocacy role of school counselors with regard to issues of sexual harassment.

If Kayla feels she is being sexually harassed by the passing of the nude pictures, then it is not for any teacher or educator to say, "it's no big deal" or "don't worry about it" or "they are just trying to get your attention." A hostile environment exists for Kayla, and school officials who are deliberately indifferent – such as Kayla's teacher – are setting the school district up for legal action.

"Title IX does not require schools to take responsibility for the actions of other students but does require school districts to respond to student actions with corrective measures" (ACA, 1997, p. 8). Corrective measures are defined as fair and equitable grievance procedures that provide: (a) clear and easily understandable instructions in filing complaints; (b) adequate, reliable and impartial investigation of complaints, including the opportunity to present witnesses and other evidence; (c) notice of the outcome of the complaint; and (d) assurances that the school will take steps to prevent recurrences of any harassment and to correct its discriminatory effects on the complainant (USDOE/OCR, 1997a, pp. 7-8).

SEXUAL HARASSMENT AND GAY, LESBIAN, BISEXUAL, AND TRANSGENDER YOUTH

Joshua, an openly gay male, is often cornered in the cafeteria by three girls who like to taunt him and mimic sexual intercourse with him. They jeer and point to his groin area while saying, "There is nothing there." Is Joshua being sexually harassed?

Points to Consider

Bullying and harassment of GLBT youth is not always considered sexual harassment, but in this case the student is being sexually harassed. Beyond making fun of Joshua's sexual identity, the harassment is sexual in nature, it occurs in an unequal relationship with the three girls having physical and psychological power over Joshua, and their behavior toward him is unwelcome. Harassment of any kind warrants a response from the school but sexual harassment is particularly grievous, as the Supreme Court has already told us. You must address it when you know about it.

ADULT-ON-STUDENT SEXUAL HARASSMENT

Your colleague is involved with a senior who is 17, the age of consent for your state. Is this sexual harassment or child abuse? Does consensual sex exist between a school counselor and a student if the student is the age of consent for his or her state?

Points to Consider

Members of our profession are outraged when they hear of a teacher or school counselor having sexual relationships with a student, yet it continues to happen. Some states, such as New York and Washington, are taking steps to make it a crime. It is a condition for a counselor's losing his or her certificate and job, and states want to make it a condition for being prosecuted as a crime. This obvious breach of trust in the school counseling position makes us all bristle. Depending on the age of the child and the state, this could be criminal child abuse or sexual harassment, but in most every state it is grounds for dismissal. The nature of our work in the personal, social and emotional arena makes this behavior especially heinous.

Following are excerpts from a newspaper article addressing the outcry to make sexual relationships a crime when it involves educators and their students.

July 27, 2001
New state law really makes sex between teachers, teens a crime
By Rebekah Denn

It was a crime, Lake Washington School District parents said: a high school counselor having sex with a student.

Except, as it turned out, it wasn't a crime – at least not at the time – because the student was 17, above the age of consent in Washington.

Professional codes of conduct bar sexual contact between school employees and all students. But, if the students were 16 or older, such contact wasn't always considered illegal until a new bill addressing the topic passed the Legislature last month.

"We had some cases (involving students who were 16 or older) we had to decline here for prosecution that were pretty egregious conduct ... " said Dan Satterburg, chief of staff for the King County Prosecutor's Office.

"You look at it and say, 'This is just wrong.'"

If the new law had been in effect earlier, it would have given the Lake Washington district other ways to pursue a case that was finally settled last month by letting counselor R. L. resign. ...
Seattle (Wash.) *Post-Intelligencer* (2001)

SCHOOL COUNSELORS AS ADVOCATES FOR A SAFE, RESPECTFUL SCHOOL CLIMATE

The principal insists that every faculty member serve on a committee. This year as your service you would like to form a committee to raise awareness about sexual harassment on the campus. Is this an appropriate role? What will be some of your considerations?

Points to Consider

Playing a role in fostering a school climate that does not tolerate sexual harassment and encourages reporting of sexual harassment incidents by students is a worthy use of committee membership and leadership. School counselors can serve as another set of eyes and ears as they put into place preventive measures to reduce harassment in the school environment before it starts (Stone, 2003). Listed below are several recommendations to help your committee get started.

1. Have the committee tackle a school policy that protects all students from sexual harassment.
A sexual harassment policy should include the following elements:

- A strong no-tolerance policy that expressly states a commitment to maintain an educational environment free of fear and intimidation to be included in a student code of conduct
- Clear disciplinary consequences for sexual harassment behavior
- Identification of specific sexual harassment behavior
- Listing of applicable laws and definitions of legal terms
- A confidentiality statement that outlines limits and protections offered to student victims, e.g., duty to protect another or potential individuals from harm
- Provision of a contact person to whom the victim can report incidents (preferably a school counselor)
- Process for grievance procedures, and
- Provision for training of school personnel and students (USDOE,1999; USDOE,1997b).

2. Make the policy widely known.
Collaborate in disseminating the sexual harassment policy through student gatherings, club meetings, bulletin boards, brochures, codes of conduct.

3. Establish safe places and mechanisms for students to report sexual harassment anonymously.

4. Develop curriculum to support the policy.
Provide lessons for teachers to present to their students that center around tolerance and openness toward differences among people.

5. Educate teachers and staff in your school.
Deliver faculty in-services to raise awareness of the issues surrounding sexual harassment. Emphasize school district culpability when educators ignore sexual harassment, and strategies to aid in creating a positive school climate within and outside the classroom. Educate everyone about the court findings in the face of deliberate indifference to harassment that is pervasive, severe and denies a child an equal educational opportunity.

In a Position to Know: A Counselor Educator Speaks

The case presented at the beginning of the chapter is revisited here and answered by a counselor educator. Compare his answer with your own approach.

CYBERSEXUAL HARASSMENT

Using computers at both the school and her home, Ashley has been sending Kenneth provocative pictures of herself and long love letters, not seeming to care that he has asked her to leave him alone. Ashley has e-mailed her communications to Kenneth and to friends, who have also sent them to other friends. She is instant-messaging people as to every move Kenneth makes, what he wears, and what his after-school activities are each day. All this attention across electronic media feels very creepy to Kenneth. Ashley has made such an issue of her "love" for him that Kenneth feels he has become the object of ridicule. Despite his embarrassment, he feels frustrated that he does not seem to have any recourse with Ashley and must simply endure, continuing to tell her that he is not interested. Is this harassment? Could this be sexual harassment? Could Ashley be breaking any laws or school board policies? What recourse, if any, does Kenneth have?

Response From a Counselor Educator

Generally, online harassment occurs when one user continually or deliberately offends another user with actions such as flaming or posting comments intended to hurt, offend or conflict with another user's beliefs. The legal definition of harassment is "a course of conduct directed at a specific person that causes substantial emotional distress in such person and serves no legitimate purpose" or "words, gestures, and actions which tend to annoy, alarm and abuse (verbally) another person" (Black's Law Dictionary, 1990).

Sexual harassment in particular occurs when the online communications or information dissemination (via a Web site or listserv) leads to unwanted sexual attention, creates a hostile environment, or becomes quid pro quo harassment. Hostile environment harassment occurs when unwelcome conduct of a sexual nature is so severe, persistent or pervasive that it affects a student's ability to participate in or benefit from an education program or activity, or creates an intimidating, threatening or abusive educational environment. A hostile environment can be created by a school employee, another student, or even someone visiting the school, such as a student or employee from another school.

Quid pro quo harassment occurs when a school employee causes a student to believe that he or she must submit to unwelcome sexual conduct in order to participate in a school program or activity. It can also occur when an employee causes a student to believe that the employee will make an educational decision based on whether or not the student submits to unwelcome sexual conduct. When a teacher threatens to fail a student unless the student agrees to date the teacher, it is quid pro quo harassment. In the case described in our scenario, quid pro quo sexual harassment could occur if Ashley promises to stop the online sexual harassment if Kenneth were to go on a date with her or perhaps even "hook up" (see Office for Civil Rights at http://www.ed.gov/about/offices/list/ocr/qa-sex-harass.html).

Is Kenneth experiencing online harassment? I think yes. His unpleasant emotions resulting from the persistent and now pervasive comments from Ashley are a key indicator. Is sexual harassment occurring in the scenario involving Ashley and Kenneth? Not sure. It is at the very least inappropriate and irresponsible. If Kenneth's experience, however, meets the criteria of hostile environment or quid pro quo harassment as previously described, it is likely then to prevent him from participating in or benefiting from his education and could easily be considered a case of sexual harassment.

Ashley is hurting Kenneth with her words and actions, although what she may not realize is that she may also be hurting herself. For instance, each school typically has an acceptable use policy which specifies what a student (or staff member) can or cannot do while using technology such as the Internet service owned and operated by the school. When Ashley uses an outside Internet service provider such as America Online, she similarly may be violating that company's policy, usually called the terms of service. As a result, she may be subjected to consequences ranging from, although not limited to, denial of service to school suspension. Worse, Ashley may be breaching state or federal anti-stalking statutes – which include stalking by electronic means – and may be subject to prosecution or litigation.

Being harassed, sexually harassed or stalked is a horrible experience for many and has proven to be a difficult issue to prevent. The Internet offers several features that seem to exacerbate the prevalence and incidence of these offenses. Among them are:

■ *Anonymity*
The Internet provides an almost unprecedented opportunity to communicate with others while remaining anonymous. In fact, some Web sites are set up to help others surf the Web and communicate without being detected (for example, http://anonymouse.ws). The relative anonymity that the World Wide Web fosters can create an outlet for outrageous, often sexist or degrading communication that would otherwise be suppressed.

■ *Instantaneous connectivity*
Anyone can now proliferate a communication, photos, video or audio over the Internet within seconds without even having to be on a computer. Cell phones, personal digital assistants, even digital cameras have the capability to post information on the Web from virtually anywhere and at any time. Once posted, the message can be automatically disseminated via blogs or listservs.

■ *Lack of nonverbal cues*

Face-to-face communication provides a context for the listener, providing the opportunity to balance actual content of a message with the facial expressions, intonations and volume of the speaker. Absent the visual clues, telephone communications provide the same features, with the added benefit of timing (for example, a middle-of-the-night phone call versus a midday call). In contrast, online communication via written text is generally one-dimensional. This problem of text-only communication often leads to misunderstandings and missteps, particularly regarding sexual issues (Bell & La Rue, n.d.?).

■ *Pile-on effect*

Speed combined with the sheer number of people one can send information to can foster a hostile environment within hours. The advanced technology of the Internet makes it much easier for a cyberstalker to encourage third parties to join in the harassing or threatening communications of a victim, triggering a pile-on effect whereby viewers of the original message will add their own caustic message to the conversation (also known as a thread), inciting further offenses.

■ *Removal of space, place and time barriers*

Offline stalking or harassment generally requires all involved (perpetrators and victims) to be located in the same geographic area; in cyberspace, they be located across the street or across the planet. The ease of the Internet's availability, where just about anyone can access the World Wide Web, lowers the barriers to harassment. A cyberstalker does not need to physically confront a victim.

Although dealing with harassment or stalking over electronic media can be frustrating and lead to a level of hopelessness, there are measures one can take to help stop it.

Following are strategies you can tell students to adopt if they are being harassed over electronic media.

1. *Get support.*

Do not deal with this potentially dangerous situation by yourself. You must tell your parents or another trusted adult (school counselor, teacher, other educator) immediately.

2. *Pay attention to the stalker or harasser — and to yourself.*

Never ignore the first signs of stalking. You have a creepy feeling about someone? Sit up and take notice. Always, always trust your instincts. It beats someday saying, "I knew there was something wrong. . . I wish I'd paid attention."

3. Archive every piece of communication relating to the situation.
Save every piece of communication you get from this person: e-mails, instant messages, postings, Web site content. Later you may need to provide copies of each harassing communication to others such as school administrators, Internet service providers, network system administrators, or even the police. In addition to your archive of communications, start a log that explains the situation in more detail. Document how the harassment is affecting your life, and document what steps you're taking to stop it.

4. Tell the harasser or stalker to cease and desist.
It's important that you contact the perpetrator directly, telling him or her in simple, strong and formal terms to stop contacting you or communicating to others about you. You must state that the communications are unwanted and inappropriate and that you will take further action if it does not stop. Don't worry about whether your letter sounds too harsh – make sure it's professional and to the point. Copy (CC:) your postmaster and the harasser's postmaster. Archive the mail you've sent, and note in your log that you saved it.

After you send this mail, your communication to this person must stop. Any further communication can feed the situation. Your attention will reward the harasser, so the behavior will continue. Also, if the case goes to court, your harasser can report that the communication was going both ways, and it could damage your case. It's best to keep quiet no matter how tempted you are to defend yourself. It's important that you tell your friends not to communicate with the harasser in your defense for the same reasons.

5. Report your experience to the appropriate people.
Report the situation to your parent(s) immediately, and together with them, your school's principal.

6. Protect your online space.
Change your password frequently. Pay attention to your files, directories and last logout information. Monitor information about yourself on the Net with Google.com and other search engines.

7. Protect your offline space.
Take all the precautions you would if an old boyfriend or girlfriend were acting inappropriately, especially if you think the harasser can find you at home or at work.

8. If necessary, take police action.
Many states have modified their stalking laws to include electronic communications. Often states will let you file for a restraining order in cases like this, and the courts will often let you ask that your harasser pay for any filing fees. You'll need the person's address if you want to serve them with a restraining order or press charges against them. The police can get this information from the harasser's postmaster if they need to. Offline charges such as defamation or libel, invasion of privacy; or infliction of emotional distress can apply in an online environment.

Russell Sabella, Ph.D., is a counselor educator at Florida Gulf Coast University and a past president of ASCA

Making Connections

1. How can you help determine the extent and prevalence of sexual harassment in your school? What are some of the strategies you can suggest to reduce sexual harassment for your students?

2. See if your school has a sexual harassment policy. Read the policy and highlight parts that you think the school could strengthen as well as sections that the school is successfully implementing.

3. Sexual harassment is emotionally costly to students. In what other ways does it take its toll on students and schools?

4. How does Title IX support students who are being sexually harassed? Why does the Office for Civil Rights recommend that you keep the identity of the victim confidential?

5. Discuss why sex between a teacher and a secondary student is not recognized by boards of education and state statutes as being consensual sex.

Key Terms

Sexual harassment
Office for Civil Rights
Sexual harassment policy
Deliberate indifference
Liability
Teacher-on-student sexual
harassment

Student-on-student sexual
harassment
Hostile environment
Quid pro quo harassment
Breach of trust

References

Alexander, K., & Alexander, D. (2005). *American public school law* (6th ed). Belmont, CA: Thomson West.

American Counseling Association. (1997). *Sexual harassment in the schools. Background on Title IX of the Education Amendments of 1972 and guidance issued by the Office for Civil Rights.* Alexandria, VA: Author.

American School Counselor Association. (2004). *Ethical standards for school counselors.* Retrieved February 13, 2005, from http://www.school-counselor.org/content.asp?contentid=173

Bell, V., & La Rue, D. (n.d.) *Gender harassment on the Internet.* Retrieved March 8, 2005, from the Georgia State University College of Law Web site at http://www2.gsu.edu/~lawppw/lawand.papers/harass.html

Black's Law Dictionary (6th ed.) (1990). St. Paul, MN: West Publishing Company.

Davis v. Monroe County Board of Education et al. 120 F.3d 1390. (Supreme Court, May 24, 1999). Retrieved July 1, 1999, from http://web.lexis-nexis.com/universe

Denn, R. (2001, July 27). New state law really makes sex between teachers, teens a crime. *Seattle* (Wash.) *Post-Intelligencer.* Retrieved June 20, 2003, from http://seattlepi.nwsource.com/local/87495_settle18.shtml

Franklin v. Gwinnett County Public Schools, Supreme Court of the United States, 1992. 503 U.S. 60, 112 S. Ct. 1028.

Harris/Scholastic Research. (2001). *Hostile hallways: The AAUW survey on sexual harassment in America's schools.* Washington, DC: American Association of University Women Educational Foundation.

Hyde, W. B., & Soronen, L. (2004). Reducing liability for sexual harassment. *Principal Leadership (Middle School Ed.), 5,* 57-61.

Stone, C. (2003). Leadership and advocacy in personal/social development: Sexual harassment. In R. Perusse & G. Goodnough (Eds.), *Leadership and Advocacy in School Counseling* (1st ed., pp. 353-377). Belmont, CA: Brooks/Cole.

Stone, M. (2004). Peer sexual harassment among high school students: Teachers' attitudes, perceptions and responses. *The High School Journal, 88,* 1-13.

Sullivan, K., & Zirkel, P. (1999). Student to student sexual harassment: Which tack will the Supreme Court take in a sea of analyses? *West Education Law Reporter, 132,* 609-628. Retrieved February 23, 2005, from http://www.ed.gov/policy/gen/guid/fpco/ferpa/index.html

Title IX of the Educational Amendments of 1972, 20 U.S.C. §§ 1681-1686.

U.S. Department of Education, Office for Civil Rights. (1997a). *Sexual harassment: It's not academic.* Washington, DC: Author.

U.S. Department of Education, Office for Civil Rights. (1997b). *Sexual harassment policy guidance: Harassment of students by school employees, other students, or third parties.* 62 Fed. Reg. 12034-12051.

U.S. Department of Education, Office for Civil Rights. (1999). *Protecting students from harassment and hate crime.* Washington, DC: Author.

Yell, M. L., & Katsiyannis, A. (2000, Spring). Student-on-student sexual harassment: What are schools' responsibilities? *Preventing School Failure, 44,* 130-132.

Zirkel, P. (2001/2002, December/January). Decisions that have shaped U.S. education. *Principal Leadership, 59,* 6-12.

CHAPTER 10

Bullying, Violence and Criminal Activity

IN THIS CHAPTER

Objectives

By the time you have completed this chapter, you should be able to:

- Discuss the incidence of school violence.
- Identify forms of peer-on-peer aggression.
- Understand the Tarasoff ruling and duty to warn.
- Understand foreseeability and how it should affect educators' behavior.
- Define a "true threat" and the implications for educators to act.
- Describe effective strategies to support a safe and respectful school climate.
- Describe the role of anonymous reporting in providing students with a safe environment.

Introduction

Schools are more complex and difficult to manage, just as the world has become more complex. It is not uncommon today for school personnel and children to witness acts of violence and aggression firsthand. Between 1992 and the current school year, 326 deaths reportedly have occurred as a result of school violence (National School Safety Center, 2004). One of the more dramatic incidents of school violence was the episode of shootings on April 20, 1999, at Columbine High School in Littleton, Colo. The Columbine tragedy heightened our nation's resolve to try to find answers to school violence (Barras & Lyman, 2000; Simmons, 2000).

Student perception is that schools are no longer safe. A report released by the Bureau of Justice Statistics and the National Center for Education Statistics reported the following opinions of 12- to 18-year-olds:

- Seven percent of students reported that they had been bullied at school, reflecting a two percent increase from 1999.
- Twelve percent of students reported that someone at school had used hate-related words against them: derogatory words related to race, religion, ethnicity, disability, gender or sexual orientation. During the same period, about 36 percent saw hate-related graffiti at school.
- Twenty-one percent reported that street gangs were present at their schools. (Bureau of Justice Statistics and the National Center for Education Statistics, 2004)

School violence can encompass a wide range of activities including physical fights, threats or destructive acts other than physical fights, robbery, harassment, dating violence, molestation, rape, bullying, hostile or threatening remarks between groups of students, assaults with or without weapons, and gang violence (Espelage, 2004). Targeted violence in schools is usually the result of a series of factors that build up over a period of time (Espelage, 2004; MacNeil & Newell, 2004).

Teasing, harassment, verbal aggression and bullying are all forms of peer-on-peer aggression and abuse that can lead to major life-threatening consequences and cannot be overlooked (Espelage, 2004; Simmons, 2000). Bullying, the most common form of school violence, is on the rise (MacNeil & Newell, 2004). A combination of researchers' findings defines bullying as verbal or physical aggression demonstrated in words, actions, or social exclusion intended to specifically hurt or harm another (Espelage, 2004; MacNeil & Newell, 2004; Olweus, 1996; Rigby, 1996). Sexual harassment is another form of bullying and is discussed in this book in Chapter 9, "Sexual Harassment."

The victim of bullying often experiences the behavior over an extended period of time and cannot defend herself or himself (Olweus, 1996). One quarter of all middle school children have reported themselves as either victims or perpetrators (sometimes both) of chronic bullying that included threats, name-calling, punching, slapping, sneering and jeering. Bullies tend to seek out a scapegoat, and many students blame victims of bullies for bringing it on themselves (Espelage, 2004). Some children see violence as a rite of passage, a part of the ritual of day-to-day living during the transition to adulthood.

The school counselor is cited as critical to receiving information about the threat of violence, identifying students who may be potential perpetrators, and educating children, families and communities about violence prevention (Hill, 1996; Simmons, 2000; Smaby, 1995). Notification of bullying may originate in an individual counseling session in which a student's disclosures may necessitate the counselor's breach of confidentiality. However, students expect and want confidentiality (Collins & Knowles, 1995), a critical consideration in the prevention of school violence and bullying. Smith-Bell and Winslade (1994) recognized that the disclosure of sensitive personal information is greatly affected by assurances of confidentiality and freedom from disclosure of private information. The guarantee of confidentiality or anonymity will greatly impact student decisions to seek the help of the school counselor in issues involving bullying (Stone & Isaacs, 2002).

In some states, school counselors have a statutory obligation to breach confidentiality if they are aware of bullying. For example, New Hampshire provides that guidance counselors may not withhold and in fact are required to report information they receive from a student that fits within the statutory definition of bullying (New Hampshire Regulatory Statutes, 2004).

Other states may have statutory obligations similar to those in New Hampshire that mandate reporting to a supervisor information from a victim of an act of theft, destruction or violence in a safe school zone. The statute explains that if not met, this duty may give rise to criminal liability on the part of the guidance counselor under N.H.R.S.A. 193-D:6.

Zero tolerance does not seem to be working (Hurst, 2005), and educators throughout the world are still trying to determine the best way to curtail bullying and violence. Courts have not been eager to address bullying in schools. The Supreme Court refused to hear a North Carolina case in which a father alleged that a school failed to protect his son who had been beaten repeatedly by school bullies. The North Carolina court concluded that the school was not required to protect the boy from harm by classmates. With the exception of cases involving civil rights, such as sexual harassment or abuse tied to racial or ethnic prejudice, legislative protection against bullying is limited. Perry Zirkel, professor of education and law at Lehigh University in Bethlehem, Penn., agrees (as cited in Coeyman, 2001): "The best remedy for bullying comes not from the courts but from an informed public. Awareness does more. It causes people to become empathetic and to help at the local level" (p.14).

Educators are grappling with the daunting task of preventing school violence by adding security devices, searches and controversial zero-tolerance policies. The effort to prevent further violence will elude us unless we do more research on the power of confidentiality, methods for anonymous reporting, and the impact of including students as vital links in violence prevention.

STUDENTS SPEAK OUT

Seven high school students enrolled in a three-week college seminar titled "Legal and Ethical Decision Making" persuasively argued that students, rather than adults, are key to curbing violence in school. These students surveyed their fellow students and reported on a number of areas. The students contended that their peers are more aware than adults of the different elements of a school's potentially dangerous social landscape: the cliques, gangs, aggressive students, isolated brooders, victims, perpetrators, carriers of weapons and so on. Furthermore, they believed that disclosure should be broad, enabling them to alert adults to any potential problems they had observed or heard about, including acts of bullying, weapons on campus, gang activity, pending fights, threats of violence and sexual harassment. According to the students who attended the seminar, certain criteria for anonymous reporting would most likely be accepted by their peers (Stone & Isaacs, 2002).

Students said they would begin with a democratic intergenerational partnership to address school violence. Truly empowered and engaged students would join forces with a team comprised of school counselors, teachers, parents and administrators. Student representatives would include nontraditional student leaders who do not necessarily serve on the student council or run for club office. The team might also benefit from the voices and insights of students who may feel alienated or on the fringe of the school (Stone & Isaacs, 2002).

Students advocated a mechanism for anonymous reporting, such as a post office box, a drop box or an identification-protected computer, so they could submit written details for selected adults to read and decide how best to proceed. They expressed concern that this might be used to harm innocent students, but their consensus was that skilled adults would be put in charge and the report would serve as an alert to gather more facts to determine the validity of each report. The students also recommended implementing confidentiality procedures so that students could disclose concerns of violence to any trusted person in the school who in turn would be allowed to report the problem without revealing the source (Stone & Isaacs, 2002).

One seminar participant explained that building open relationships is not a job exclusively for school counselors, but that every teacher should make it a point to establish bonds with students (Broder, 2001). College students and peer helpers were other suggestions for those who could provide a listening ear. The point was that there needs to be those who could listen, and then maybe anonymous reporting would no longer be needed (Broder, 2001).

Students believed that school counselors are an optimum choice to be among the "trusted adults," but only if students are allowed to choose the counselor with whom they are willing to share personal and sensitive topics such as being victimized (Broder, 2001). Students expressed strong opposition to having a counselor assigned to them for personal matters, as opposed to nonthreatening matters such as college admissions and academic advising. Students want to be able to choose the counselor whom they perceive will ask the right questions and, when appropriate, urge the student to allow adults in the school to intervene on behalf of all students. Students also recommended providing more staff development to help faculty understand confidentiality, anonymous reporting, warning signs of potentially violent students, a school's cliques, social strata, gangs, and the need to create a school climate that strives to eliminate increased violence (Stone & Isaacs, 2002).

CONFIDENTIALITY WITH MINORS: THE NEED FOR POLICY TO PROMOTE AND PROTECT

Policy making regarding confidential reporting should be a top priority. A starting point for addressing the issue might include developing a management team comprised of students, school counselors, teachers, and parents and administrators to join forces to address violence prevention and to promote an atmosphere whereby students will know that their identity will not be revealed and their confidences will be respected.

Confidentiality is not only a widely held ethical standard but also a variously accorded legal right of clients and responsibility of counselors (ASCA, 2004). The ASCA Position Statement on Confidentiality reminds us that:

> Confidentiality ensures that disclosures will not be divulged to others except when authorized by the student or when there is a clear and present danger to the student and/or to other persons. ... It is the counselor's responsibility to provide notice to students regarding the possible necessity for consulting with others. This confidentiality must not be violated by the professional school counselor except where there is a clear and present danger to the student and/or to other persons. (ASCA, 2002)

However, client rights and counselor responsibilities remain open to professional judgment when the subject involves a client's report of behaviors that may be dangerous to self and others. Handling such cases can be complicated when the client is a minor in a school setting, since school counselors are charged with balancing the rights and needs of their minor clients with their obligations to the school community and their clients' families. There are times when school counselors must protect or breach confidentiality in order to act in their students' best interest. Concurrently, school counselors must respond to teacher and administrator requests for information or mandates for sharing among community or law enforcement agencies, since such requests are in keeping with ethical and administrative agreements.

Balancing client rights and professional standards with responsibility to protect one's client and legitimately interested third parties (families, victims or the broader society) necessitates counselor discretion and professional judgment. This is especially true in view of the numerous recent incidents of school shootings (Collins & Knowles, 1995). As a result of those tragedies, school safety and school violence are important topics for every educator and for every family sending a child to school each day. Efforts to stave off further violence in our schools should include developing policy regarding confidentiality when students want to discuss or report violent behavior or the potential of violent behavior.

Adolescents see themselves as entitled to confidentiality rights similar to adults, although they acknowledge that parents should be made aware of information about sexuality, pregnancy, physical or sexual abuse, substance abuse, crimes against property and danger to self or others (Collins & Knowles, 1995). Similarly, Milne (1995) noted that adolescents recognize that their rights to privacy may at times appear to conflict with counselors' obligations to parents and other third parties.

Milne (1995) recommends a specific procedure for counselors of minor clients to follow when their clients express concerns for confidentiality. If the counselor determines that confidentiality must be breached, he or she should work with the minor client to obtain consent for breaching confidentiality. Finally, in the face of an adolescent who refuses such consent, the counselor acts in the best interests of the child's welfare. Such a procedure continues to place great responsibility on the counselor for the welfare of a minor client where there are proximate and immediate competing interests.

An informed consent policy can help protect and promote good communication between counselors and students. With the assurance of confidentiality, students will be more forthcoming in revealing critical information. Schools nationwide are implementing policies and programs aimed at encouraging students to report potentially dangerous students (Barras & Lyman, 2000; Simmons, 2000). "In order for these programs to work, students must feel confident that their identity will remain strictly confidential to avoid any retaliation" (Barras & Lyman, 2000, p. 4). The school counselor's role of being the recipient of critical information will be far less complicated with a policy or guideline to help protect minors while also respecting the inherent rights of parents and the larger society.

Ethical Standards Addressed in This Chapter

Professionalism means knowing your professional associations' codes and adhering to them. Those ethical standards from American School Counselor Association that are most germane include the following:

- The professional school counselor supports and protects the educational program against any infringement not in students' best interest. (D.1.a)
- The professional school counselor informs appropriate officials in accordance with school policy of conditions that may be potentially disruptive or damaging to the school's mission, personnel and property while honoring the confidentiality between the student and counselor. (D.1.b)
- The professional school counselor assists in developing: (1) curricular and environmental conditions appropriate for the school and community, (2) educational procedures and programs to meet students' developmental needs and (3) a systematic evaluation process for comprehensive, developmental, standards-based school counseling programs, services and personnel. The counselor is guided by the findings of the evaluation data in planning programs and services. (D.1.g)

The full text of the ethical codes for the ACA and the ASCA can be found at the organizations' Web sites, http://www.counseling.org and www.schoolcounselor.org, respectively.

Getting Started: What Would You Do?

The following case is discussed for you at the end of this chapter by a school counselor. Before you read her responses, formulate in your own mind how you would approach this ethical dilemma.

SUPPORTING A SAFE AND RESPECTFUL SCHOOL CLIMATE

The discipline referral rate for fighting and conflict at your school is really high and your perception is that there is a great deal of bullying taking place in the school. You conduct an anonymous school-wide survey with a class on each grade level and learn that bullying is a problem for many students in the fourth and fifth grades. What would you consider your ethical responsibility in this situation?

Working Through Case Studies

WARNING POTENTIAL VICTIMS

Phillip, one of your students, has difficulty managing his frustration and is prone to violent outbursts. Phillip told you today that he hates Kimberly, that she annoys him: "Talk, talk, talk, is all she does. I am going to drive the heel of my hand upwards under her chin and snap her neck." Additionally disturbing to you is that Phillip has spent years learning martial arts and describes the techniques he intends to use. What are your legal and ethical obligations in this situation? Do you inform the administration? Do you notify Kimberly, Kimberly's parents and/or Phillip's parents?

Points to Consider

Confidentiality is an important component of counseling. However, this is a situation that demands a breach of confidentiality because of the possibility that a student might be in harm's way.

A counselor's duty to warn potential victims arises from the court case *Tarasoff v. Board of Regents of California* (1976). Posenjit Poddar killed Tatiana Tarasoff in 1969. Two months earlier, in a University of California hospital at Berkeley, Poddar had advised his psychologist, Dr. Moore, of his intention to kill Tarasoff. Tarasoff's parents filed a lawsuit charging negligence, with the claim that Moore had a duty to warn Tarasoff and her parents of the impending danger. The crux of the case was whether or not Moore had a duty to warn. The California Supreme Court ruled that the psychologist-parent relationship is a special one and, as such, requires the duty to warn. The California court stated that the potential danger to Tarasoff outweighed the psychologist's obligation of confidentiality to his client.

According to Fischer and Sorenson (1996), "Historically, under common law, one is not duty bound as a general rule to control the conduct of another or to warn those endangered by such conduct" (p. 27). A member of the general public who sees something dangerous has a moral duty but not necessarily a legal duty to warn a potential victim. However, due to the special relationship school counselors have with their students, they are required by law to exercise the same skill, knowledge and care that other members of their profession would demonstrate under similar circumstances (Fischer & Sorenson, 1996).

Since the *Tarasoff* ruling, a number of state courts have sought to limit or expand the scope of the counseling professional's obligation of duty to warn. Some state legislatures have enacted laws granting greater privilege. Maryland is an example of a state in which there is no legal duty to warn in similar situations. In contrast, Nebraska courts have expanded duty to warn to include duty to attempt to detain. Generally, a duty to warn is extended to identified potential victims and possibly to other people who might be in harm's way because they are involved in a close relationship with the intended victim. In some states (New Hampshire) this can be expanded to include other threats such as damage to real property and other violent acts. Some states (Florida) have refused to adopt the *Tarasoff* ruling because of the inherent difficulties of predicting dangerousness and the importance of confidentiality.

The exact limits of the duty to warn from the *Tarasoff* case are uncertain because of the differing statutes in respective states. Different state statutes address (1) who is subject to the duty to warn or take precautions; (2) the type of threats that will activate the duty; (3) the required identifiability of the victim; and (4) the acceptable means of satisfying the duty (Fischer & Sorenson, 1996, p. 29).

Cases that have followed the *Tarasoff* case have both broadened and narrowed the strength of the ruling. *McIntosh v. Milano* (1979), the first case decided after the *Tarasoff* decision, more broadly held the practitioner's obligations "to protect the welfare not only of the client as in *Tarasoff* but also of the community." *Thompson v. County of Alameda* (1980) limited the extension of the duty to warn. The Thompson court specified that a duty to warn depends on a prior threat to a "named or readily identifiable victim or group of victims." Other courts have extended the duty to situations in which there are classes of identifiable potential victims (Gilbert, 2003).

In *Boynton v. Burglass* (1991), a court in Florida completely rejected the Tarasoff ruling. The court based its rejection of a duty to protect on its belief in the inexact science of psychiatry and the near-impossible task of predicting violence. In *Nasser v. Parker* (1995), the Virginia Supreme Court held that a therapist-patient relationship does not qualify as a "special relation" unless the doctor has taken "charge" of the patient and, therefore, according to the Virginia Supreme Court, a duty to protect or warn does not exist unless the therapist actually has "charge" of the patient (Gilbert, 2003).

In Phillip's case, a breach of confidentiality is necessary because Kimberly is vulnerable, and you have a "special legal relationship" to protect her. Also, you need to support Phillip by ensuring that he receives additional help to manage his anger and by helping him understand the seriousness of threatening harm to another student. However, not all the steps that should be taken are within the realm of school counseling. In my opinion, an administrator or law enforcement official should be responsible for notifying Kimberly's parents of the threat, if such notification is deemed necessary. The gravity of the obligations and responsibilities that may ensue is enormous.

Foreseeability is a critical consideration in cases where school officials are accused of negligence. In this case school officials have been apprised of the potential for harm and foreseeability will easily be established if something happens to Kimberly at Phillip's hands, regardless of whether or not it happens on school grounds. In *Durant v. Los Angeles Unified School District* (2003), a case involving a student who was shot by a classmate off school grounds, the court said, "The vigilant and effective school supervision of our children on and near school grounds is an increasing component of child safety. Thus, it is reasonable to expect that school officials will be under a greater, not a lesser, duty to take reasonable steps to protect students from harm that may befall them. This is the result of increasingly foreseeable risks to children at school as well as the special relationship between student and school that exists due to the compulsory nature of education" (*Durant v. Los Angeles*, 2003).

Meanwhile, the counselor must maintain as much loyalty to the student as possible. To do so, you need to explain to Phillip why the administration, faculty, parents and outside counselors must be informed and involved. As the school counselor, you must take the duty to warn seriously and know it is imperative to breach confidentiality when a student is in imminent danger.

PROTECTING POTENTIAL VICTIMS

Two students stop by your office before homeroom to tell you that they heard that there was going to be a fight. You know one of the students allegedly involved is a fighter and the other student is a fairly quiet, seemingly mild-mannered young man. You send for both of the students and review school board policy related to student fighting. Your impression is that the mild-mannered student is scared and does not want to fight. You detain him, and in your questioning he expresses fear and says that he is being bullied into this fight. Is there anything more you must do as the school counselor?

Points to Consider

School counselors are often the first members of the school staff to become privy to student situations in which someone may be at risk of harm or danger. The ethical obligation is obvious; however, the legal responsibility to protect potential victims also guides the school counselor's response and behavior.

More than 25 years ago, an Illinois Appellate Court reversed a lower court's decision and sent it back to be tried (*Gammon v. Edwardsville Community Unit School District*, 1980). The lower court found a school counselor negligent for not taking appropriate action to protect a student from intentional injury by another student. In the situation, friends and acquaintances told an eighth-grade student that another student who was making threats against her wished to see her in the restroom. The student went to her school counselor for help. The counselor testified that she had worked extensively with the offending student and had established a good rapport with her. The counselor brought in the threatening student and gave the two girls a chance to air their differences. The school counselor testified that the threatening student's considerable anger was very apparent and did not diminish as a result of the joint counseling sessions or later when the counselor met privately to warn her that suspension would result if any fighting occurred. The counselor subsequently conferred with the apprehensive student and recommended that she avoid any encounter with the other girl. The student continued to express her apprehension and indicated clearly that her difficulties with the aggressor were not over. The counselor did not notify the administration or playground supervisors, who would have both girls on the playground at the same time later in the day. During playground time, the aggressor struck the victim in the left eye with her fist, producing a skull fracture so serious it required corrective surgery (*Gammon v. Edwardsville Community Unit School District*, 1980).

The victim contended that the school's response to a known threat of violence on school premises was inadequate under the circumstances. The counselor was well aware of the offending student's prior conduct, and there was evidence that school officials knew of prior fighting on her part. Since the assailant was a known disciplinary problem, the victim argued that steps should have been taken to guarantee that no altercation would occur. More specifically, she contended that direct supervision of both students was indicated and that immediate steps should have been taken to sequester and discipline the student who threatened her following the morning counseling session (*Gammon v. Edwardsville Community Unit School District*, 1980).

There was ample proof that the risk of harm was brought to the attention of the counselor and that school officials did not provide the supervision necessary to maintain discipline aimed at avoiding a confrontation between these pupils. The court cited the school counselor's *in loco parentis* status: "In all matters relating to the discipline in and conduct of the schools and the school children, they [educators] stand in the relation of parents and guardians of the pupils. This relationship shall extend to all activities connected with the school program and may be exercised at any time for the safety and supervision of the pupils in the absence of their parents or guardians" (Illinois Rev. Statute, 1977).

Situations involving threats between students are commonplace, and it is always better to err on the side of caution. You should fully investigate, to the best of your ability, all potential incidents brought directly to your attention. The knowledge that the student involved is a known offender may in itself warrant additional investigation and involvement of other school personnel. When in doubt, it is always best to consult with other professionals about possible precautionary measures, keeping in mind the predictable and yet unpredictable nature of teen behavior. *In loco parentis* can hold us legally responsible if negligence is proved. Although we cannot eliminate every altercation that comes to our attention, we can to the best of our ability investigate, involve others, and initiate appropriate precautionary measures (Illinois Rev. Statute, 1977).

THREATS OF VIOLENCE AGAINST EDUCATORS

A student well known to you for her violent propensities threatens you with bodily harm when you fail to comply with her schedule change requests. You perceive it as a real threat and report it to the assistant dean for student services. He dismisses your concerns, saying, "Let's see if anything else transpires." Knowing that every time this student gets into trouble her parents give the assistant principal a difficult time, you believe that he just wants to avoid another scene with this family. However, you feel very unsafe. Is there anything else you can do?

Points to Consider

The First Amendment to the U.S. Constitution states that Congress "shall make no law…abridging the freedom of speech," but the U.S. Supreme Court has held that certain types of speech are not entitled to constitutional protection. They include fighting words, obscenities, defamation and true threats (Missouri Center for Safe Schools, 2001).

In a court case involving a student threat against a school counselor, the court found in favor of the school district when the student sued citing a violation of her First Amendment rights. The 9th Circuit Court of Appeals in 1996 heard the case (*Lovell v. Poway Unified School District*, 1996). A high school student was sent back and forth between her school counselor and the school administration for approval to change her schedule. Once she received the authorization, she returned to her counselor, who could not make the change because the courses were already filled. The student told the counselor, "If you don't give me this schedule change, I'm going to shoot you." The student was suspended for three days, then challenged the suspension as a violation of her First Amendments rights. The 9th Circuit Court held that the statement was a true threat that any reasonable person would foresee as a serious expression of intent to harm or assault. The court noted that in light of the violence prevalent in schools today, school officials are justified in taking student threats against faculty or other students very seriously.

CODE OF SILENCE

A student in your school was caught carrying a gun that discharged, injuring another student. In an optional anonymous survey, 37 students gave convincing details that indicated that they had seen the gun but failed to notify school officials. Furthermore, 64 percent of the school's students reported that they had seen other students with weapons at school at least once during the past year. The principal has given you the task of heading a committee to try to determine what policies and practices should be established to ensure student reporting of weapons, violence and bullying. You accept this task willingly because of your strong desire and professional commitment to promoting a safe, respectful school climate. Beginning with the end in mind, what policies and procedures do you hope will emerge from this committee?

Points to Consider

In nearly every case of reported school violence, students saw warning signs in advance but did not report what they saw to adults because of peer pressure, fear of retaliation and absence of a sense of personal responsibility to help keep their school safe (Barras & Lyman, 2000; Lamberg, 1998). In one dramatic example in Texas, 54 students saw a weapon prior to its being used to shoot two fellow students, but no one reported it (Cromwell, 2000). According to a survey by Stone & Isaacs (2002), students are apprehensive about trusting adults to skillfully handle confidential information about potential violence.

Furthermore, these same students overwhelmingly expressed the opinion that anonymous reporting is the most likely means of securing critical information from teenagers. Anonymous reporting is a communication system whereby students can report concerns about violence through a mechanism that does not require that they reveal their identity. This manner of revealing potentially incriminating information enables students to report to a school counselor or other trusted adult crimes, harassment or violence, without fear of being hurt by angry students or being labeled an outsider or one who discloses information to adults (Lamberg, 1998).

BULLYING THAT IS DIFFICULT TO STOP

Last school year, a group of high school girls took harassment to a new level. The school district has a policy in place that defines harassment and the steps to take when dealing with it. School officials followed the policy and brought the parents and students in to meet. In spite of the fact that they were caught on the school's security camera vandalizing the bathrooms and threatening other students, the girls still declared their innocence. At the meeting attended by the principal, counselor, students and parents, the girls refused to acknowledge their guilt and didn't agree to end the harassment.

All staff efforts to stop the harassment have been unsuccessful, and the negative behavior continues. Now the counselors are fearful for the upcoming school year, with many of the aggressors' younger siblings entering as freshmen. What steps can you take to eliminate harassment in the building? What is the role of the counselor when dealing with harassment? What other considerations must be addressed in seeking a solution?

Points to Consider

No Child Left Behind (2002) has focused considerable attention on creating and maintaining educational environments that are safe, drug-free, and conducive to learning, an especially difficult task in some of America's schools. This all-too-real scenario of ongoing harassment evokes few answers and many questions. How can school officials effect positive change in the school climate when the offending students and their parents are unwilling to acknowledge the existence of the harassing behaviors?

We know children can't learn if they don't feel safe, but just telling educators and school counselors they have to provide a safe environment does not guarantee that they will be able to comply. How realistic is the expectation that school personnel will be able to watch this group of girls' every move throughout the school day?

This situation may call for drastic measures, such as suspension or expulsion of the harassers, separating them by sending them to different schools, or possibly involving law enforcement officials. As educators and counselors, we must recognize that we cannot always change attitudes and beliefs within the school community, but we must do our best to protect the victims of bullying. It is possible that the harassing students will continue to look for victims, perhaps on an even larger scale. However, we hope they will eventually have a change of heart and stop their bullying.

The school counselor may be able to facilitate change through the use of leadership and advocacy skills. By engaging the administration, faculty and students in collaborative problem solving, the school counselor can be instrumental in helping determine the underlying causes of the harassment. The group may find, for instance, that race is indeed a factor in this case. While staff training on how to address bullying will certainly help mitigate the damages if someone is injured by a school bully, a schoolwide focus on harassing behaviors can make a great difference in the attitudes and responsiveness of the adults.

Educators have found that providing students and parents with mechanisms for reporting harassment increases the frequency of reporting incidents that students have either witnessed or experienced firsthand (U.S. Department of Education, 1998). Empowering the entire student body may help to isolate the girls' behavior and bring peer pressure to reduce some of their power. Mediation may also be an option to address some of the underlying causes that, as previously mentioned, may in actuality be racially motivated.

While strategizing ways to reduce harassment, all adults in the school should closely monitor the threatening girls. It would be a good idea to remove perpetrators from the classes they share with the targeted students in order to minimize disruption. Furthermore, all teachers must be alerted to be watchful and to intervene when necessary.

BULLIED STUDENT WHO WANTS TO CHANGE SCHOOLS

Ryan, one of your ninth-grade students, struggles with feelings of inadequacy. Ryan's parents are asking the district to allow their son to go to a different high school to get away from bullies who have followed him since elementary school. Despite their efforts, school officials have not been able to stop the harassment. The principal does not want to allow this special assignment, saying that to do so would to teach children to run away from their problems. What, if any, might be your role in this situation?

Points to Consider

Shore Regional High School Board of Education v. P.S. (2004) ruled that a district court judge failed to give "due weight" to an administrative law judge's determination that a school district's failure to protect a student from bullying constituted a denial of a free appropriate public education required by the Individuals with Disabilities Education Act (1990). P.S., a New Jersey ninth grader, had been teased and bullied throughout elementary school, to the point that he displayed suicidal tendencies and became eligible for special education on the basis of emotional disturbance. P.S.'s parents wanted him to go to a different high school than the one to which he was assigned so he could avoid being with the same children who had previously emotionally and physically abused him.

Despite repeated complaints, the school administration failed to remedy the situation. After the district refused to place P.S. at the requested high school, the parents unilaterally placed him at that school and requested a due process hearing to obtain reimbursement for the placement. The new high school's plan was to mainstream P.S. for all his classes, and it included a program intended to combat bullying through discipline and diversity seminars.

As the district court noted, P.S. thrived both academically and socially at the requested high school. The plaintiffs presented testimony that the home high school could not provide P.S. with a free appropriate public education, as required by the IDEA. The administrative law judge ordered the school district to reimburse the parents for the out-of-district placement. However, the 3rd Circuit Court reversed the lower court's decision, saying that the inability of the elementary school administration to successfully discipline its students did not make the home high school an inappropriate placement; the risk that the harassment would continue was not so great as to render the high school inappropriate.

Once again, the courts were unwilling to go against a school district in a bullying situation. Planning and developing anti-bullying policies is an important message school officials can send to parents and students in the effort to address the problem of bullying. This creates a system of accountability for the students who bully as well as for those who look the other way when witnessing a bullying incident (MacNeil & Newell, 2004).

In this case the school counselor might have taken a different path than the principal by advocating for the student to be allowed to attend a new school. Special assignments for students are frequently made for far less critical reasons. As ASCA states:

> It is the professional school counselor's role to support programs and provide leadership emphasizing prevention and intervention related to violence, weapons and gangs. Programs for students must be designed to teach nonviolent alternatives to resolve differences. Inherent in these programs is an emphasis on the teaching of communication skills and an awareness of and an acceptance of diversity. The professional school counselor encourages and supports the shared responsibility of ensuring and providing a safe school environment and the development of policies to support a safe environment. (ASCA, 1994, p. 1)

School counselors have a responsibility to support students who are being bullied as well as to help them acquire the coping and resiliency skills necessary to regain a sense of safety and control. Students of all ages need to feel comfortable asking their counselor to help them through difficulties that can do harm physically as well as emotionally. As counselors, we must praise our students for having the courage to talk about their fears and help them identify what will make them feel safe. Also let them know that you will seek the assistance and support of other adults in the school building but not breach their confidentiality.

As we have learned from the *Shore* case, it may not be legally possible to provide a school transfer but, as the school counselor, you can use the resources available to you to help this student make new friends, help educators monitor bullying incidents, enforce related policies, and do what is within your power to ensure that the student feels supported and protected.

CYBERBULLYING

As you wander into the library during passing time, you notice a small group of boys and girls huddled over a computer giggling and whispering to one student to type faster. As you approach them, some of the students quickly begin to scurry away. You get closer to the computer and catch the open IM box out of the corner of your eye. The student at the keyboard quickly pushes the power button off. Later that morning, three girls walk into to your office and break into tears. It seems that they have been the topic of discussion

on everybody's instant and text messages. Last period in social studies class, one of their friends discreetly showed them some of the
messages on her cell phone, with at least 50 sexually derogatory
statements and hate messages from just that morning. One of the
girls breaks the school policy banning cell phones and turns on her
phone to show you. The girls have no idea why this has happened.
They refuse to go to class and beg you to make it stop. What can
you do?

Points to Consider
Technology has expanded the social lives of teenagers but has also offered
more opportunities for student-to-student bullying and harassment.
Bullying is no longer confined to the lunchroom or face-to-face contact;
cyberbullies are on 24/7. Students have taken cyberbullying to new
heights, often not realizing the implications of their actions. Technology
has brought a disturbing, dark side to bullying because it allows a student
to inflict pain anonymously without being forced to see the effect on the
victim.

In a recent *New York Times* article titled "Internet Gives Teenage Bullies
Weapons to Wound From Afar" (2004), Amy Harmon presents scenarios
from real life, all of which reveal the extensive nature of cyberbullying. E-
mail messages, IMs (instant messaging), chat rooms, and blogs (Web logs
or journals) enable the harassment to be both less obvious to adults and
more publicly humiliating, as gossip, put-downs, and embarrassing pictures are circulated among a wide audience of peers with just a few clicks
(Harmon, 2004). The new weapons in the teen-age arsenal of cruel social
bullying include stealing each others' screen names and sending inflamma-
tory messages to friends, forwarding private material to people for whom
it was never intended, and anonymously posting derogatory comments
about fellow students on blogs.

Online bullying has a particular appeal for girls, who often practice emotional rather than physical harassment and strive to avoid direct confrontation (Harmon, 2004). Boys also bully online, often in the form of
betraying the trust of adolescent girls. School officials and other caring
adults must struggle with ways to protect students from being cyberbul-
lied by their peers (Harmon, 2004). In the same article, a school psychologist reveals the frequency of students seeking her help because of what

happened on the Internet the night before. The psychologist said the students complain, "'We were online last night and somebody said I was fat.,' or 'They asked me why I wear the same pair of jeans every day,' or 'They say I have Wal-Mart clothes.'" She also has intervened in situations in which explicit sexual comments appeared online (Harmon, 2004).

ASCA reminds us that the authors of Internet information in chat rooms, pen pal services, and on home pages have anonymity. These factors allow for potential victimization of students. Professional school counselors know children's developmental stages and can provide Internet guidelines to parents and school personnel (ASCA, 2000) and take a leadership role in implementing policies and practices that encourage students to respect each other online or off.

Although it would be impossible to put an immediate end to the cyberbullying of the three students in the case above, you have both legal and ethical obligations to do what you can to curtail and eliminate the harassment that interferes with every student's right to an education in a safe environment. The "In a Position to Know" case at the end of the Sexual Harassment chapter gives you specifics as to how to address cyber-bullying.

THE CRITICAL NEED FOR CONFIDENTIALITY

Sandra meets with you to discuss her poor academic performance this semester. During the conversation, she reveals that she has been become involved with a group of popular students of whom several are gang members. She knows that hanging with this group is affecting her grades but she says it is more important to be a member of the group. She also is privy to information that involves petty larceny, weapons, drug sales and harmful threats. If she doesn't go along with the group, she will be socially isolated and subject to overt and covert harassments. She asks you not to tell anyone what she has revealed to you. What do you do?

Points to Consider

Confidentiality is complicated in a school setting where counselors are charged with balancing the rights and needs of their students with obligations to protect the school, community and students' families (ASCA, 2004). Confidentiality is an issue for students, especially in reporting potential violence by their peers. The perceived or real possibility that their identity may be revealed to others has contributed to the violence in our schools because students will not risk reprisals that would come from being informants (Lamberg, 1998).

Confidentiality related to curbing violence is also a concern for educational policy makers. When students are confident that their school counselor is empowered to protect their confidentiality, they are more likely to confide in the counselor when faced with violence or when possessing knowledge of others who are in danger. However, there will always be times when school counselors must breach confidentiality, such as when they know that a child is suicidal, planning violence against another person, or acting in ways that will harm self or others. A plea for total confidentiality is not appropriate, but a policy to protect the identity of informants and mechanisms to provide for anonymous informants is not only appropriate but necessary.

School counselors and other educators must join forces to establish policies that will enable them to help solve the problem of school violence. The task of preventing future acts of violence is insurmountable without student informants. An examination of the facts surrounding past incidents of violence on school campuses reveals that almost without exception, the perpetrator told other students about the pending violence before it happened (Stein, 1999; Woods, 2002).

Much of the literature (Lamberg, 1998; Stein, 1999; Woods, 2002) advocates for school districts to establish policy and best practice that would prohibit retaliation against those who report threats of violence. Students do not believe that it is possible to prevent retaliation in the absence of a guaranteed mechanism for anonymous or confidential reporting (Stone & Isaacs, 2002). The risk of social isolation or physical retaliation would therefore continue to deter student cooperation.

SHOPLIFTING

A 16-year-old student tells you about her compulsive shoplifting behavior. She gives you the dates, times and places of her previous shoplifting. Her confession of committing a criminal act creates an ethical dilemma for you, who must decide either to keep the matter confidential or inform her parents. You realize that you must be extremely cautious about breaching confidentiality by involving the parents, but you are concerned about the student getting caught and the very real possibility of her being arrested. Do you have a duty to report this to the authorities? To her parents?

Points to Consider

School counselors do not have a legal duty to report a crime that has already been committed (Fischer & Sorenson, 1996). However, working with a minor in a school setting necessitates that a school counselor pay close attention to parental rights to be involved in their children's lives, especially in value-laden issues.

Even though a student's telling you about criminal activity does not always require a breach to law enforcement agencies, you are still faced with the issue of how much parental involvement is necessary. Do parents need to be informed? There is a likelihood that the shoplifting student may be caught, arrested and spend time in jail. What needs to be discussed are the root causes of her illegal behavior. Why does she continuously feel the need to shoplift?

The school counselor is ethically obligated to discuss the nature and severity of this problem with the student and to educate her about the ramifications of shoplifting, pointing out the seriousness of having a permanent criminal record. Referral to a community agency would probably be appropriate. Depending upon her age and the agency's policy, the student may not need to have parental consent for counseling services. Although the girl's parents should be involved in the counseling process, it is not a legal obligation to report her prior shoplifting to them. The best recourse is to encourage the student to talk to her parents and to offer to meet with her and her parents to discuss the issues together.

The professional school counselor has certain responsibilities to his or her students, and they are clearly stated in the ASCA Ethical Standards (2004). By connecting the shoplifting student to the resources and support offered in her community, the school counselor can try to ensure that the student will understand the ramifications of her actions and modify her behavior to avoid future acts of shoplifting.

School counselors can advocate for the development and implementation of measures to help students navigate materialism, fear, pressures, insensitivity, failure, intimidation and conflicting values. School counselors, as responsible and caring adults, play a key role in the lives of youth (Daniels, 2002).

In a Position to Know:
A School Counselor Speaks

The case presented at the beginning of the chapter is revisited here and answered by a school counselor. Compare her answer with your own approach.

SUPPORTING A SAFE AND RESPECTFUL SCHOOL CLIMATE

The discipline referral rate for fighting and conflict at your school is really high and your perception is that there is a great deal of bullying taking place in the school. You conduct an anonymous survey with a class on each grade level and learn that bullying is a problem for many students in the fourth and fifth grades. What would you consider your ethical responsibility in this situation?

Response From a School Counselor

Being an elementary counselor for more than 1,000 students, I was outnumbered, and in order to tackle the bullying problem at my school I involved all the resources I could muster from inside and outside the school. I established a committee primarily of parent volunteers, and we set our sights on reducing the number of discipline referrals that involved fighting, name-calling, verbal harassment and other forms of bullying. Support and teamwork came from every part of the school: teachers, paraprofessionals, custodians, principal, physical education teachers, and music and art teachers.

Classroom teachers were especially active, and their buy-in for a bullyproofing program was strong because they could immediately see that the program resulted in reduction of conflict among students. The teachers were consistent in implementing various conflict resolution strategies, such as teaching the students to identify bullying behavior and charting it as a class, until they extinguished the behavior. Navy pilots helped mentor students with a history of discipline referrals for conflict. The art, music and physical education teachers and the media specialist coordinated with me and others in the bully-proofing program and made their lessons and activities coincide.

At the end of the year, the efforts reduced the number of discipline referrals from 183 to 98 – almost a 50 percent reduction. I believe the ethical counselor uses his or her time and talents to try to help create a safe, respectful school climate so that all students can come to school and not feel molested or abused by others. Bullying is a form of child abuse, just at the hands of other children instead of adults. I believe that in working with others who want to see bullying reduced we can make a difference.

Mary Ann Dyal, newly retired Jacksonville, Fla., elementary counselor and a consultant for anti-bullying programs

Making Connections

1. Zero tolerance is a controversial topic in education, with some contending it is the only fair way to mete out discipline and curtail violence, and others finding that it does not work. Develop a paper on the subject and decide for yourself, after being informed by research, whether or not you believe it works.

2. With the exception of cases involving civil rights, such as sexual harassment or abuse tied to racial or ethnic prejudice, legislative protection against bullying is limited. What is your opinion on this? Do you think legislation is the key link to solving the bullying problem? Why or why not?

3. You have just been told that three students are planning to fight just off school grounds that afternoon. This is one of those dreaded days when all administrators are out of the building and you are the principal designee for the day. What do you do?

4. Discuss duty to warn and the limits of duty to warn as you understand them. Do some additional research on your own to find a case in your state that has ruled on a counselor's duty to warn. What does your state say counselor's obligations are with regard to duty to warn?

5. There is a group of students at your school who are chronic offenders with regard to bullying. Discipline referrals, pleading and behavior modi-

fication have worked only as long as someone is watching these students. You want to try to change their attitudes and beliefs about their right to bully those less able to defend themselves. What approach do you use?

Key Terms

Zero tolerance

Safe school zone

Violent propensities

Real threat

Mediation

Social bullying

Peer-on-peer aggression

Bullying

School violence

Verbal aggression

Physical aggression

Statutory obligation

Anonymous reporting

Duty to warn

Special relation

Identifiability of the victim

References

American School Counselor Association. (1994). *The professional school counselor and the promotion of safe schools*. Alexandria, VA: Author.

American School Counselor Association. (2000). *The professional school counselor and student safety on the Internet*. Alexandria, VA: Author.

American School Counselor Association. (2002). *The professional school counselor and confidentiality*. Alexandria, VA: Author.

American School Counselor Association. (2004). *Ethical standards for school counselors*. Alexandria, VA: Author.

Barras, B., & Lyman, S. A. (2000). Silence of the lambs: How can we get students to report pending violence? *Education*, 12(3), 495-502.

Boynton v. Burglass, 590 So. 2d 446, 448-49 (Florida Dist. Ct. App. 1991)

Broder, J. (2001, September). *Learning how to deal with the information: Violence within these walls*. Unpublished paper presented as a class assignment for the Yale Summer Exploration Program, New Haven, CT.

Bureau of Justice Statistics and the National Center for Education Statistics. (2004). *Indicators of school crime and safety: 2004.* Retrieved January 9, 2005, from http://www.ojp.usdoj.gov/bjs/

Coeyman, M. (2001, December 4). Schools still working to rein in bullies [Electronic version]. *Christian Science Monitor.* Retrieved January 12, 2005, from http://www.csmonitor.com/2001/

Collins, N., & Knowles, A. D. (1995). Adolescents' attitudes towards confidentiality between the school counselor and the adolescent client. *Australian Psychologist, 30,* 179-182.

Cromwell, S. (2000, November 29). *Anonymity spurs students to report potential violence. Education World.* Retrieved January 15, 2005, from http://www.education-world.com/a_admin/admin202.shtml

Daniels, J. (2002). Assessing threats of school violence: Implications for counselors. *Journal of Counseling and Development, 80,* 215-218.

Durant v. Los Angeles Unified School District, Court of Appeal of California, 2nd Appellate District, Div. 8, B155739 (2003).

Espelage, D. L. (2004). An ecological perspective to school-based bullying prevention. *The Prevention Researcher, 11*(3), 3-6.

Fischer, L., & Sorenson, P. (1996). *School law for counselors, psychologists, and social workers.* White Plains, NY: Longman.

Gammon v. Edwardsville Community Unit School District 79-433, Appellate Court of Illinois, March 26, 1980.

Gilbert, M. (2003). "Time-out" for student threats? Imposing a duty to protect on school officials. *UCLA Law Review, 49,* 685-941.

Harmon, A. (2004, August 26). Internet gives teenage bullies weapons to wound from afar [Electronic version]. *The New York Times.* Retrieved March 3, 2005, from http://www.nytimes.com/2004/08/26/education/26bully.html?ex=1113969600&en=907969af6c53617d&ei=5070

Hill, M. S. (1996). Making students part of the safe schools solution. *NASSP Bulletin, 80*(579), 24-30.

Hurst, M. (2005, February 9). When it comes to bullying, there are no boundaries: Nations try various strategies to eradicate such behavior in schools. *Education Week, 24*(22), 8.

Illinois. Rev. Statute. 1977, ch. 122, par. 24 — 24.) n1.

Individuals with Disabilities Act. (1990). 20 U.S.C. 1400-1485.

Lamberg, L. (1998). Preventing school violence: No easy answers. *Journal of the American Medical Association, 280*(5), 404-407.

Lovell v. Poway Unified School District, 90 F.3d 367 (9th Cir. 1996).

MacNeil, G., & Newell, J. (2004). School bullying: Who, why, and what to do. *The Prevention Researcher, 11*(3), 15-17.

McIntosh v. Milano, 403 A.2d 500 (NJ, 1979).

Milne, J. (1995). Analysis of the law of confidentiality with special reference to the counseling of minors. *Australian Psychologist, 30*, 169-174.

Missouri Center for Safe Schools. (2001). *Legal issues pertaining to student threats at school.* Retrieved January 8, 2005, from http://www.umkc.edu/education/safe-school/downloads/index.asp

National School Safety Center. (2004). *School associated violent deaths.* Retrieved January 23, 2005, from http://www.nssc1.org/savd/savd.pdf

Nasser v. Parker 249 Va. 172 (455 S.E. 2d 502) March 3, 1995.

New Hampshire Regulatory Statutes (2004). H.R.S.A. 193-F:3(II).

No Child Left Behind Act of 2001, 20 U.S.C. § 6301 (2002).

Olweus, D. (1996). Bully/victim problems in school: Facts and effective interventions. *Reclaiming Children and Youth, 5*(1), 15-22.

Rigby, K. (1996). *Bullying in schools: And what to do about it.* London: Jessica Kingsley.

Shore Regional High School Board of Education v. P.S., No. 03-3438 (3d Cir. August 20, 2004).

Simmons, J. (2000, October). Kids' mental health tackled. *Counseling Today*, 1 & 22.

Smaby, M. H. (1995). The school counselor as leader of efforts to have schools free of drugs and violence. *Education, 115*, 612-623.

Smith-Bell, M., & Winslade, W. J. (1994). Privacy, confidentiality, and privilege in psychotherapeutic relationships. *American Orthopsychiatric Association, 64*, 180-193.

Stein, N. (1999). *Classrooms and courtrooms: Facing sexual harassment in K-12 schools*. New York: Teachers College Press.

Stone, C., & Isaacs, M. (2002). Involving students in violence prevention: Anonymous reporting and the need to promote and protect confidences. *National Association of Secondary School Principals Bulletin, 86*(633), 54-65.

Tarasoff v. Board of Regents of California 551 P.2d 334 (Cal.1976).

Thompson v. County of Alameda, 167 Cal. Rptr. 70 (1980).

U.S. Department of Education. (1998). *Preventing bullying: A manual for schools and communities*. Washington, DC: Author.

Woods, J. (2002). Hostile hallways, *Educational Leadership, 59*(4), 20-23.

CHAPTER 11

Gay, Lesbian, Bisexual and Transgender Students

IN THIS CHAPTER

Objectives

By the time you have completed this chapter, you should be able to:

- Discuss your leadership and advocacy role in creating a more humanistic environment for the GLBT students.
- Discuss the cost of dangerous school climates to GLBT students.
- Discuss case law, statutes and federal guidelines that can influence positive change for GLBT students.
- Give specific strategies for acting as a systemic change agent for unhealthy school climates.
- Identify the legal and ethical ramifications for school counselors and school districts that do not intervene on behalf of GLBT students.

Introduction

A fair and inclusive education is not possible for a student whose physical and emotional safety is routinely compromised. School climates can adversely impact educational opportunities for gay, lesbian, bisexual and transgender (GLBT or LGBT) students by being, at best, indifferent to the vulnerability of this at-risk minority, and, at worst, hostile and dangerous (Stone, 2003b). Gay, Lesbian and Straight Education Network conducts a national biennual survey of experiences of GLBT students in America's schools. In 2003, The National School Climate Survey shed new light on the experiences of GLBT students in America's schools and clearly demonstrated that despite modest measurable gains, "violence, bias and harassment of GLBT students continues to be the rule, not the exception, in America's schools" (GLSEN, 2003b).

The GLSEN survey found that more than four out of five GLBT students report being verbally, sexually or physically harassed at school because of their sexual orientation. "Harassment continues at unacceptable levels and is too often ignored: 84 percent of LGBT students report being verbally harassed because of their sexual orientation; 82.9 percent of students report that faculty never or rarely intervene when present" (GLSEN, 2003b).

Unchecked harassment correlates with poor academic performance and diminished aspirations (GLSEN, 2003b). "For the first time, the biennual study reports a direct relationship between in-school victimization, grade-point averages (GPAs) and the college aspirations of LGBT students."

Other findings included the following:

- Unchecked harassment correlates with poor performance and diminished aspirations: LGBT youth who report significant verbal harassment are twice as likely to report they do not intend to go to college and their GPAs are significantly lower – nearly a full letter grade lower, in fact (2.9 or C+ versus 3.3 or B/B+).
- Supportive teachers can make a difference: 24.1 percent of LGBT students who cannot identify supportive faculty report they have no intention of going to college. That figure drops to just 10.1 percent when LGBT students can identify supportive staff at their school.
- Policymakers have an opportunity to improve school climates: LGBT students who did not have (or did not know of) a policy protecting them from violence and harassment were nearly 40 percent more likely to skip school because they were simply too afraid to go (GLSEN, 2003b).

When schools ignore GLBT students or say they do not have any GLBT students, then the school is probably not a safe place for those students to be (Carroll & Serwatka, 1999; Frankfurt as cited in Bart, 1998). The implication is that if students are afraid to let it be known that they are gay, lesbian, bisexual or transgender, then the logical assumption is that they must believe their school is not a safe place. When school counselors are advocating for a safe, harassment-free environment, they need to give time and attention to this population.

Schools need advocates and change agents to promote a safer, more inclusive school climate (Stone, 2003a). Although laws and court cases have protected the educational issues of inequality by gender, race or handicapping conditions for years, the courts have remained largely mute with regard to GLBT students until the latter half of the 1990s, which culminated with the *Davis v. Monroe County Board of Education* (1999) case. This ruling, coupled with recent interpretations of the Title IX statute, strengthens the position for a more humane school environment. School districts are liable in cases where harassment is so "severe" and "pervasive" that it denies equal access to education. In these cases, it must be proven that the school district knew about the harassment and was deliberately indifferent (for more details, see Chapter 9, "Sexual Harassment").

In 1997, the Office for Civil Rights of the U.S. Department of Education released new guidelines for educators on Title IX (Lambda Legal, 2005). Title IX, the federal statute barring sex discrimination in schools that receive federal funding, supports GLBT youth as well as heterosexual youth when the harassment creates a sexually hostile environment (Title IX, 1972). Sexual orientation was not included, but harassing conduct of a sexual nature directed toward gay or lesbian students may create a sexually hostile environment. For example, while calling a student "gay" is not considered sexual harassment, grabbing at the crotch of a student perceived to be gay (or other sexually suggestive gestures or language) might be considered sexual harassment and prohibited by Title IX.

State and local laws may prohibit discrimination on the basis of sexual orientation. In its 2004 State of the States Report, the Gay, Lesbian & Straight Educators Network found that 75 percent of students in America's schools do not have legal protection in state statutes against anti-LGBT harassment. Eight states and the District of Columbia "currently have statewide legal protections for students based on sexual orientation. Only California, Minnesota and New Jersey include protections based on "gender identity or expression" (GLSEN, 2004).

However, a significant case in Arkansas involving harassment of a gay student, Willi Wagner, changed the interpretation of a Title IX violation with regard to how the courts view harassment of GLBT students (Fischer, Schimmel, & Kelly, 1999; Title IX, 1972). After Wagner filed a complaint stating that he had endured two years of abuse from other students, the Fayetteville (Ark.) School District signed an agreement with the U.S. Department of Education to hold sexual harassment workshops to raise educators' awareness of their legal obligations to protect students from sexual harassment, and to take disciplinary action against any student who engages in sexual harassment (Fischer et. al., 1999; Lambda Legal, 2005). This case is significant because it opened the door for students to seek legal remedy under Title IX for sexual harassment (Lambda Legal, 2005). The Willi Wagner case was highly significant but several other early court cases contributed to supporting GLBT students:

- *Wisconsin, 1996:* The court awarded Jamie Nabozny $962,000 for injuries he suffered while in middle and high school. Nabozny v. Podlesny (1996) used the federal equal protection law to challenge public school officials' failure to take action against anti-gay abuse in a school, resulting in a near-million-dollar recovery from the officials.
- *Illinois, 1996:* The Riverside-Brookfield School District settled a lawsuit filed by the family of a gay student who alleged that school officials did not act on the student's complaints of abuse from his peers (Fischer et. al., 1999; Lambda Legal, 2005).

School counselors are committed to facilitating and promoting the fullest possible development of each individual by reducing the barriers of misinformation, myth, ignorance, hatred and discrimination based on sexual orientation (Stone, 2003a). In "A Family's Guide to Handling Anti-Gay Harassment" by the Safe Schools Coalition, school counselors are recognized as advocates for students. Parents are urged to find information and support by calling "a trusted school counselor, nurse, teacher, administrator or social worker" (The Safe Schools Coalition, n.d.)

A consortium of national organizations under the leadership of the National School Boards Association has issued a resource document to help school leaders address legal issues surrounding students' sexual orientation and gender identity. Aimed at school policymakers and administrators yet a valuable resource for school counselors, the guide, "Dealing with Legal Matters Surrounding Students' Sexual Orientation and Gender Identity," provides practical guidance on the legal rights of lesbian, gay, bisexual and transgender students (NSBA, n.d.). The guide is significant, not just for the important information it contains but because more than 20 professional organizations such as the American School Counselor Association sponsored and contributed to it. This guide makes a strong statement about the need for advocacy for these heretofore largely neglected minorities.

Ethical Standards Addressed in This Chapter

Professionalism means knowing your professional associations' codes and adhering to them. Those ethical standards from American School Counselor Association that are most germane include the following:

- Each person has the right to be respected, be treated with dignity and have access to a comprehensive school counseling program that advocates for and affirms all students from diverse populations regardless of ethnic/racial status, age, economic status, special needs, English as a second language or other language group, immigration status, sexual orientation, gender, gender identity/expression, family type, religious/spiritual identity and appearance. (Preamble)
- The professional school counselor respects the rights and responsibilities of parents/guardians for their children and endeavors to establish, as appropriate, a collaborative relationship with parents/guardians to facilitate the student's maximum development. (B.1.a)

- The professional school counselor is knowledgeable and supportive of the school's mission and connects his/her program to the school's mission. (D.1.c)
- The professional school counselor assists in developing: (1) curricular and environmental conditions appropriate for the school and community, (2) educational procedures and programs to meet students' developmental needs and (3) a systematic evaluation process for comprehensive, developmental, standards-based school counseling programs, services and personnel. The counselor is guided by the findings of the evaluation data in planning programs and services. (D.1.g)
- The professional school counselor affirms the diversity of students, staff and families. (E.2.a)

The full text of American Counseling Association ethical codes and ASCA ethical codes can be found at these Web sites: ACA at http://www.counseling.org and ASCA at www.schoolcounselor.org.

Getting Started: What Would You Do?

The following case is discussed at the end of this chapter by a practicing school counseling candidate. Before you read her response, formulate in your own mind how you would approach this ethical dilemma.

A COUNSELOR'S ATTITUDE AND BELIEFS

Alexia Huart had been taught in religious training and at home that homosexuality is a choice and that people who make the choice to be homosexuals are misguided. She never really questioned her beliefs, and she thought that as a school counselor in training it really did not matter how she felt about gays. Huart's preparation program pushed her to examine her biases.

Why must school counselors continuously take inventory and confront their own prejudices and beliefs about others with regard to diversity issues such as sexual orientation and gender identity?

At the end of the chapter you can read Huart's words describing her own self-analysis and eventual change of heart. "I was so challenged and moved by all that has transpired in this graduate program that it pulled at my heart to really take personal inventory of my attitudes, values and prejudices on homosexuality" (A. Huart, personal communication, August 2003).

Working Through Case Studies

HARASSMENT OF GAY, LESBIAN, BISEXUAL AND TRANSGENDER STUDENTS

A 15-year-old openly gay student asks you to help stop the daily harassment she has been enduring from other students. She tells you she receives approximately 25 anti-gay remarks a day and at least twice in the last five months she has been kicked and punched while on school grounds. She tells you the harassment is especially bad in Mrs. Smith's class, and that she has experienced other students calling her a "she-he" and a "queer," but the teacher pretends not to hear. She also tells you she has gone to the assistant principal for disciplinary action for these students, giving names of the students who have verbally and physically attacked her, but the assistant principal just tells her to "stop wearing your lesbianism on your sleeve." What do you do?

Points to Consider

A safe and respectful school climate is a mandate for all students and is part of the No Child Left Behind legislation in the reauthorization of the Elementary and Secondary Education Act of 1965. Part A of Title IV issues a directive for safe and drug-free schools and communities (No Child Left Behind Act, 2002).

School counselors are integral to the mission of creating safe and respectful schools and can contribute in a variety of ways. By creating and delivering anti-bullying programs and inviting speakers who have been bullied to present at assemblies, counselors can convey the message that the school community will not permit intolerance of its group members (Stone & Isaacs, 2002a).

School counselors can also be at the forefront of diversity training for students and staff to raise awareness of the gay, lesbian, bisexual and transgender population. Raising awareness in the school community by holding seminars, assemblies or other functions can go a long way toward creating the type of environment in which all students can learn and feel safe. Indeed, the counselor might implement effective yet simple measures like prominently posting rights and responsibilities of students as citizens of the school to help one another learn and grow in an accepting climate (Stone & Isaacs, 2002b).

Educate administrators and staff about the legal ramifications of ignoring harassment of GLBT students, including the possibility that judicial decisions may make school systems responsible for monetary damages. Present court cases that have found both individual educators and school districts negligent and levied monetary damages. *Davis v. Monroe County Board of Education et al.* (1999) raises as many questions as it answers, but it unarguably encourages school districts to protect this currently disregarded minority against harassment by fellow students (Stone, 2003a).

Other ways to support GLBT students include discussing the research demonstrating that GLBT students are at greater risk than their peers for suicide, as well as for physical and emotional abuse in schools. School counselors can partner with administrators to create disciplinary committees to handle discipline referrals and oversee punitive action for offenders of anti-harassment policies (Stone, 2003a).

Expanding awareness and sensitivity to the consequences of homophobia and heterosexism is an indispensable aspect of working toward a harassment-free environment. This education, directed to both offenders and nonoffenders, encourages everyone to re-examine thoughts and beliefs, and recognizes that respecting human dignity rises above prejudicial feelings (Stone, 2003a).

In a position statement the American School Counseling Association affirms the school counselor's role in the schools:

"The professional school counselor is sensitive to ways in which attitudes and behavior negatively affect the individual. School counselors are called to provide constructive feedback on the negative use of exclusive, presumptive language and inequitable expectations toward sexual-orientation minorities. The school counselor places emphasis on a person's behavioral choices and not on his or her identity and uniqueness. Demonstrations of sexual-orientation-minority equity also include fair and accurate representation of sexual identities in visible leadership positions as well as other role positions" (ASCA, 2000).

A Football Team Captain's Revelation

In an article by Robert Lipsyte on April 30, 2000, entitled "An Icon Recast: Support for Gay Athlete," *The New York Times* recounted family, school and community reactions to a Masconomet (Mass.) High School football team captain's revelation of his homosexuality.

Corey Johnson's story is one that provides a "hopeful model" amid schools that struggle with issues such as "diversity, tolerance and jock culture."

Corey Johnson had suppressed thoughts about his homosexuality since the sixth grade, and expressed pain at his desire to live a "normal life." His fear intensified as he imagined reactions of others to the revelation of his secret, often losing sleep at night or being unable to get out of bed in the morning. Johnson's decision to reveal his homosexuality to his guidance counselor and biology teacher had its roots in slurs towards gays put forth by two uncles at a family Super Bowl party. Corey Johnson could no longer hold the secret of his sexual orientation.

The reactions of Corey's parents ranged from unreserved love to fear of harm to their son by others. In fact, Corey's father already knew of his son's homosexuality after reading an e-mail between his son and a gay e-pal, and yet had not shared this knowledge with his son. At the end of a sports workshop led by Jeff Perrotti challenging the entitlement of athletes during a conference of the Gay Lesbian and Straight Education Network, a national organization that works with Massachusetts' Safe Schools program, Corey Johnson raised his hand and told those gathered that he was a football captain, wanted to share his secret, and needed help.

Johnson's mother, the school staff and Jeff Perrotti orchestrated a controlled coming out for Corey. The reaction to Johnson's news by the football coach and teammates ranged from support to meekness to curiosity. A few in the school community scrawled gay slurs, and opposing linemen in football games attempted to intimidate Johnson by shouting gay slurs in his face. When the president of Masco's active booster club demanded that Johnson be removed as captain in the name of "unit cohesiveness," the coach rejected it as a nonissue. Many imagined problems never materialized due to commitment of school personnel to diversity and alternative education (Lipsyte, 2000).

COMMUNITY STANDARDS

You receive a notice that a new program called "No Name-Calling Week" will be implemented at schools across the nation. You want to bring it into your own school, thinking that this will be a great kickoff to your own program to create a safe and respectful school climate for all students. You are confident that any program aimed at reducing bullying will be highly supported and respected by your administrators, teachers, parents and community. What criticism could a bully-proofing program encounter, and how might you be informed and prepared for those criticisms?

Points to Consider

Gay, Lesbian & Straight Education Network is in the second year of a middle school initiative called "No Name-Calling Week" (No Name-Calling Week Coalition, 2005). The program is supported by a partnership of more than 40 national education and youth service organizations, including the National Middle Schools Association and the Girl Scouts, but also has been criticized by some for its inclusion of harassment of LGBT youths. LaBarbera, a senior policy analyst at the Culture and Family Institute, opposes programs designed to support sexual orientation because "homosexual acts are unhealthy – especially for males. Like smoking, alcohol and drug abuse, they should be discouraged. Dangerous behavior that shortens a person's life should never be promoted to impressionable students" (LaBarbera, 2002). Responding to the criticism, GLSEN argues that it seeks to safely accommodate students of all sexual orientations and that No Name-Calling Week is a comprehensive program of which LGBT issues represent only a small part.

The "No Name-Calling Week" was inspired by *The Misfits*, a book by openly gay author James Howe (2003). The book deals with four much-taunted middle schoolers – one of them gay – who runs for the student council on a platform advocating an end to nasty name-calling. Howe responds that the criticism of No Name-Calling Week is unwarranted, as all students are potential targets of harassment.

Communities have a wide range of views on their support of certain programs in schools such as reading The Misfits. The outcry from parents in Iowa prompted the Pleasant Valley School Board to rule that teachers could no longer read it aloud. Colorado lawmakers rejected a proposal to declare a statewide "No Name-Calling Week," as House Majority Leader Keith King said he was concerned about fostering a "victim's mentality" and argued that children should be taught to ignore taunts (No Name-Calling Week Coalition, 2005). In contrast, Michigan Gov. Jennifer Granholm fully supported the initiative with an official proclamation endorsing and recognizing the event (No Name-Calling Week Coalition, 2005).

As advocates, school counselors are educated about the prevailing community standards, and they learn to predict and skillfully negotiate the political landscape. To rush headlong into programs without understanding the potential for criticism is to risk being stopped dead in one's tracks in an effort to improve the school environment for students. It is always best to review materials with administrators to ensure their support and to anticipate possible concerns – and be prepared to address them – should they arise.

REALIZATION OF SEXUAL IDENTITY

John, an 11-year-old sixth-grade boy, has stuffed his desk to overflowing with papers, library books, supplies from the teacher's closets and more. One afternoon as the teacher is lining up the desks, the contents of John's desk begin to spill when she moves it. The teacher turns the desk on its side, empties the contents, and proceeds to sort through the pile. Some of John's papers catch her eye and she starts to read his words describing his pain over sexual identity issues and expressing his love for a classmate. The teacher immediately brings six papers to you to read. You are convinced that this child is in a great deal of pain. How will you proceed in this situation?

Points to Consider

The school counselor in this complex case will need much sensitivity. A child in pain needs help, and there are no black-and-white answers as to how to provide it. In fact, there are more questions than answers. Should John's parents be involved? Will they be supportive of him or make his pain worse? The younger the child is, the greater our responsibility to his parents; but what do we do if his parents react negatively? Most importantly, is John in such pain that he may be contemplating suicide?

The American School Counselor Association reminds us that "identity is determined by a complex mix of nature and nurture" (2000). For adolescents, the development of sexual identity is a natural process, but it can be much more stressful for homosexual adolescents because of the way society views homosexuality (Harrison, 2003). Adolescence, as difficult as it is, requires GLBT and questioning youth to hide their sexual identities, resulting in problems of isolation, depression, and real or imagined fear of discovery or rejection by their families and friends (Harrison, 2003). The psychological difficulties become a daily challenge when hiding one's true self (Wittmer, 2000).

The fact that John is in pain is a common scenario for GLBT youth because of "hush-hush" attitudes. He is expressing pain and seems to be calling out for help. We know that there is a potential danger for John here, because statistics have shown that gay, lesbian, bisexual and transgender students have a higher rate of depression and are more likely to consider suicide than other students (Harrison, 2003).

Something must be done to address the child's pain and confusion before it is too late. The question is, how do you go about it? Who should be involved and what should be done? Some may believe it is the parents' right to know what is going on their child's life. However, how can we be sure that this will make things better for the child? Maybe the parents are unwilling to accept that their child might be gay, and the child is experiencing pain and confusion because he is afraid they will find out. Coming out is not always easy for GLBT students, and their own families may reject them.

Research in this area focuses primarily on older children and the consequences of disclosure to family members. Harrison (2003) indicates that prior positive family relations and family cohesion usually predict a good outcome for adolescents who decide to disclose. Harrison (2003) found that a safe sibling is often told first and mothers are disclosed to before fathers. However, the age of the young man in the case and his self-proclaimed pain over his sexual identity makes it premature to predict that he will decide to disclose to his parents or siblings.

While studies of LGBT youth show that they recognize their sexual orientation between ages 8 and 11, the age at which they "come out" is between 15 and 17, indicating that for many years they feel too afraid to be honest about the issue. But the fact is that many students are increasingly "coming out" while still in high (or even junior high) school, increasing the necessity for school counselors to consider how to support students (American Psychological Association, 2004; National Mental Health Association, 2005; Parents, Family and Friends of Lesbians and Gays, 2005).

Before notifying John's parents or guardians, you need to establish a relationship with John to address the pain he is experiencing (Harrison, 2003). Let John know that you are there for him to listen to his concerns.

Without labeling him, drop clues that you are prepared to address these issues by saying phrases like "gay and lesbian" or "sexual orientation" as part of your conversation. Accept whatever language he is using to describe himself and move on from there. Establishing a relationship with this student will benefit him.

Although 37.3 percent of GLBT students do not feel comfortable discussing issues with their teachers, GLBT students who can identify with school counselors or other supportive faculty or staff do better in school than those who cannot, with grade-point averages that are a full letter grade higher than their peers (GLSEN, 2003b). It might be a good course of action to suggest that the student reach out to an adult relative who is a constant in his life and can help him for the next six years, and who can help him think through his options in this regard (J. Van Nostrand, personal communication, January 17, 2005).

After you form a relationship with John, you could inquire how he believes his parents would react to finding out he is gay or bisexual. Considering his age, even if John is reluctant to tell his parents, you should encourage him to do so. Offering John support by being present when he talks to his parents or offering to talk to them yourself might help. *Eisel v. Montgomery* (1991) has shown that if we question whether this child's pain will lead to causing himself harm, we have a duty to warn. In addition, parents may want their religious beliefs to be taught and upheld in schools. They also may firmly believe in parents' rights to complete authority over their offspring, including knowing and controlling what their children experience in school and choosing disciplinary methods (Gysbers & Henderson, 2000).

Although we would like to provide the parents with all the information to relieve our own anxiety, this is not always the best course of action. Disclosing the content of John's papers to his parents might not be feasible, but the counselor could discuss his emotional distress with his parents. Making a strong recommendation for outside counseling might be the best way to help John, while still preserving his confidentiality. Protecting John's privacy can demonstrate that you are his ally and are available to assist in any way.

To protect the counselor-counselee relationship, schools should provide parents with an explanation of the professional school counselor's role that emphasizes the confidential nature of counseling. Parents should know that counselors provide accurate, comprehensive and relevant information in a manner consistent with all ethical guidelines and make reasonable efforts to honor the requests of parents and guardians for information while protecting the counselee (Cobia & Henderson, 2003).

Besides the legal implications, there can be several benefits to involving parents in the student's personal life. One principle that school counselors endorse is that children's personal and educational well-being is best served when school counselors and other educators work together as partners with parents on the behalf of the children and youth (Gysbers & Henderson, 2000). Many parents, in fact, want to be supportive of their LGBT child, but simply lack the knowledge and expertise as to how to be an effective parent on this subject. Sharing resources with them, as well as directing them to places where they can turn for support – Parents, Families and friends of Lesbians and Gays at www.PFLAG.org is one excellent suggestion – may be a great relief to them. Parent involvement can boost students' grades and achievement, improve their social skills and behavior, and keep their attitudes about school more positive (Bluestein, 2001).

Four nonschool counselors shared their opinions with the author about how they would want the school counselor to help them if they were the child in the case study.

Julie A. is a 27-year-old bisexual who lives in New York. When asked if she believed the boy's parents should be involved, her answer immediately was "absolutely not." She believes the boy needs someone to talk to who can help him become more comfortable with himself. Telling others when he might not be ready to reveal his sexual identity could be the worst thing to do.

Fred B. is a gay 27-year-old male who lives in New York. He does not believe parents need to be involved right away and maybe not. He believes that the counselor should meet the parents and develop a relationship with them. By doing so, the counselor might be able to determine how John's parents would take the news about his sexuality and decide at that point how to move forward.

Melissa C. is a 28-year-old lesbian. When asked if she believes that John's parents should be notified, she struggles to respond. Her struggle comes from her own painful experience and the isolation she felt upon realization of her sexuality. Melissa says she did not feel comfortable telling anyone about her sexuality until after high school graduation, and all those years she felt completely alone. Melissa says she became someone she did not want to be because she thought otherwise people would judge her and treat her differently. In an effort to disguise her sexuality, Melissa says she had boyfriends. Melissa respects a person's decision to keep his or her sexuality a secret. However, if the counselor is aware of a child in pain and is able to discuss this and ensure the confidentiality between them, she believes it would benefit the child. "John needs at least one person to talk to, and be able to open up to be himself."

Janet D., a lesbian and mother of three, has revealed her sexual identity only recently, since her divorce. She has a slightly different reaction to the scenario about John, saying she believes there are many more open-minded parents than some seem to think. She believes that the counselor should speak with John first and then his parents. She would not at once tell his parents about his sexuality, but she would work with John on trying to get him to tell them himself. She does, however, believe it is important for John's parents to become aware eventually. "Living in secrecy is very painful," she explains.

REPARATIVE OR CONVERSION THERAPY

A school counselor and her student are talking just outside her door. As you walk by, you see the counselor hand the student a copy of the book, You Do Not Have to Be Gay, and hear her say to the student, "I know where you can go to get better. You do not have to go through life like this." You strongly suspect that the school counselor is talking to this young man about reparative or conversion therapy in an attempt to change him. You know with certainty that this school counselor attends a church espousing the belief that gay, lesbian and bisexual youth have a choice in their sexual preference, and that they should choose to be heterosexual. You have heard her talk about individuals her church has "saved" through reparative therapy. What would you do?

Points to Consider

The term "reparative therapy," also known as "conversion" therapy, refers to psychotherapy aimed at eliminating homosexual desires. People who use it do not think homosexuality is a variation within human sexual orientation, but rather a mental disorder. "Reparative therapy is based upon the assumption that homosexuality is a mental disorder and thus needs to be cured" (American Psychological Association, n.d.). In response to the danger posed to young people by this quasi-scientific "treatment," the APA and a coalition of several other groups issued in 1999 "Just the Facts About Sexual Orientation and Youth" to clarify the appropriate actions by professionals working with LGBT youth. You can find it on the Interet at http://www.glsen.org/binary-data/ GLSEN_ATTACHMENTS/files/446-3.pdf.

This very sensitive situation requires professionalism and tact. Questioning another professional about her interactions with a counselee can be treading in deep water, but there are some things you can do. Depending on your relationship with your colleague, perhaps you could have a private conversation respectfully reminding her of her ethical obligations with regard to this student. Specifically, the American School Counseling Association Code of Ethics A.1.c states that the professional school counselor "respects the student's values and beliefs and does not impose the counselor's personal values" (ASCA, 2004).

ASCA's position statement says, "Many internal and external obstacles exist in school and society that inhibit students from accurately understanding and positively accepting their sexual orientation. Professional school counselors need to become accurately informed and aware of the ways communication limits the opportunities and infringes upon the development of self-acceptance and healthy esteem. Harm is perpetrated against gay, lesbian, bisexual and transgender youth through language, stereotypes, myths, misinformation, threat of expulsion from social and institutional structures and other entities and from beliefs contrary to their identity. These youth begin to experience self-identification and the 'coming out' process, both essentially cognitive activities, during adolescence. Such identification is not indicative of sexual activity" (ASCA, 2000, p.1).

The statement concludes, "The professional school counselor is committed to the inclusion and affirmation of youths of all sexual orientation. The professional school counselor supports consciousness-raising among school counselors and increased modeling of inclusive language, advocacy and equal opportunity for participation for all. This is done to break through individual, social and institutional behaviors and expectations limiting the development of human potential in all populations" (ASCA, 2000, p.1).

Explore the regulations set forth by the school district and inform your colleague if she is in jeopardy of punitive action by the district for noncompliance. If your relationship with your colleague is not at that level, make information about reparative or conversion therapy part of your overall educational message about gays, lesbians, bisexuals and transgendered individuals. Present both sides, with research supporting both views, and encourage students to explore their own feelings about the practice.

The American Psychiatric Association, publishers of the Diagnostic and Statistical Manual of Mental Disorders, declassified homosexuality as a mental disorder in 1973 (APA, 1996). Numerous mental health and health organizations, including the American Academy of Pediatrics, the American Counseling Association, the American Psychiatric Association, the American Psychological Association, the National Association of School Psychologists, and the National Association of Social Workers, all take the position that an individual is not mentally ill if he or she has sexual feelings for a person of the same gender.

Several of these organizations have declared that reparative therapy is not a useful tool for counseling persons confused about their sexual orientation. According to the American Academy of Pediatrics (2000), using reparative therapy will most likely result in little or no change in orientation, leaving the person feeling more anxious and guilty than before.

The American Academy of Pediatrics (2000) explains that confusion about sexual orientation is common during adolescence and that counseling is a helpful tool for young people who are uncertain about their sexual orientation or for those who are uncertain about how to express their sexuality and might profit from an attempt at clarification through counseling.

As these statements make clear, health and mental health professional organizations do not support efforts to change young people's sexual orientation through reparative therapy and have raised serious concerns about its potential to do harm. Many of the professional associations mentioned in this chapter are able to provide helpful information and local contacts to assist school administrators, health and mental health professionals, educators, teachers and parents in dealing with school controversies.

EQUAL ACCESS AND GAY-STRAIGHT ALLIANCE CLUBS

Johnston, one of your high school juniors, has often been to see you during his struggles toward adulthood. He is coming to you now for advice because he is being ignored by the administration in his efforts to start a gay-straight alliance club for gay/lesbian/bisexual/ transgender youth and their straight friends. He says he met with the teacher in charge of student activities, who told him to get permission from the assistant principal, who sent him to the principal for an answer. The principal told him he "would get back with him." Three months have gone by and each time Johnston tries to see the principal, his secretary says she will call when the principal is ready to talk. Johnston is coming to you for advice, since he believes his next step is to complain at the district office. What do you do?

Points to Consider

Administrators' reluctance to support a student's desire to establish a school club for GLBT and straight students is a situation that has been addressed in countless school districts across the country. This dilemma presents an opportunity for you to use your knowledge of court findings and legislation to benefit a minority student population. The establishment of a school club that sensitizes all students to diversity issues will further efforts to build a school climate embracing all students no matter what differences exist among them.

Having in your knowledge bank the Equal Access Act (1984) and other legal guidance from court cases will help you assist Johnston and other students who need the support of a GSA student club. From a legal perspective, the Equal Access Act has primarily been used in court cases involving establishment and protection of GSA school clubs. The Equal Access Act was originally proposed to ensure that student religious clubs could meet in public schools, although subsequent court rulings have extended its application to a broad array of student groups. The Equal Access Act requires schools that receive federal funds to provide GLBT clubs the same access to school facilities that other student groups enjoy.

These student clubs must be student-initiated. In other words, the Equal Access Act dictates that community members outside the school community may not direct, conduct, control or regularly attend activities of student groups. Guests may occasionally attend student meetings, and school faculty and staff may regularly attend and supervise meetings. If a school staff member is provided to monitor noncurricular student clubs, a staff member should be assigned to the gay student association as well (Equal Access Act, 1984).

Certain limitations apply with regard to equal access. For example, a limitation would apply if the school denies access based on a substantive possibility that it will interfere with the orderly conduct of educational activities within the school. A complete guide on the Equal Access Act can be found at http://www.usdoj.gov/crt/cor/byagency/ed4071.htm.

School administrations do not always support formation of gay-straight alliance clubs, often dragging their feet about establishing these groups in their schools. The courts have not looked favorably on efforts of some school districts to change district policies or finesse legal definitions in order to defeat requests to establish student groups that address GLBT issues (Equal Access Act, 1984).

One Utah school district attempted to eliminate all student noncurriculum-related organizations after students tried to hold a GSA meeting. This would be legal only if the new policy applied equally to every student club. However, the school district reconsidered such a drastic measure. In order to avoid potential future legal problems, many school districts have put into place a uniform set of policies regarding establishment of student organizations.

The school administration has the responsibility of addressing Johnston's desire to form a GSA club. As the school counselor you have an opportunity for advocacy by talking to the administration about the Equal Access Act and encouraging them to learn more from their school district's legal counsel to avoid a legal misstep. Your advocacy role would serve two purposes: It would position you as supporting the principal by drawing his attention to the appropriate federal legislation; and you would be providing support for Johnston and his need to form a GSA club.

For the skillful advocate, this could open up important dialogue about diversity and support by the administration for all groups, especially minority or disenfranchised groups. Your advocacy can go a step further if you volunteer to help the principal gather information about the issues, such as how many students might want a GSA club and which specific school district policies would affect its formation.

Explore your own emotional comfort level with the variety of issues that may arise regarding GLBT student populations. Reflect on your own personal knowledge of the professional literature dealing with GLBT issues in school settings. Be aware of the attitudes of persons within and outside the school community in reference to GLBT issues and the support or resistance expected in setting up a GSA student club.

ORGANIZATIONS PERCEIVED AS ANTI-GAY

Johnston has been able to form a Gay-Straight Alliance Club at your school. His parents have become very supportive and verbal on Johnston's behalf and are helping him become informed and confident that he can stand up for himself. Johnston and his family are asking you and the school's administration to reconsider allowing the Boys Scouts of America to have access to the schools. Their argument is that they believe this organization discriminates against gay, lesbian and bisexual students, and Scout leaders should not be allowed to meet on school grounds or visit the school campus to talk to students. How would our legal system respond?

Points to Consider

The No Child Left Behind Act (2002) contains a provision called the Boy Scouts of America Equal Access Act. Public schools receiving federal funds must provide the Boy Scouts of America with the opportunity to meet in school facilities if the school district makes school facilities available to other outside groups (Jones, 2001). The district is not required to sponsor a Boy Scout troop, but a school district that receives federal funds must make its facilities available to the Boy Scouts on the same basis it does to other organizations. Therefore, the counselor can best support Johnston, his parents and all students legally and ethically by creating an inclusive school climate that teaches tolerance and celebrates diversity.

In a Position to Know:
A School Counseling Candidate Speaks

The case presented at the beginning of the chapter is revisited here and discussed further by a practicing school counseling candidate. Compare her thoughts with your approach.

A COUNSELOR'S ATTITUDE AND BELIEFS

Alexia Huart had been taught in religious training and at home that homosexuality is a choice and that people who make the choice to be homosexuals are misguided. She never really questioned her beliefs, and she thought that as a school counselor in training it really did not matter how she felt about gays. Huart's preparation program pushed her to examine her biases.

Why must school counselors continuously take inventory and confront their own prejudices and beliefs about others with regard to diversity issues such as sexual orientation and gender identity?

Excerpts of comments written by Alexia Huart

I never had to "confront" my values or what I thought of others' values and lifestyles prior to entering the school counseling program. The more courses I took, the more challenged my values, biases and prejudices. At first, my reaction was, "So, what's the big deal? My thoughts and opinions are mine and should not matter or impact my ability to become a successful school counselor."

But I began to realize that confronting my values was of extreme importance. I learned that when it comes to a student's issues and situations, what I think, my nonverbal behavior (i.e., my reactions: empathy, shock, horror, concern or indifference), as well as what I say, could make a crucial difference in the student's life! I think about students who could be spared pain or brought back from the brink of suicide just by a caring look, empathy or unconditional support from an educator.

My entire life I believed I was trying to be vigilant in respecting beliefs and cultural differences. I had a great desire to learn more about others, regardless of race, ethnicity or religion. Now the professors in my school counseling preparation program were adding to the pot sexual differences, beliefs and identifies ... Uh-oh! I had no idea as to the challenge it would bring to my doorstep. Now I have to look into myself and address my beliefs and biases concerning homosexuality. I felt I respected the rights of others to be different from me, but did I really? Did I ever consider their actual pain? Not until I watched "The Laramie Project," the moving story of Matthew Shepard (Home Box Office, 2002).

Matthew was beaten, tied to a fence and left for dead because he was gay. After watching "The Laramie Project" and seeing Matthew's father give his impassioned speech during the sentencing phase of the trail, I was changed. Anyone who has a heart would realize that it doesn't matter about Matthew's skin color or sexual orientation. He was a son, a classmate, a neighbor, a friend, a person...a human being. This man and his family suffered pain and devastation, like so many who have experienced the cruelty of hatred, prejudice and ignorance.

Joe Wittmer says, "In addition to creating a more positive environment for teenagers, counselors must become aware of the unique personal pressures facing gay and lesbian teenagers....Those gay/lesbian youth who decide to come out may face immediate rejection from their peers. Rejection by one's peers is always difficult, but this type of rejection can be devastating" (Wittmer, 2000, p. 18). Wittmer notes that gay and lesbian students are sometimes rejected by their own families. "Sadly, such blatant, overt, non-acceptance by family and peers can lead to alienation, abandonment, and even physical abuse by family members...Can [these] teenagers get help in their schools? As noted, very few counselors have been appropriately trained and courses that confront attitudes and beliefs about homosexuality are still almost nonexistent in counselor education programs. School counselors are the ones most counted on in this issue" (Wittmer, 2000, p. 18).

After much pondering and soul searching on my own, I have come to the conclusion that there are a plethora of qualities which a counselor should possess in order to do an adequate job in his or her field. Chief among them are fairness, loyalty and a tolerance and appreciation for diversity. In the world in which we live, one must do a personal inventory of where he or she stands in view of these most necessary attributes. There are some things that cannot be acquired from a book. One can study forever and still not possess the qualities needed to work with people successfully or compassionately. This takes personal effort and determination to improve your character and view of the world at large. I'm determined to grow daily through my interactions with others regardless of race, creed, ethnicity or sexual orientation....It's not a pat on the back by any means, just a "charge to keep" to myself...personally.

Alexia Huart, staff development teacher at P.S. 224 in Brooklyn, N.Y.

Making Connections

1. Discuss 10 strategies you would like to implement to reduce harassment of GLBT students in your school.

2. What are the human costs to gay, lesbian and bisexual students in dangerous school climates? Cite some statistics to show their peculiar vulnerability.

3. View the videotape titled "The Laramie Project." What is your reaction? Pick a character in the movie and write your reaction about the barriers or contributions that person made to acceptance of diversity. There are recent revelations from the defendants that Matthew Shepard may not have been a victim of a hate crime, but a target for robbery; does this change the impact of the reenactment for you?

4. What are your personal beliefs about homosexuality? How will your attitudes and beliefs be manifested in your work? Is this a problem? If so, what will you do to minimize harm to your students?

5. Why should the school counselor be the one person everyone in the school can count on to promote diversity and respect for all students?

6. Courts will rule more quickly in students' favor in sexual harassment and cultural or ethnic discrimination cases. Why do you think this is the practice of the courts?

Key Terms

Dangerous school climates
Physical and emotional safety
Gay-Straight Alliance Club
Sexual orientation
Community standards
Adversely stratified educational
  opportunities
Title IX of Educational
  Amendment of 1972
Homophobia

Heterosexism
Reparative or conversion therapy
Equal Access Act
Homosexuality
Gay, Lesbian & Straight Education
  Network
Lambda Legal
Parents, Family and Friends of
  Lesbians and Gays
The Safe Schools Coalition

References

American Academy of Pediatrics (2000, July 21). *Parity, scope-of-practice issues in spotlight at AMA meeting.* Retrieved on February 18, 2005, from http://www.psych.org/pnews/00-07-21/parity.html

American Psychiatric Association. (1996). *Diagnostic and statistical manual of mental disorders* (4th ed.). Arlington, Va: Author.

American Psychological Association. (2004). *Healthy lesbian, gay and bisexual students project.* Retrieved January 11, 2005, from http://www.apa.org/ed/hlgb/

American Psychological Association. (n.d.). *Just the facts about sexual orientation & youth: A primer for principals, educators and school personnel.* Retrieved January 31, 2005, from http://www.apa.org/pi/lgbc/publications/justthefacts.html

American School Counselor Association. (2000). *The professional school counselor and sexual orientation of youth.* Retrieved January 18, 2005, from http://www.schoolcounselor.org

American School Counselor Association. (2004). *Ethical standards for school counselors.* Alexandria, VA: Author.

Bart, M. (1998, September). Creating a safer school for gay students. *Counseling Today,* 26, 36, 39.

Bluestein, J. (2001). *Creating emotionally safe schools: A guide for educators and parents.* Deerfield Beach, FL: Health Communications, Inc.

Carroll, L., & Serwatka, T. J. (1999). No safe places: Lesbian, gay, and bisexual adolescents at risk. In D. Rea & R. Warkentin (Eds.), *Empowering youth-at-risk with skills for school and life* (pp. 160-165). New York: McGraw Hill.

Cobia, D. C., & Henderson, D. A. (2003). *Handbook of school counseling.* Upper Saddle River, NJ: Merrill Prentice Hall.

Davis v. Monroe County Board of Education et al. 120 F.3d 1390 U.S. (Supreme Court, May 24, 1999).

Equal Access Act, 20 U.S.C. § 4071-74 (1984). *Title 20—Education, Chapter 52—Education for economic security, Subchapter VIII—Equal access*. Retrieved February 6, 2005, from http://www.usdoj.gov/crt/cor/byagency/ed4071.htm

Eisel v. Board of Education of Montgomery County. 324 Md. 376, 597 A. 2d 447 (Md. Ct. App. 1991). Retrieved December 27, 2002, from LexisNexis database.

Fischer, L., Schimmel, D., & Kelly, C. (1999). *Teachers and the law*. New York: Addison Wesley Longman.

Gay, Lesbian & Straight Education Network. (2003a). *Resources on GSAs and anti-bullying and anti-harassment efforts*. Retrieved January 13, 2005, from http://www.glsen.org

Gay, Lesbian & Straight Education Network. (2003b). *The 2003 national school climate survey*. Retrieved on December 20, 2004, from http://www.glsen.org

Gay, Lesbian & Straight Education Network. (2004). *State of the states report*. Retrieved February 6, 2005, from http://www.glsen.org

Gysbers, N. C., & Henderson, P. (2000). *Developing and managing your school guidance program* (3rd ed.). Alexandria, VA: American Counseling Association.

Harrison T. (2003). Adolescent homosexuality and concerns regarding disclosure. *The Journal of School Health*, 73(3), 107-12.

Home Box Office. (2002). *The Laramie project*. Warner Brothers Entertainment. Los Angeles, CA: Author.

Howe, J. (2003). *The misfits*. New York: Simon & Schuster.

Jones, R. (2001, April). Be prepared: What your school board needs to know about Boy Scouts, school policies, and the law. *American School Board Journal*. Retrieved January 12, 2005, from http://www.asbj.com/2001/04/0401ASBJjones.pdf

LaBarbera, P. (2002). 15 good reasons to oppose sexual orientation (homosexuality) codes in schools. Concerned Women for America's Culture and Family Institute. Retrieved January 27, 2005, from http://www.cwfa.org

Lambda Legal. (2005). *Defending gay/straight alliances and other gay-related groups in public schools under the Equal Access Act – Questions and answers.* Retrieved January 11, 2005, from http://www.lambda legal.org/cgibin/iowa/cases/documents.htm/?record=251

Lipsyte, R. (2000, April 30). An icon recast: Support for gay athlete. *The New York Times*, p. A14.

Nabozny v. Podlesny. 92 F. 3d 446 (7th Cir. 1996).

National Mental Health Association. (2005). *What does gay mean? How to talk with kids about sexual orientation and prejudice.* Retrieved January 25, 2005, from http://www.nmha.org/whatdoesgaymean/

National School Boards Association. (n.d.). *Dealing with legal matters surrounding students' sexual orientation and gender identity.* Retrieved February 6, 2005, from http://www.nsba.org/site/docs/34600/34527.pdf

No Child Left Behind Act of 2001, 20 U.S.C. § 6301 (2002).

No Name-Calling Week Coalition. (2005). *No name-calling week kicks off in schools nationwide.* Retrieved January 19, 2005, from http://www.nonamecallingweek.org/cgi-bin/iowa/home.html

Parents, Family and Friends of Lesbians and Gays (2005). *From our house to the schoolhouse.* Retrieved January 11, 2005, from http://www.pflag.org/publications/schools.pdf

The Safe Schools Coalition. (n.d.). *A family's guide to handling anti-gay harassment.* Retrieved January 11, 2005, from www.safeschoolscoalition.org

Stone, C. & Isaacs, M. (2002a). Involving students in violence prevention: Anonymous reporting and the need to promote and protect confidences. *National Association of Secondary School Principals Bulletin*, 86 (633), 54-65.

Stone, C., & Isaacs, M. (2002b). Confidentiality with minors: The effects of Columbine on counselor attitudes regarding breaching confidentiality. *The Journal of Educational Research*, 96(2), 140-150.

Stone, C. (2003a). Counselors as advocates for gay, lesbian, and bisexual youth: A call for equity and action. *Journal of Multicultural Counseling and Development*, 31(2), 143-155.

Stone, C. (2003b). Leadership and advocacy in personal/social development: Sexual harassment. In R. Perusse & G. Goodnough (Eds.), *Leadership and advocacy in school counseling* (1st ed., pp. 353-377). Belmont, CA: Brooks/Cole.

Title IX of Educational Amendments of 1972, 20 U.S.C. §§ 1681-86.

Wittmer, J. (Ed.). (2000). *Managing your school counseling program: K-12 developmental strategies*. Minneapolis: Educational Media Corporation.

CHAPTER 12

The Ethics of Advocacy

IN THIS CHAPTER

Objectives

By the time you have completed this chapter, you should be able to:

- Explain the ethical standards relating to advocacy for all students.
- Define the philosophy of a social justice school counseling program.
- Understand the role of the school counselor as advocate.
- Understand the role of the school counselor as a social change agent.
- Describe your own behavior that promotes equity and opportunity for all your students.
- Develop plans to responsibly challenge the institutional barriers that deny equal access and success for all students.

Introduction

The ethical codes of the school counseling profession give us permission – no, not just permission, they issue us a directive – to envision a better world for our students, and to seek ways to bring that vision to reality. If the vision is ethical, it seeks to challenge the institutional and environmental barriers that impede student success (American School Counselor Association, 2003; Stone, 1998). If all students are to realize brighter futures, the ethical school counselor will need to take up the charge to promote a social justice agenda (Martin, 2002).

Ethical school counselors act intentionally and strategically to increase each student's opportunity to participate fully in the economic and social rewards of our society (Stone & Martin, 2004). The ethical counselor acts as an advocate, providing support and encouraging students to challenge their future by tackling the barriers that hinder their success.

Counselors who couple the ethical imperative of social justice with an understanding of the issues that impact equity and opportunity can help change systems that continue to adversely stratify opportunities. They can influence attitudes and beliefs regarding equitable practices; provide attention to equity and access issues; and provide resources designed to improve opportunities (Martin, 2004; Stone & Martin, 2004).

Students are either advantaged or disadvantaged by what we do (Martin, 2004). The ethical school counselor makes certain that he or she creates advantages for students by challenging the status quo and questioning the rules and regulations that deny students access to coursework that will allow them to choose from the widest array of educational opportunities (ASCA, 2004; Dahir & Campbell, 1997; Stone & Dahir, 2004).

Problems that individuals face can often be traced to the systems in which they live, work and play such as schools, families, social agencies, neighborhoods and many others (Stone & Dahir, 2004; Stone & Martin, 2004). Embracing a social justice agenda requires school counselors to "possess the awareness, knowledge, and skill to intervene not only at the individual level, but at the system-wide level" (Lee & Walz, 1998, p. 9). School counselors are in an influential position to challenge the status quo, and to assist those who have been victims or are potential victims of social and educational problems (Kiselica & Robinson, 2001). The practice of counseling is more complete and effective when the counselor helps students learn to negotiate through the systems in which they must move. The counselor who extends that philosophy by acting as a social change agent offers a more powerful position and increases his or her effectiveness in multiple ways (Lee & Walz, 1998; Stone & Martin, 2004).

Ethical behavior is not limited to the traditional role of school counseling, which relies on helping individuals resolve problems and make decisions. The language of the American School Counselor Association's Ethical Standards for School Counselors (2004) clearly defines our role as catalysts for change. The notion of social change, in whatever capacity necessary to assist students to reach their maximum development, lies at the heart of the school counselor's role (Stone, 1998) and ASCA Ethical Standards (2004).

The Ethical Standards for School Counselors (2004) recognize that the origin of students' problems can often be traced to an impaired school environment (Stone, 1997). As the Preamble indicates, the counselor's job is to ensure that "each person has the right to receive the information and support needed to move toward self-direction and self-development and affirmation within one's group identities, with special care being given to students who have historically not received adequate educational services: students of color, low socio-economic students, students with disabilities and students with nondominant language backgrounds" (ASCA, 2004). Social change agents attend to empowerment and advocacy for students with the belief in the possibility of a better world for their students. Part of a counselor's philosophical orientation should be a commitment to the idea of social change and his or her role as catalyst for such change (Lee & Walz, 1998).

Attitudes and beliefs determine our behavior toward students, and the counselor who believes in the dignity and worth of each individual and the right to participate fully in society will behave in a way that assertively supports this belief (Stone, 1998; Stone & Turba, 1999). Working from a social justice mindset requires school counselors to give special care to those who historically have not received adequate educational opportunities, including students of color, students from low socioeconomic backgrounds, students with disabilities, and students with nondominant language backgrounds (ASCA, 2004). Responsibly attacking entrenched inequities in schools is part of the ethical imperative of the ASCA Ethical Standards (2004).

Most of the cases presented in this chapter will focus on student access and how students' future opportunities will be advantaged or disadvantaged by school practices and procedures. As you work through these cases involving the ethics of advocacy, identify how students' opportunities are being adversely limited and how school officials are contributing to an environment marked by a stratified social order. For example, opportunities in schools are stratified in that predominately white, middle-class, and relatively high-achieving students are offered more chances for enriched and rigorous academic experiences (Education Trust, 2000; Haycock, 1998; House & Sears, 2002; Oakes, 1997). Despite tests of academic ability that often determine the assignment of educational offerings, ethnic minority students and low-income students are less likely to be placed in college preparatory or high-ability courses (College Entrance Examination Board, 1986; Education Trust, 2003; Hart & Jacobi, 1992; Lee & Ekstrom, 1987; Stone, 1998).

In a study by Stone (1998), analyses revealed a strong association between socioeconomic background and placement in algebra for 6,000 eighth-graders in one large urban school district. In examining the records of all students who scored in the upper quartile on a nationally normed mathematics test, Stone found that high-socioeconomic students were three times more likely to be placed in algebra than low-socioeconomic students. Low-income students were accessing higher-level academics in dismal proportions even though they had achieved the standards set for admissions into rigorous academics.

As you read the cases that follow, place yourself in the role of agent of social change and recognize discrimination. As you determine how best to solve the ethical dilemmas of each case, make a conscious effort to hone your own skills, strengths and strategies to advantage all students who are fortunate to have you for their school counselor.

Ethical Standards Addressed in This Chapter

Professionalism means knowing your professional associations' codes and adhering to them. Those ethical standards from ASCA that are most germane include the following:

- Each person has the right to receive the information and support needed to move toward self-direction and self-development and affirmation within one's group identities, with special care being given to students who have historically not received adequate educational services: students of color, low socio-economic students, students with disabilities and students with nondominant language backgrounds. (Preamble)
- Each person has the right to understand the full magnitude and meaning of his/her educational choices and how those choices will affect future opportunities. (Preamble)
- The professional school counselor advocates for counseling plans supporting students' right to choose from the wide array of options when they leave secondary education. Such plans will be regularly reviewed to update students regarding critical information they need to make informed decisions. (A.3.b)
- The professional school counselor assesses the effectiveness of his/her program in having an impact on students' academic, career and personal/social development through accountability measures especially examining efforts to close achievement, opportunity and attainment gaps. (A.9.g)
- The professional school counselor advocates for equal access to technology for all students, especially those historically underserved. (A.10.b)
- The professional school counselor provides professional personnel with accurate, objective, concise and meaningful data necessary to adequately evaluate, counsel and assist the student. (C.2.b)
- The professional school counselor extends his/her influence and opportunity to deliver a comprehensive school counseling program to all students by collaborating with community resources for student success. (D.2.b)
- The professional school counselor possesses knowledge and understanding about how oppression, racism, discrimination and stereotyping affects her/him personally and professionally. (E.2.c)

The full text of American Counseling Association ethical codes and ASCA ethical codes can be found at these Web sites: ACA at http://www.counseling.org and ASCA at www.schoolcounselor.org.

Getting Started: What Would You Do?

The following cases are answered for you at the end of this chapter by practicing school counselors. Before you read their responses, formulate in your own mind how you would approach these ethical dilemmas.

PLACEMENT IN EXCEPTIONAL STUDENT EDUCATION

You are a new counselor in an urban school that has many challenges: 98 percent of the students are on free/reduced lunch, 78 percent of the students are from single-parent homes, 54 percent are students of color, 29 percent are English Language Learners, and 39 percent of the students are in Exceptional Student Education. Your predecessor's practice was to refer every student who had any academic problems for ESE placement testing. Teachers and administrators are entrenched in the practice of seeking ESE as a first line of intervention for students who are struggling academically, and any student who is in danger of failing is placed on the priority list for testing. The district requires two solid, meaningful, sustained interventions before testing for ESE placement can be considered.

In your review of the past interventions, you are shocked at what the Child Study Team accepted as a "solid, meaningful, sustained" intervention: such actions as "moved the student's desk"; "explained the math concepts to the student"; and "spoke to the student's mother." In checking with the district ESE department, you learn your school has a disproportionate number of students in ESE and you are four times more likely to test minorities for ESE than the district average. Is there an ethical dilemma in this school's practice? If so, how would you address this dilemma?

PARENTS VERSUS STUDENTS' ASPIRATIONS

Xing Le is a 16-year-old junior who has been a dedicated student throughout high school. She has built a resume that will easily get her into any state university and you will encourage her to seek scholarships and support for schools that demand much of her, as this is the environment in which Xing Le appears to thrive. In your first of many classroom guidance lessons with your juniors about preparing for the future, you are listing college admissions tasks they need to complete during the year. You

THE ETHICS OF ADVOCACY

notice that Xing Le keeps her eyes averted and appears withdrawn and sad throughout the lesson. Xing Le, usually so eager to learn all that is being presented to her, drifts off into another place during your talk. You are disturbed; something is not right.

You invite Xing Le to your office to talk and over the next few days during the course of three conversations you piece together her worries. Her parents are not allowing Xing Le to pursue higher education. She explains that they need her to take over the family's small business that is conducted on the first floor of the building where they live. Xing Le says she will not abandon the needs of her family and that after graduation she will obey her parents' wishes and work full time so her father and mother can work fewer hours. She is adamant that her place is to care for a family that has always cared for her, even though she admits that she would love to go to college. You want so much to see Xing Le have a chance through education and to have an easier life than the one you know lies ahead of her. What can you do?

Working Through Case Studies

EDUCATING VERSUS DIRECTING

You are a high school counselor in an urban school with a diverse student population. One of your seniors comes to you and requests your help with her application to Harvard. This senior has an 86.6 average, is on the yearbook staff, has spent two years on the track team, and is enrolled in four Advanced Placement classes. Kimberly says, "I know Harvard may not be a sure thing, but I have to try." Your frustration rises as once again you are forced to look a student in the eye and explain that it is the practice and policy of the school's administration that only the top five students in each graduating class may apply to an Ivy League school. How do your profession's ethical codes support you to advocate for a change of policy?

Points to Consider

The New York Times article, "Amid Policy Confusion, Senior Is Allowed to Apply to Harvard" (Herszenhorn, 2004) describes the all-too-real case of Kimberly Cummins, a senior in a Brooklyn, N.Y., public high school. Kimberly, ranked 11 out of 400 seniors in her class, had a solid academic and extracurricular activity record. Kimberly sought help for her Harvard application only to be told she could not apply, as the officials of her high school allowed only the top five students to seek an Ivy League education. Shocked, Kimberly's older sister rallied her fellow NYU law school students and together they raised the issue with school and government officials and advocacy groups. Kimberly was allowed to apply – but what about the other "Kimberlys" who have had their dreams deferred with no savvy advocates to help them?

The just-retired principal of Kimberly's school said that it is school officials' obligation to discourage students from applying to colleges out of their reach. This is the "gatekeeper" behavior often pinned on school counselors, sometimes rightly so. In many instances, however, it is the perception of the listener and not the reality of the counselor's spoken words. This is a warning to us to be vigilant about conveying the message of hope to all our students.

After Dr. Condoleezza Rice was appointed U.S. Secretary of State on Nov. 16, 2004, we learned from her biographer that her school counselor told her that she was not college material. In today's schools, this counselor would be the exception, not the rule; our profession bristles at the idea of shifting and sorting students, relegating some to narrow options. Measurable success resulting from these efforts can be documented by an increased number of students completing school with the academic preparation, the career awareness, and the personal and social growth essential to choose from a wide range of substantial postsecondary options, including college (Education Trust, 2003).

This *New York Times* article came just a few months after the ASCA membership overwhelmingly declared at the June 2004 delegate assembly that it is our ethical imperative to provide all students with equity of service. The delegates revised the ethical standards to add equity and emphasize that school counselors will survey the school landscape for practices and policies that adversely stratify students' opportunities and we will responsibly tackle those policies to make changes to benefit students. School counselors must call attention to situations in schools that are defeating or frustrating students, thereby hindering their success (Dahir & Stone, 2004).

Self-awareness, autonomy and independence are watchwords for school counselors who value their role in helping students move toward becoming functioning, self-directed adults (Lapan, 2001). School counselors work with students to help them see the potential of their lives and gently push them toward being informed, solid decision makers. It is infinitely easier to mete out advice and to just "tell" students what they need to do in personal, social, career and academic issues. However, our professional ethics tell us to eschew the easy way and to help students make informed choices while being careful to promote their dreams (ASCA, 2004).

Dreams without preparation are hollow. Helping students realize their dreams is a critical and essential component of the work of school counselors (Dahir, 2001). School counselors at all levels, behaving as advocates, systemic change agents, and career and academic advisers, help students dream from the time they are in elementary school and assist them in understanding what they need to do in school to fulfill their dreams. When students discover their passion and see the connection between dreams and education, it serves to motivate them for higher grades, better attendance, and a stronger commitment to their education (Schwallie-Giddis, Maat, & Park, 2003).

Basic to self-direction and autonomy is students' right to understand the full weight and meaning of their decisions, as well as the interrelatedness between what they do in school and their future economic opportunities. Moreover, students have the right to be supported when choosing a program of study, and to have the safety nets to be able to fulfill their dreams (Maddy-Bernstein, 2000). Providing educational and career planning from elementary school to graduation will present students with quality postsecondary opportunities and help close the information gap (Feller & Davies, 2003). Productive adults come to self-awareness and self-understanding not by walking smooth roads but by trial and error (Mitchell, Levin & Krumboltz, 1999). Perhaps Kimberly will suffer the disappointment of not being accepted to Harvard. A bigger travesty would occur if she decided not to risk the possibility of rejection; it would be unthinkable if school officials, who are in the business of promoting student's self-direction and autonomy, told her she must always take the road of least resistance.

EQUITY OF SERVICES

You love being a school counselor, especially for a select group of students that you describe as very bright, engaging and accomplished. It is this group of students that receive most of your time and attention. You believe these students have tremendous potential and are destined to make a considerable contribution to society. Further, you believe that with your limited time, it is in the best interest of society to give most of your time and attention to the students that you consider to be the future of America. For this select group you seek optimum schedules with the best teachers and frequent academic advising sessions. Because of your efforts these students have all the information they need to choose from a wide array of postsecondary education opportunities. Is your behavior ethical?

Points to Consider

As school counselors we are offended by the blatant prejudicial behavior described in the above scenario. Deliberate selective service in school counseling is a clear case of unethical behavior; but what about unintentional selective service? School counselors are so outnumbered that there are certain students to whom we give more attention than others and many students we rarely or never see. We all must engage in the struggle to reach as many students as we can, not just the top five percent or most at-risk five percent of our student population, but all students. The struggle is not an easy one, but ethical behavior requires us to grapple with equitable service delivery and be unwilling to ignore the other 90 percent of our students.

School counselors have over the years spent an inordinate amount of energy and time working for change, support or success for a small fraction of the students for whom they are responsible. This work is important, but has not had sufficient positive impact for the many students whose futures are left to chance without strong advocates or savvy guardians. No Child Left Behind (2001) calls for school counselors to accept the responsibility to advocate for every student to experience success (Stone & Dahir, 2004). This effort to transform our practice for the purpose of reaching our total student body has been the focus of work by the National Office for School Counselor Advocacy (College Board, 2004), The Education Trust's Transforming School Counseling Initiative (1997), and ASCA's National Model (2003) and National Standards (Campbell & Dahir, 1997). These organizations have brought us guidance with strategies and techniques to deliver programs aimed at caring for all students.

There are so many unalterable factors in students' lives that cause them hurt and harm. School counselors cannot change the parents for those who don't have security and comfort, or give them a loving home or establish for them optimal conditions for their time away from school. Although school counselors cannot give to every child what they would seek for their own children, they can offer every child optimum opportunities in school. School counselors can fervently influence the school environment so that students have equitable, ethical school counseling programs that seek through education to better students' circumstances and to ensure development of skills and knowledge needed for them to become productive citizens.

Optimum learning is the gift school counselors can give students, the best gift we can give them in the thirty-five hours a week we have them. As unwilling as we are as a profession to engage in preferential treatment for just a select few of our students as described above, let us as a profession become just as intolerant of programs that fall short for some students (Stone & Martin, 2004).

In a Position to Know: School Counselors Speak

The cases presented at the beginning of the chapter are revisited here and answered by practicing school counselors. Compare their answers with your own approach.

PLACEMENT IN EXCEPTIONAL STUDENT EDUCATION

You are a new counselor in an urban school that has many challenges: 98 percent of the students are on free/reduced lunch, 78 percent of the students are from single-parent homes, 54 percent are students of color, 29 percent are English Language Learners, and 39 percent of the students are in exceptional student education. Your predecessor's practice was to refer every student who had any academic problems for ESE placement testing. Teachers and administrators are entrenched in the practice of seeking ESE as a first line of intervention for students who are struggling academically, and any student who is in danger of failing is placed on the priority list for testing. The district requires two solid, meaningful, sustained interventions before testing for ESE placement can be considered.

   In your review of the past interventions, you are shocked at what the Child Study Team accepted as a "solid, meaningful, sustained" intervention: such actions as "moved the student's desk"; "explained the math concepts to the student"; and "spoke to the student's mother." In checking with the district ESE department, you learn your school has a disproportionate number of students in ESE and you are four times more likely to test minorities for ESE than the district average. Is there an ethical dilemma in this school's practice? If so, how would you address this dilemma?

Response From a School Counselor

When students are unable to make adequate progress, the professional school counselor endeavors to establish collaborative relationships with parents, students and teachers. Students present diversity and we cannot expect teachers to go it alone to provide all the answers. When they lose hope in their ability to reach a student, teachers may call out for help, which often starts with parents and teachers meeting to discuss a means of resolving a student's academic or behavioral problems. At times, for whatever reason, the student shows no improvement. Teachers may want to start testing immediately if they suspect a learning or behavioral disability. Unfortunately, special education testing can be a lengthy process that may or may not in the long term meet the needs of individual students. Those students who do become eligible for special education eventually receive remediation through the use of an Individual Education Plan, but as the testing referral process begins, there are no immediate solutions. We must begin the collaboration process so we do not set up for a loss of valuable learning time, or even worse, run the risk of a child's early years being ones of frustration and discouragement.

Accomplished school counselors seek to facilitate systemic changes that cultivate communication between students, parents, and school staff. For example, the school counselor can strategically institute equity, equality and fairness by coordinating a collaborative study of the child's needs, including significant understanding of the child's self-management skills. Counselees need help understanding how to set goals and little by little see growth in themselves. Parents and teachers provide a structured environment that meets the unique learning styles of the child. Working together we can realign resources on behalf of students.

Since 1998, I have implemented this kind of collaborative academic intervention team approach. In 2002, with the support of my principal, we named the student support group CARE, or Considering Available

Resources for Everyone. CARE meetings facilitate the academic goal setting and prescriptive action plans outlining responsibility for all team players, which may or may not include a referral to Exceptional Student Education.

Prior to the CARE meeting, I look at education records, talk with teachers and parents, and usually meet with the student. Then I establish a CARE team meeting date for the parents, perhaps the student, myself, the teacher of the student, and any other person who has significant input or concern regarding the student's academic or behavioral needs. We meet at a time that is convenient for everyone interested in participation. CARE meetings last about 30 minutes to an hour.

The CARE team utilizes data to determine a plan of action. Team members look at the student's records and current daily work, discuss teacher and family concerns, share success stories, and consider a child's self-management ability level. We discuss student academic strengths and weaknesses, interventions attempted, and learning gains or progress over time. Often we discuss student learning styles, personalities, extracurricular interests and career goals. Then we develop, document and implement the plan. We establish a monitoring routine and we look for immediate results. After a designated time, the team reevaluates, considers ways to fine-tune the action plan, and considers alternatives.

I have found this team approach to be an effective means of providing immediate interventions for low-performing students long before we consider Exceptional Student Education referrals. But there are other benefits as well.

As a result of our CARE team's proactive collaboration with teachers, parents and students, my school's ESE screening outcomes have shown improvement. Our CARE meetings began during the 2002-2003 school year, but it was very much a transitional year and as might be expected, change was difficult. Yet by the end of the 2003-2004 school year we saw significant impact on ESE screenings. The percentage of screenings that resulted in Handicapped Eligible has increased and the percentage of Handicapped Ineligible has decreased (see chart).

We have seen other benefits as well. When a child's case is referred to ESE because of continued poor progress, we have been able to demonstrate to the ESE Child Study Team that our CARE team has made every effort to exhaust all available resources to maximize student learning for all stu-

SUMMARY OF CST SCREENINGS

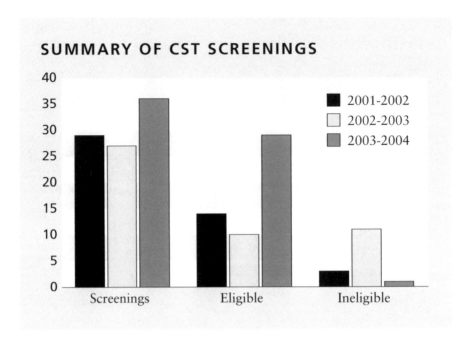

dents. We continue to achieve an equitable balance of minority and non-minority children as handicapped eligible. For 2003-2004 our data indicates 18 children of European descent and 16 ethnic minority children (black, Hispanic, mixed) received ESE services either through the specific learning disabilities or emotionally handicapped programs. That's an indication of fair balance when you consider our population is made up of approximately 39 percent white and 61 percent nonwhite.

Finally, the ESE admissions team depends on school personnel to adequately utilize ESE resources. For each referral, the teacher, parents, student, ESE teachers, admissions personnel, school psychologists and social workers as well as administrators invest time and materials necessary to screen ESE candidates. Professional school counselors respecet these resources and use them prudently.

I continue to evaluate ways to collaborate with staff, students and parents to monitor student progress on a regular basis. The CARE team provides a systematic routine for managing purposeful and attainable improvement for all low-performing students in our school.

Claire Wayne, elementary counselor in Jacksonville, Fla.

PARENTS VERSUS STUDENT'S ASPIRATIONS

Xing Le is a 16-year-old junior who has been a dedicated student throughout high school. She has built a resume that will easily get her into any state university and you will encourage her to seek scholarships and support for schools that demand much of her, as this is the environment in which Xing Le appears to thrive. In your first of many classroom guidance lessons with your juniors about preparing for the future, you are listing college admissions tasks they need to complete during the year. You notice that Xing Le keeps her eyes averted and appears withdrawn and sad throughout the lesson. Xing Le, usually so eager to learn all that is being presented to her, drifts off into another place during your talk. You are disturbed; something is not right.

You invite her to your office to talk and over the next few days during the course of three conversations you piece together her worries. Her parents are not allowing Xing Le to pursue higher education. She explains that they need her to take over the family's small business that is conducted on the first floor of the building where they live. Xing Le says she will not abandon the needs of her family and that after graduation she will obey her parents' wishes and work full time so her father and mother can work fewer hours. She is adamant that her place is to care for a family that has always cared for her, even though she admits that she would love to go to college. You want so much to see Xing Le have a chance through education and to have an easier life than the one you know lies ahead of her. What can you do?

Response from a School Counselor

Within the atmosphere of the large urban high school with its diverse student population, counselors meet many challenges. In addition to academic matters, there are cultural and social issues that one anticipates in counseling work, and there are unexpected and surprising situations that arise as well. These less-than-ordinary cases can challenge our ready responses and demand thoughtful, original solutions. Here, too, outside the boundaries within which we usually work, we are confronted with perhaps more ethical concerns.

Xing Le's story seems to fit this unusual profile. She sits there in the classroom without demonstrating the typical interest or enthusiasm for college that one would expect in a student of her ability. Some students declare confidently that going to college is not in their immediate plans. Xing Le has presented us with a more unexpected dilemma: She will sacrifice her education for her family. As school counselors we naturally ask, doesn't Xing Le deserve the chance to make a better life for herself, and possibly her family, if she were to attend college? From our perspective, if we do nothing, we see her future as limited. Aren't we obligated to help her recognize her broader options within the expectations of her family? It is a delicate matter demanding that we balance cultural sensitivity and ethical responsibility.

The counselor's ethical responsibility is to advocate for Xing Le by allowing her to make an informed choice about her future. The ethical standards for school counselors state that the student has the right to understand the full magnitude and meaning of educational choices and how those choices will affect future opportunities (ASCA, 2004).

To permit Xing Le simply to accept her fate would be wrong. That would amount to giving up on her without any concern for her own development and self-direction. The counselor's role is critical: An idea or suggestion, a plan or question can alter a young person's vision of the future. In the case of Xing Le, the meetings the counselor holds with her must accomplish several things. The counselor must affirm her worth as a student who would be valued by a college, acknowledge her culture and duty to her parents and encourage her to be open to other possibilities that maximize her potential. The meetings cannot push her away through lack of understanding or coercion on the counselor's part.

An attempt would be made to invite Xing Le's parents to join us for an informational meeting, but Xing Le's insistence against that idea – perhaps because of language barriers – takes that step out of the process. If parents don't participate, the counselor must beware of exerting too much pressure on Xing Le. The counselor's responsibility is to constantly remind her that the values and beliefs of her parents are not in question, but that her own nascent college aspirations are also valuable and worth exploring.

My goal would be to assure Xing Le that there might be practical solutions that satisfy her parents' expectations as well as her own desire for an education. These solutions might involve choosing a part-time university program close to home, or perhaps weekend college classes or some online classes. Literally opening up college catalogs and reading about courses and designing an imaginary schedule of classes would be very appropriate. I might emphasize the need to start off slowly, devoting time to the family business with the hope that more classes could be taken later. The important point to emphasize for her is that by taking some college classes, she would not be forsaking her parent's wishes, nor would she be sacrificing her own.

Xing Le needs to see how the choices she makes in the present, to reject college or accept it in a limited way, will affect her in the very near future. Should she go to college as I have counseled, her future may be more successful. Who knows? Perhaps her parents will recognize that their daughter has profited from college, and they will be more supportive. Perhaps some deus ex machina will change the equation altogether, and Xing Le will be permitted to choose her path freely. The counselor helps to point the student down the road or helps draw the map. The rest is up to her.

To advocate on Xing Le's behalf means to defy knee-jerk responses. Helping her involves the counselor's dedication to advocate for and affirm Xing Le's right to an education, offered with compassion for her struggle and an application of ethical principles. All work toward one end: Xing Le makes her decision in the most informed and respected manner.

Robert Weiss, high school counselor at John F. Kennedy High School in New York City

Making Connections

1. Your school encourages students to take the AP exam if they are considered likely candidates for scoring a 3 or above on it. District administrators compare AP test results for schools, and it is widely understood that it is considered a black mark against you if you have too many students in your school scoring below a 3. Many high schools in the district including yours consider it best to covertly select students to take the AP exam and gingerly dissuade others from it. Are there any legal or ethical obligations involving this practice by your school district? With fellow professionals, discuss or debate the following positions:

- It is ethical to limit the students who can take the AP test so that the school can enhance its standing and test scores.
- Regardless of AP exam results, students always benefit by taking the AP exam.

- Other test scores such as the state test are likely to be positively impacted by students taking AP exams.
- If a student knows at the beginning of the school year he or she will be expected and supported to take the AP exam, with the hope that this will encourage the student to more actively prepare for the exam.
- Students will strengthen their resume and college applications by taking the exams.
- We should not be narrowing any opportunity that might possibly lead to scholarship dollars or college credit.

2. Discuss your beliefs about how an equitable and ethical school counseling program can serve all students. Describe the characteristics and behaviors of a systemic change agent. Discuss a time when you exhibited these characteristics.

3. Discuss ways that a school counselor who is committed to equity for all students might avoid spending too much time with students who are among the top five percent of the class and those who are in the lowest five percent of the class.

4. Review the American School Counselor Association's Ethical Standards for School Counselors (2004) and identify which ethical code that deals with equity may be difficult to attain and maintain. Discuss the code.

5. Consider the student population in your building. Are some students underserved in achieving an equitable education? What first step can you take to begin to remedy the situation?

Key Terms

Advocacy
Social justice
Social change agent
Equity and opportunity for all
  students

Equal access
Challenging the status quo
Entrenched inequities
Unalterable factors

References

American School Counselor Association. (2003). *The ASCA national model: A framework for school counseling programs.* Alexandria, VA: Author.

American School Counselor Association. (2004). *Ethical standards for school counselors*. Alexandria, VA: Author.

Campbell, C. A., & Dahir, C. A. (1997). *The national standards for school counseling programs*. Alexandria, VA: American School Counselor Association.

The College Board. (2004). *National Office for School Counselor Advocacy*. Retrieved January 30, 2005, from http://www.collegeboard.com/prof/counselors/nosca.html

College Entrance Examination Board. (1986). *Keeping the options open. Recommendations: Final report of the commission on precollege guidance and counseling*. New York: College Entrance Examination Board. (ERIC Document Reproduction Service No. ED275948).

Dahir, C. A. (2001). The national standards for school counseling programs: Development and implementation. *Professional School Counseling, 4*, 320-327.

Dahir, C. A., and Campbell, C. A. (1997). *Sharing the vision: The national standards*. Alexandria, VA: American School Counselor Association.

Dahir, C., and Stone, C. (2004). Leaving no school counselor behind. *VISTAS – Perspectives on counseling 2004*, 177-182. Greensboro, NC: CAPSpress.

The Education Trust. (1997, November). *Transforming school counseling: DeWitt Wallace-Reader's Digest Grant* [Request for grant proposal]. Washington, DC: Author.

The Education Trust. (2000). *Achievement in America*. Washington, DC: Author.

The Education Trust. (2003). *Education watch*. Washington, DC: Author.

Feller, R. W., & Davies, T. G. (2003). Contemporary issues changing the career planning context. In T. Harrington (Ed.), *Handbook of career planning for students with special needs* (pp. 345-374). Austin, TX: ProEd.

Hart, P. J., & Jacobi, M. (1992). *From gatekeeper to advocate: Transforming the role of the school counselor.* New York: College Entrance Examination Board.

Haycock, K. (1998). Good teaching matters: How well-qualified teachers can close the gap. *Thinking K-16, 3,* 1-2.

Herszenhorn, D. (2004, October 18). Amid policy confusion, senior is allowed to apply to Harvard. *The New York Times.* Retrieved December 5, 2004, from http://query.nytimes.com/gst/abstract.html?res= FA0A11FB3F5E0C758DDDA90994DC404482&incamp=archive:search

House, R., & Sears, S. (2002). Preparing school counselors to be leaders and advocates: A critical need in the new millennium. *Theory Into Practice, 41,* 154-162.

Kiselica, M., & Robinson, M. (2001). Bringing advocacy counseling to life: The history, issues, and human dramas of social justice work in counseling. *Journal of Counseling and Development, 79,* 387-397.

Lapan, R. T. (2001). Results-based comprehensive guidance and counseling programs: A framework for planning and evaluation. *Professional School Counseling, 4,* 289-299.

Lee, C. C., & Walz, G. R. (Eds.). (1998). *Social action: A mandate for counselors.* Alexandria, VA: American Counseling Association.

Lee, V. E., & Ekstrom, R. B. (1987). Student access to guidance counseling in high school. *American Educational Research Journal, 24,* 287-310.

Maddy-Bernstein, C. (2000). *Career development issues affecting secondary schools.* Columbus, OH: National Dissemination Center for Career and Technical Education.

Martin, P. (2004, July). *Our little red wagon.* Unpublished speech. Rhode Island School Counselor Conference.

Martin, P. J. (2002). Transforming school counseling: A national perspective. *Theory Into Practice, 41,* 148-153.

Mitchell, K., Levin, A., & Krumboltz, J. (1999). Planned happenstance: Constructing unexpected career opportunities. *Journal of Counseling and Development, 77*, 115-124.

No Child Left Behind Act of 2001, 20 U.S.C. § 6301 (2002).

Oakes, E. J. (1997). Detracking: The social construction of ability, cultural politics, and resistance to reform. *Teachers College Record, 98,* 482-510.

Schwallie-Giddis, P., Maat, M., & Park, M. (2003). Initiating leadership by introducing and implementing the ASCA national model. *Professional School Counseling, 6*(3),170-173.

Stone, C. (1997). Extending the reach of academic counseling in middle schools. *Principal Journal, 76,* 48-51.

Stone, C. (1998). Leveling the playing field: An urban school system examines access to mathematics curriculum. *Urban Review, 30*(4), 295-307.

Stone, C. (Speaker). (2001). *Legal and ethical issues in working with minors in schools* [Film]. Alexandria, VA: American School Counseling Association.

Stone, C., & Dahir, C. (2004). *School counselors and accountability: A MEASURE of student success.* Upper Saddle River, NJ: Merrill Prentice-Hall.

Stone, C., & Martin, P. (2004). School counselors using data driven decision making. *ASCA School Counselor, 41*(3), 10-17.

Stone, C., & Turba, R. (1999). School counselors using technology for advocacy. *The Journal of Technology in Counseling, 1,*1.

Conclusion

We are our ethical codes. We have professionalized ourselves by assigning core ethical characteristics that distinguish us from all other professions. Our special skills, competence and application of knowledge have guided the development of an ethical code, just as our code of ethics guides the acquisition of new knowledge. This symbiotic relationship requires continual vigilance if we are to stay informed and current.

We perform our school counseling role in an institution that both empowers and hinders our efforts to be legal and ethical. The personal, social and emotional aspects of education compound the legal complexities. I hope one of the primary objectives of this book was accomplished, namely to demystify some of these complexities that impact school counselors' daily work. If you found this book to be user-friendly and if it helped you gain a better understanding of the law and the practical application of your ethical codes, then another primary objective of the book was met.

Unlike public education systems in most countries, the system in the United States is decentralized, so that there are very few one-size-fits-all laws prevailing in every state and affecting every school counselor. Laws and legal precedents that govern school counselors are dependent on 50 different states, each with their own approach to the educational process. Federal legislation and Supreme Court decisions can give the bottom-line directive regarding some educational issues but there are really few legal imperatives that can be uniformly applied to all school counselors; we have more exceptions than rules established by the variation in philosophies, perspectives, school law and community standards.

This book does not propose to do the impossible: to exhaustively review the law for each state. Instead, we set forth general guiding principles of law that have been established by federal legislation and courts. The court cases presented here do not apply to all situations and certainly not to all states. Each case in the book is intentionally followed not by answers, but by "Points to Consider." This book does not suggest hard-and-fast rules but a range of less-than-definitive responses for your contemplation and application to the context of your own particular school.

Thus, this book is not the last word. School counselors must always be consumers of their specific state statutes and school board rules. It cannot be overemphasized that you should always consult with local authorities and seek supervision from local professionals before drawing any conclusions based on what is stated here.

America is a litigious society. Almost every facet of schooling, from slogans written on a T-shirt to a student's right to access an appropriate education, has been the subject of judicial discourse. We have attempted here to help school counselors learn about some of the judicial debates that inform their practice. By raising our awareness, we can practice prevention and become legally literate.

More importantly, if we raise our awareness of the law we may also prevent the paralysis that can come from fear and anxiety about slipping up and becoming the subject of a lawsuit. This book was written to also dispel the myth that we should view the law with fear and trepidation. Yes, we are a litigious society but a lawsuit is a rare occurrence for a school counselor, especially those who make an honest attempt to act legally and ethically. The truth is that school counselors have a better chance of winning the lottery than of becoming the subject of a lawsuit if they practice as reasonably competent professionals. School counselors who are empowered to identify policies, practices or sources of potential legal and ethical conflict are better equipped to serve students and to reduce their own chances of becoming the center of a stressful lawsuit.

I hope that you will not put this book aside after reading it, but actively discuss and debate the cases and the issues presented with your colleagues or classmates. Remember, in the legal and ethical arena of our human services profession, there is rarely a single right answer to the dilemmas we face as school counselors.

Public schools have become increasingly important as the one institution in our country that is supposed to level the playing field for all Americans. Throughout this book the ethics of advocacy have been a primary focus. The extraordinary challenges, rewards and obligations of being an ethical educator require that we work to provide each student with an education that will allow him or her to participate in the global economy. Such a tremendous imperative carries additional legal and ethical obligations, and I hope this book has helped us to understand that even though we cannot do everything, we have to try to do everything we possibly can. It is my sincere hope that this book empowered you.

Key Terms

abortion termination of a pregnancy and expulsion of an embryo or fetus that is incapable of surviving.

addressing a known danger a situation requiring a public officer or employee to act in a particular way based on what the danger is.

adversely stratified education opportunities education opportunities that are unfavorably arranged in a school, especially unequal opportunities for historically disadvantaged students such as minority and low income students.

advocacy intervening on behalf of a particular group of people.

age of consent the age minors can legally engage in sexual activity; age of consent varies from state to state.

anonymous reporting reporting of a situation without revealing the identity of the reporter; it is an effort to protect the identity of informants, and it is a mechanism to provide for anonymous informants.

autonomy promoting students' ability to choose their own direction.

beneficence promoting good for others. Ideally, counseling contributes to the growth and development of the student.

breach of trust a betrayal of a person's trust; breach of a student's confidence.

breach violation of the duty owed, such as confidentiality. Whether or not a breach occurred is based on reasonableness and the standard of care.

bullying verbal or physical aggression demonstrated in words, actions, or social exclusion intended to specifically hurt or harm another; the most common form of school violence.

case law laws pronounced by the courts.

case notes sole-possession records that act as a memory aid or professional opinion or observation for the creator. They are to be kept separate from education records, but may become education records when they are 1) shared with others in verbal or written form, 2) include information other than professional opinion or personal observations and/or 3) are made accessible to others.

causal connection connection between the school counselor's breach of duty and the injury that the student suffered.

challenging the status quo stimulating change in conditions that are already established or currently in existence.

child abuse physical or psychological mistreatment of a child by his or her parents, guardians, or other adults.

child neglect lack of care that risks or causes harm to a child, including lack of food, clothing, supervision, or medical attention.

Child Protective Services a constituted authority and agency in the state providing protection from harm to children and providing services to meet the needs of the child and family.

chronological level the level at which a student has reached based on actual age.

civil wrong a wrong against another person that causes physical, emotional, or monetary damage and for which the plaintiffs can seek compensation.

civil law the set of rules governing relations between persons.

classroom guidance leading, advising, and informing students on appropriate topics in a classroom setting.

clear imminent danger a known or perceived danger to a student or others that has a high risk danger of resulting in damage, injury, and/or death if an action is not taken. School counselors have an ethical obligation to breach confidentiality and inform parents and administrators if a student indicates a clear imminent danger to himself/herself or others.

common law judge-made law based on legal precedents developed over hundreds of years; also referred to as the "body of general rules prescribing social conduct" and "unwritten" law.

community standards written and unwritten standards in which the community and those who work in it must behave consistently and ethically within its parameters, while working to change those standards that are detrimental to its members.

confidentiality in group counseling confidentiality cannot be guaranteed in a group; counselors use extraordinary care when putting young people together in groups where highly sensitive and personal materials may be disclosed.

consequences a result that occurs from an action or condition.

constitutional law consists of two major categories: criminal law and civil law.

corporal punishment deliberate infliction of pain intended as a disciplinary action or punishment; used in judicial, domestic and/or education settings.

counselors' values counselors must not impose values on students and must remain objective or avoid value-laden issues.

Court of Appeals a court having jurisdiction to review the actions of an inferior court (such as trial court) but not having the power to hear a legal action initially.

court order an order that requires a person to do a specified act, such as producing material or appearing in court. The government has the right to obtain a person's information by court order.

criminal law a crime against society; criminal law can be categorized as either a felony or a misdemeanor.

custodial parent a term used for the parent having primary physical custody of a child.

dangerous school climate atmosphere of a school that is unsafe or unwelcoming for one or more students; atmosphere of harassment, violence, crime, and/or bullying.

defamation injuring a person's character or reputation by false or malicious statements.

defendant the person against whom a legal action is brought. School counselors become defendants in cases such as defamation, qualified privilege, abortion, academic advising, failure to report child abuse, or unauthorized disclosure of information.

deliberate indifference intentional unresponsiveness or lack of concern.

deposition testimony under oath, especially a statement by a witness that is written down or recorded for use in court at a later date.

developmental level the level at which a student has reached based on maturity, behavior, and competency. Developmental levels cannot be attached neatly to chronological age.

developmentally delayed maturity, behavior, and competency level that is below that person's chronological level.

directory information basic public information about a student such as name, address, telephone number, date and place of birth, etc.

dogmatic solution a black-and-white answer to a problem, without examining multiple perspectives in the context of a situation.

domestic violence violence toward or physical abuse of one's spouse or domestic partner.

dual relationship a relationship where professional distance is violated and impairs a school counselor's objectivity and increases the risk of harm to the student (e.g., counseling one's family members, close friends, or associates).

duces tecum a Latin term meaning "you shall bring with you;" a court order issued by a clerk of court, justice of the peace, notary public, or lawyer, usually signed by a lawyer; a lawyer signed subpoena.

due process hearing procedures or steps that the school district and parents must take to settle disagreement. FERPA requires that parents be given due process in order to protest when they disagree on the accuracy of education records.

duty to warn obligation to notify members involved in a potential harmful or dangerous situation; school counselors have a duty to warn parents if clear and imminent danger is perceived from a student.

educational malpractice a comparison between the acceptable standard of care for the school counseling profession and the specific act or conduct claimed to be malpractice.

emotional harm harm to a person's ability to think, reason, or have feelings, such as cruel acts or statements, intimidation, rejection, and indifference.

entrenched inequities established injustice or unfairness.

equal access access to rights, privileges, opportunities, and social institutions by all people or groups, especially those who have historically been disadvantaged such as minority and low income individuals.

Equal Access Act originally proposed to ensure that student religious clubs could meet in public schools; however, court rulings have extended its application to a broad array of student groups; requires schools that receive federal funds to provide GLBT clubs the same access to school facilities as other student groups.

equity and opportunity for all students equal access to rights, privileges, opportunities, and social institutions by all students or groups, especially those who have historically been disadvantaged such as minority and low income students.

ethical standards guidelines developed by ASCA, used to clarify the ethical responsibilities of its members to students, parents, colleagues, the profession, the community, and to themselves.

ethics agreed upon values, norms, customs, and mores that have withstood the test of time; provide a general framework for professional conduct.

expert witness a person called to testify because he or she has a recognized competence in an area.

falsifying student records fraudulently altering a student's education record with or without a reasonable cause or authorization.

Family Education Rights and Privacy Act (FERPA) federal legislation that governs education records and dictates how all written information regarding a student will be handled and disseminated for the protection of the student and her or his family.

Family Policy Compliance Office administers the Family Education Rights and Privacy Act.

federal court litigates cases involving citizens of several states and cases involving federal statutes.

federal statutes laws issued by the federal government.

Gay, Lesbian, & Straight Education Network a national network of parents, students, teachers and others that wish to put an end to discrimination based on sexual orientation and gender identity/expression in K-12 schools.

Gay-Straight Alliance Club a student club for the support of gay, lesbian, bisexual, and transgender youth and their straight friends.

governmental immunity protection from civil or tort liability while engaged in school functions of a governmental nature.

group counseling sessions counseling multiple members at the same time based on mutual needs and goals of the members; counselors avoid putting young people together in groups where highly sensitive and personal materials may be disclosed.

guardian ad litem a guardian appointed by a court to represent a minor unable to represent himself or herself.

heterosexism a belief or argument that male-female sexuality is the only natural or moral mode of sexual behavior.

homophobia fear of homosexuality or homosexual individuals.

homosexuality a sexual orientation characterized by attraction, romantic love, and sexual desire for members of the same sex or gender identity.

hostile environment involves *student-on-student sexual harassment,* in which a student feels the environment is not a safe place.

identifiability of the victim in sexual harassment cases, school counselors are obligated to report the harassment, but the identity of the victim does not have to be revealed.

immune from liability incapable of being held legally responsible; school counselors are immune from liability for parents or guardians who have been erroneously reported to Child Protective Services.

in loco parentis Latin term for "in place of parent" in which the person or entity acts as a parent with respect to the care, supervision, and discipline of a child. School counselors act *in loco parentis* with minors in a school setting.

Individual with Disabilities Education Act federal legislation for Exceptional Student Education (ESE) administered by the Office of Special Education, which spells out parents' and students' rights with regards to ESE records.

informed consent counselee chooses to enter a counseling relationship after given direct information about the purposes, goals, techniques, rules of procedure, and limits of confidentiality in which he or she may receive counseling.

injury suffered harm an individual suffered such as injury, lost scholarship, or death.

institutional standards written and unwritten standards in which members of that institution must behave consistently and ethically within its parameters, while working to change those standards that are detrimental to its members.

intervening, superseding cause breaks the line of causation from the wrongful act to the injury suffered and does not render liability.

judicial bypass a process by which minors can get state approval to have an abortion without parental consent or notification in states requiring parental involvement.

justice providing equal treatment to all people regardless of age, sex, race, ethnicity, disability, socioeconomic status, cultural background, religion, or sexual orientation.

Lambda Legal a nongovernmental organization devoted to promoting the legal rights of gays, lesbians, bisexuals, transgender, and people with HIV or AIDS, through impact litigation, education, and public policy work.

laws the minimum standards that society will tolerate; used to codify a value or set of values. Laws and their interpretations differ from one geographic location to another.

legal status of minors minors, generally under age 18, are legally unable to make decisions on their own behalf.

legitimate educational interest access of an education record for the purpose of performing appropriate tasks within job description; performing a task related to a student's education; performing a task related to discipline; or providing a service or benefit related to the student or to the student's family such as counseling, health care, or job placement.

liability legal responsibility; liability in a sexual harassment case may be imposed if harassment is so severe, pervasive, and objectively offensive that is deprives a student of an equal educational opportunity.

loyalty staying connected with students and being available to them to the extent possible.

maintaining student records keeping, organizing, and updating student education records throughout years of schooling.

malicious, willful and intentional torts occurs when one acts in a determined way to harm another individual such as assault, battery, wrongful death, fraud, and theft.

malpractice improper or unethical conduct by a professional that results in injury, damage, or loss.

mandated reporter a person who is required by law to report a situation or reasonable suspicion; school counselors are mandated in all states to report suspected child abuse to proper authorities under penalty of criminal charges.

mediation an attempt to bring about a peaceful settlement or compromise between disputants through the objective intervention of a neutral party.

ministerial a duty that is plainly laid out and requires no discretion.

moral principles the principles of right and wrong that are accepted by an individual or a social group.

negligence civil liability if a school counselor is found to owe a duty to another person, breaches that duty by not living up to expected standards, and as a result of the breach of duty causes damages to another person.

noncustodial parent term used for the parent that has physical custody of a child for a lesser amount of time than the custodial parent. Typically the child does not reside with the noncustodial parent except when that parent exercises his or her visitation rights.

nonmaleficence avoiding doing harm, which includes refraining from actions that risk hurting students.

Office for Civil Rights the arm of the federal government that requires compliance with anti-discrimination policy and practice for school districts.

opacity of law laws are often defined case by case and interpreted in different ways; school counselors often must practice in the absence of clear-cut guidelines.

parental permission written consent from a parent or guardian for a student to participate in services such as small group counseling.

Parents, Family, and Friends of Lesbians and Gays promotes the health and well-being of gay, lesbian, bisexual, and transgendered persons and their families and friends.

peer-on-peer aggression aggression between peers that includes teasing, harassment, verbal aggression, and bullying.

personal bias a subjective preference or behavior based on personal values and beliefs.

physical aggression hostile or abusive behavior toward another person or group.

physical and emotional safety an atmosphere or condition free from physical or emotional harm.

plaintiff one who initiates a lawsuit; the party bringing the suit.

Planned Parenthood health service organization that provides reproductive health care and sexual health information to men, women, and teens.

potential courses of action possible strategies or procedures.

precedents a court decision that serves as a rule of guide or direction on how to decide future cases with similar facts or legal questions.

prevailing community standards written and unwritten standards in which the community and those who work in it must behave consistently and ethically within its parameters, while working to change those standards that are detrimental to its members.

privacy rights rights given to the parents of a minor student in which the parents make critical decisions regarding disclosure of personal information.

privileged communication a term by which school counselors can deny courts their testimony and refuse to disclose confidential communications made for the purpose of counseling a client; decided by state statutes whether or not school counselors are granted privileged communication or privileged communications with exceptions.

privity having an interest in a transaction, contract, or legal action to which one is not a party, but where the interest arises out of a relationship to one of the parties of the legal action.

process of discovery process in which the attorneys may require an oral or written deposition; written interrogatories requiring written responses to questions; certain documents or materials; a request to submit a listing of facts that are not in dispute; and/or physical or mental examination of one of the parties of the lawsuit.

professional communication choosing words judiciously and in an effort to maintain optimal communication with those who have the "need to know."

professional distance the appropriate familiarity and closeness that a school counselor engages in with students and their family members.

professionalism internal motivation to perform at the level of practice that represents the ideals of the profession. For school counselors, professionalism is used to maintain a counselor's standing with his or her peers, teachers, staff members, administrators, parents, and students and adhering to local, state, and federal laws, school board policy, ethical standards, and community standards.

qualified privilege the right to say things about students that are not flattering but necessary to fulfill a school counselor's duty in the context of the situation at hand.

quid pro quo harassment involves *teacher-on-student sexual harassment*, in which a teacher gives a better grade or a favor in exchange for a sexual act.

real threat a danger that can be validated with evidence of a written threat, the presence of a weapon or other indicators that point to serious intent to harm.

reasonableness person acted within the reasonable standard of care and took necessary precautions; person-specific and depends on an individual's background, education, profession, culture, nationality, and experiences.

reasonable suspicion having a notion about a certain situation or person. School counselors who merely have a reasonable suspicion that a child is being abused or neglected are mandated to report the situation to officials.

reparative therapy psychotherapy aimed at eliminating homosexual desires; also known as conversion therapy.

safe haven law a law that allows birth mothers to leave their newborns at hospitals, fire stations, or police stations anonymously, mostly with no questions or legal repercussions.

The Safe Schools Coalition partnership of organizations that seek to promote tolerance in schools by providing resources for students, parents, and schools.

school board policy a guideline or procedure developed by the school board relating to an issue or situation in schools that all schools in that district must follow.

school violence encompasses a wide range of violent activities including physical fights, threats, destruction, robbery, harassment, dating violence, molestation, rape, bullying, hostile or threatening remarks, assault with or without weapons, and gang violence.

screening members assessing the suitability of students for their appropriateness and commitment to participate in small groups and formulating individual goals with each student. A preferred method of screening is an individual interview.

self-direction direction that is guided by oneself; autonomous action.

separation of power each division of government functions freely within the area of its responsibility.

sexual harassment conduct that is sexual in nature or related to the gender of the person; the behavior occurs in an unequal relationship where one person has more power over another; and the behavior is unsolicited or unwelcome.

sexual harassment policy a procedure that protects all students from sexual harassment; school counselors are required by law to report sexual harassment to school officials.

sexual orientation the focus of a person's desires, fantasies, and feelings; the gender(s) that one is primarily oriented towards.

sexually active students students who are intimate in a sexual way such as touching someone's genitals, oral sex, or intercourse.

slander oral defamation; the speaking of false and malicious words that injure another person's reputation, business, or property rights.

social change agent a representative in a position to affect and bring about change in society regarding unequal procedures, policies, and regulations.

social justice promotion of equity for all people and groups in society; working from a social justice mindset requires school counselors to give special care to those who historically have not received adequate educational opportunities.

special relation is a legal relationship such as in loco parentis.

standard of care what the reasonably competent professional would do. School counselors behaving within the standard of care follow laws, ethical standards and school board policies; courts also consider expert witnesses, length of career and professional development to show that a school counselor behaved within the standard of care.

state court from highest to lowest: a system that includes the court of last resort such as state supreme courts; intermediate appellate courts; courts of general jurisdiction; and courts of limited jurisdiction or small claims courts. State courts decide most cases for public school districts.

state legislature provides the basis for public school law and the courts, through litigation, interpret the laws; gives school boards authority to create their own rules and regulations.

state statutes laws issued by the state.

statutory obligation an obligation based on a statute or law passed by a unit of federal, state, or local governments.

statutory rape adults, usually 18 years or older, who have a sexual relationship with a minor of a certain age; the age of both the victim and the perpetrator are variable depending on the state.

STEPS Solutions To Ethical Problems in Schools; a nine step model adapted from the seven-step, ACA Ethical Decision Making Model that addresses the emotional influence of a problem and considers chronological and developmental appropriateness as well as parental rights.

student-on-student sexual harassment one student is harassed by another student and doesn't feel safe in that environment, also known as *hostile environment*.

subpoena a Latin term meaning "under penalty"; a court order requiring the recipient to perform a specified act such as appearing in court to answer questions about something he or she has witnessed or heard, or producing records as evidence. There are penalties if a person fails to respond to a subpoena.

teacher-on-student sexual harassment a student is harassed by a teacher; typically a teacher gives a better grade or favor in exchange for a sexual act, also known as *quid pro quo*.

testimony all such declarations, spoken or written, offered in a legal case or deliberative hearing.

threat of harm activities, conditions, or persons that place a child at risk of abuse. Threats, domestic violence and drug or alcohol abuse fall into this category.

Title IX of Educational Amendment of 1972 requires educational institutions to maintain policies, practices and programs that do not discriminate against anyone based on sex.

tolerance for ambiguity acceptance and open-mindedness of situations that will not contain clear-cut solutions.

unalterable factors factors that are stable and very difficult to be changed in a person's life; there are many unalterable factors in students' lives that cause them hurt and harm.

Uniform Marriage Act followed by many states when deciding custody, which encourages custodial decisions in part to favor the parent that is most likely to keep the other parent involved in the child's life.

value-laden counseling counseling students who need assistance with controversial issues that are surrounded by a person's value and belief system; school counselors must be objective and not impose their own values or beliefs when dealing with value-laden issues.

verbal aggression hostile or abusive language used toward another person or group.

vested with rights having the legal rights of ownership.

violent propensities tendencies to act in a violent manner.

witnesses school counselors act as witnesses for the court usually in cases of child custody, child abuse, or disciplinary action.

written interrogatories written responses to questions; required under process of discovery.

zero tolerance a strict approach to rule enforcement that states absolutely no deviation will be allowed. Zero tolerance policies allow no levels of tolerance or compromise for violators of the rule or law in question, such as bullying, harassment, drug use, etc.

Name Index

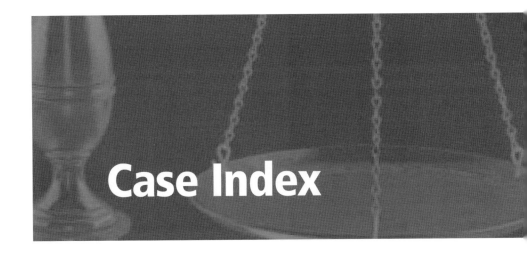

Case Index

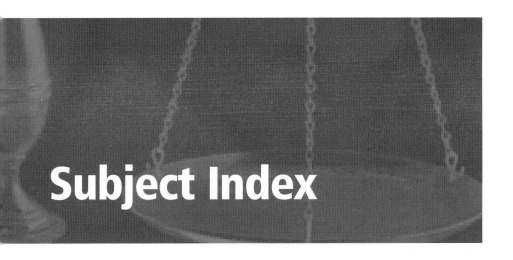

Subject Index

D

H

I